Spanish for Gringos

Level Two

William C. Harvey

About the Author

William C. Harvey is founder of Language Services Institute, a highly successful conversation Spanish program aimed specifically at meeting the needs of today's busy adult learner. For the past 14 years he has taught Spanish and ESL (English as a Second Language) in school districts and community colleges, as well as in private industry. He has also traveled extensively throughout the West Coast giving workshops and seminars to teachers and professional organizations. Mr. Harvey holds a bachelor's degree in Spanish and a master's degree in Bilingual-Bicultural Education from Cal State University, Fullerton, where he received the "Project of the Year" award for his work in ESL Curriculum Development.

Five of his books already have been published by Barron's: *Spanish for Gringos, Inglés para Latinos, Household Spanish, Spanish for Law Enforcement Personnel,* and *Spanish for Health Care Professionals*.

All inquiries should be addressed to:
Barron's Educational Series, Inc.
250 Wireless Boulevard
Hauppauge, New York 11788

International Standard Book Number 0-8120-9743-2

Library of Congress Catalog Card Number 96-78503

Printed in the United States of America

9 8 7 6 5 4 3 2

Contents

INTRODUCTION
Presentación

¡Hola, compañeros gringos!

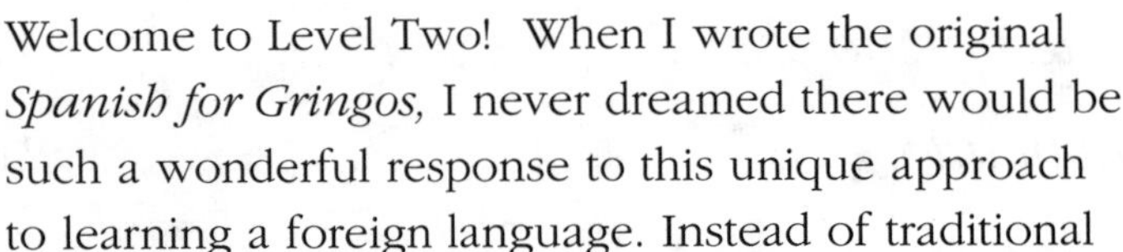

Welcome to Level Two! When I wrote the original *Spanish for Gringos,* I never dreamed there would be such a wonderful response to this unique approach to learning a foreign language. Instead of traditional units and lessons, my books, audiocassettes, and videos offer a variety of practical suggestions and easy-to-follow shortcuts to successful communication. The idea seems to have caught on, because now there is a demand for more!

Spanish for Gringos—Level Two is designed for beginning Spanish students who are ready to "travel" beyond the basic fundamentals. If you are able to understand some Spanish, and can speak a little in return, then this is the program for you.

Like space travelers, we will venture from one "planet" to the next, picking up intermediate and advanced skills along the way. By following more shortcuts and tips, in no time, you will be able to communicate in Spanish at a whole new level. All aboard!

Su profesor y amigo,

Bill

READY TO GO!
¡Listo para irse!

Prior to your travels into unfamiliar territory, make sure that you're properly equipped. There's plenty to double check, so take your time with the following pieces of information. These are real keys to your progress and success:

- **Keep listening to Spanish!** Listen to fluent speakers of Spanish regularly, and both your grammar and pronunciation will improve! Try listening to Spanish radio stations or music tapes and CDs. Find out which TV stations also air in Spanish, or watch Spanish movies on videocassette. Come up with your own creative ways to take in Spanish without having to spend a lot of money.

- **Use Spanish that you already know!** Speak aloud familiar words and phrases in Spanish. Gradually experiment with new vocabulary and verb forms, but don't force yourself to speak more fluently. You must build confidence first before moving ahead, so add to your skills only when you feel ready to do so.

- **Learn all you can about the cultural differences between English and Spanish speakers!** In any language, there's a lot more to communication than just the spoken word. Hand and body gestures, along with facial expressions, speak volumes in countries everywhere. Find out about non-verbal messages in Spain and Latin America. While you're at it, inquire about certain customs and traditions. Learn more about the Hispanic culture, and your conversational skills in Spanish will drastically improve!

- **As always, relax, and try to have a good time!** Don't overload your circuits! Study and practice Spanish at your own pace. Becoming fluent in a new language takes time, so plan to play with it as often as possible. Try not to panic. Just remember—the Spanish speaker you're talking to is probably having as much trouble as you are. Lighten up, believe in yourself, and everything you learn will somehow begin to make sense.

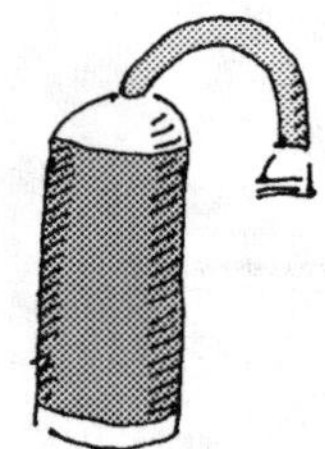

• **Practice, Practice, Practice!** Get together with a fluent Spanish speaker, and try out your new language skills as often as you can. One-on-one practice is best, but remember that it must be in a light, comfortable setting. Obviously, the more you read, write, speak, or listen to Spanish, the more proficient you'll become. Believe it or not, practice does make it **perfecto**!

• **Follow these helpful shortcuts to successful communication:**

✔ Be friendly and use all the courteous expressions you know. People with pleasant personalities seem to communicate better!

✔ When you listen to Spanish, try to recognize words that sound like their English equivalents.

✔ Express comprehension by pointing, moving, or touching things.

✔ Repeat new words and phrases that you learn several times before trying them out in public.

✔ Ask questions often during conversations, and don't give up when you feel confused.

More suggestions before we start:

✔ If you can't remember a word, try another way to explain yourself.

✔ As with every language, Spanish is full of informal idiomatic expressions. People often use slang, so it's always a good idea to ask about words or phrases that you don't understand.

✔ Let others correct you, since natural mistakes actually help you to learn faster.

✔ Dialects may vary, so don't get discouraged when certain words or sounds seem unfamiliar to you.

HOW TO USE THIS GUIDEBOOK
Cómo usar este libro

Spanish for Gringos—Level Two is divided into eight chapters, each one exploring a different realm of Spanish verb conjugations and useful terminology. Since action words play an integral part in language development, an extensive list of verbs is found at the back of this book. You can quickly look up any verb you don't understand. To look up any vocabulary item, simply use the Spanish-English or English-Spanish glossary.

This book also provides students with numerous specialized segments, which are scattered on pages throughout the text. Don't just skim over this material. Everything you read is important, and will assist in accelerating the language learning process. Here are the areas we'll need to cover:

Hot Tips! (Language details that can't be overlooked)

How Do You Write It? (Insights on Spanish writing skills)
¿Cómo se escribe?

Demand It! (How to utilize Spanish command words)
¡Ordénelo!

Verbal Advice (Suggestions on the use of verb infinitives)
Consejos verbales

I Remember! (Practice and review activities)
¡Yo recuerdo!

1

CHAPTER *UNO*
El gran repaso

THE GREAT REVIEW
El gran repaso

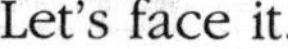

Let's face it.

Level Two will be pretty difficult if you're clueless about *Level One.*

I hope you have looked through the original *Spanish for Gringos* program carefully, so that the following information is nothing more than a review. If you have not, don't fret. Here are all the fundamentals you'll need to know.

How Do You Pronounce It?
¿Cómo se pronuncia?

Let's review the Spanish sounds first. Since you'll have to pronounce everything you read correctly, it's mandatory that you know all of these sounds by heart. Start by repeating the BIG FIVE. That is, the five main vowels:

a (ah)	like yacht	**mañana**
e (eh)	like met	**excelente**
i (ee)	like keep	**dividir**
o (oh)	like open	**tono**
u (oo)	like spoon	**Lulú**

Keep going. These are the consonant sounds you'll need to know.
Don't forget—these sounds are pronounced the way they're written:

Spanish Letter	*English Sound*
c (after an **e** or **i**)	s as in Sam (**cigarro**)
g (after an **e** or **i**)	h as in Harry (**general**)
h	silent, like the k in knife (**hola**)
j	h as in hot (**Juan**)
ll	y as in yes (**llama**)
qu	k as in kit (**tequila**)
rr	the rolled r sound (**carro**)
v	v as in Vincent (**viva**)
z	s as in sun (**cerveza**)

The rest of the letters in Spanish are very similar to their equivalents in English, so pronunciation guides aren't necessary. However, pronouncing complete words and phrases is a different story. In some cases, you'll need extra help, so be on the lookout for any side notes on Spanish pronunciation. To review the secrets on how to sound like a native speaker, follow the simple pronunciation tips below.

Pronunciation Tips
Consejos para mejorar su pronunciación

• Spanish is pronounced the way it's spelled, and vice-versa. So pronounce each sound the same way every time the corresponding letter appears.

• Watch for exceptions. In some cases, for example, the letter **u** doesn't make the "oo" sound (**guitarra, guerra**).

• Spanish sounds are usually made toward the front of the mouth instead of back—with little or no air coming out. And, short, choppy sounds are better than long stretched-out ones.

• Accented (´) parts of words should always be pronounced LOUDER and with more emphasis (**olé**). If there's no accent mark, say the last part of the word LOUDER and with more emphasis (**español**). For words ending in a vowel, or in **n** or **s**, the next to the last part of the word is stressed (**importante**).

• This information is repeated at the end of the book just before the Glossary. You can never have enough support when it comes to pronunciation!

How Do You Write It? ¿Cómo se escribe?

Take a few moments to review the alphabet. At *Level Two,* you'll have to know how to spell what you are trying to say. Special segments labeled **¿Cómo se escribe?** will provide you with all the insights that you will need. Note the accent indicating the stress. For now, say each letter aloud:

a (ah)
b (beh)
c (seh)
ch (cheh)*
d (deh)
e (eh)
f (éh-feh)
g (heh)
h (áh-cheh)
i (ee)
j (hóh-tah)
k (kah)
l (éh-leh)
ll (éh-yeh)*
m (éh-meh)
n (éh-neh)
ñ (éhn-yeh)
o (oh)
p (peh)
q (koo)
r (éh-reh)
rr (éh-rreh)
s (éh-seh)
t (teh)
u (oo)
v (veh)
w (veh dóh-bleh)
x (éh-kees)
y (ee-gree-éh-gah)
z (séh-tah)

Hot Tips!

- This one-liner is definitely required:

How do you spell it?	**¿Cómo se deletrea?**
How do you spell your name in Spanish?	**¿Cómo se deletrea su nombre en español?**

I Remember! ¡Yo recuerdo!

Pronounce these common words. Remember to sound out each letter:

amigo	**excelente**	**macho**	**plaza**
amor	**general**	**mujer**	**zapato**
carro	**grande**	**pollo**	**señor**
español	**hombre**	**poquito**	**vino**

---

* Recently, these letters were cut from the official Spanish alphabet. However, people do refer to them when spelling out a word.

MY FIRST WORDS
Mis primeras palabras

Letters form words, and where we're going you'll need to know a lot of them. For starters, look over these popular greetings and exchanges, and then highlight the ones you know:

And you?	**¿Y usted?**
Excuse me	**Con permiso**
Go ahead	**Pase**
Good afternoon	**Buenas tardes**
Good evening, good night	**Buenas noches**
Good morning	**Buenos días**
Good-bye	**Adiós**
Hi	**Hola**
How are you?	**¿Cómo está?**
How's it going	**¡Qué tal!**
I'm sorry	**Lo siento**
May I come in?	**¿Se puede?**
My name is...	**Me llamo...**
Nice to meet you!	**¡Mucho gusto!**
Nothing much!	**¡Sin novedad!**
Please	**Por favor**
Same to you	**Igualmente**
Thank you very much	**Muchas gracias**
Very well	**Muy bien**
What's happening?	**¿Qué pasa?**
What's your name?	**¿Cómo se llama?**
You're welcome	**De nada**

Hot Tips!

- A little expression at the end of a statement often is meant to confirm, question, or emphasize the message. Try out one of these examples:

  It's your car, right? **Es su carro, *¿no?***

Es su carro, *¿verdad?*

Es su carro, *¿no es cierto?*

- You won't find every Spanish one-liner in this guidebook. Start a specialized list of your own!

How can I help you?	**¿Cómo puedo ayudarle?**	More or less!	**¡Más o menos!**
What's the matter?	**¿Qué pasó?**	No problem!	**¡Ningún problema!**
Who's calling?	**¿Quién habla?**	No wonder!	**¡Con razón!**
All the better!	**¡Tanto mejor!**	Of course!	**¡Por supuesto!**
Good idea!	**¡Buena idea!**	Really?	**¿Verdad?**
I agree!	**¡De acuerdo!**	That depends!	**¡Depende!**
I hope so!	**¡Ojalá!**	That's the way it is!	**¡Así es!**
I see!	**¡Ya veo!**	That's for sure!	**¡Es cierto!**
I'm so glad!	**¡Me alegro!**	That's OK!	**¡Está bien!**
Maybe!	**¡Quizás!**	I think so!	**¡Creo que sí!**
Me, neither!	**¡Yo tampoco!**	Whatever you want!	**¡Cómo no!**
Me, too!	**¡Yo también!**	Why not!	**¡Cómo no!**

The Same Thing
La misma cosa

Every language has synonyms, that is, words that carry the same meaning. They will be necessary as we travel through second level Spanish, because our conversations will be longer. Study these examples:

Nice to meet you	**Mucho gusto** **Encantado** **A sus órdenes**
Thanks a lot	**Muchas gracias** **Mil gracias** **Muy amable**
You're welcome	**Por nada** **De nada** **No hay de qué**

Look-Alikes!
¡Las palabras afines!

A pleasant surprise to discover is that many Spanish words are very similar to English words. For extra pronunciation practice, dive into this selection of cognates:

banana	**final**	**natural**
chocolate	**hospital**	**popular**
color	**idea**	**terror**

These aren't spelled exactly the same, but you should be able to figure out what they mean:

inteligente	**universidad**
interesante	**posibilidad**
momento	**vocabulario**
rápido	**diccionario**
conversación	**especial**
televisión	**estúpido**

Hot Tips!

- Here's a trend that's always good to remember. You can often guess at the meanings of Spanish words by focusing on the few last letters! Note these consistent patterns:

ic	***ico***	*ous*	***oso***
romantic	**romántico**	delicious	**delicioso**
ent	***ente***	*ty*	***dad***
different	**diferente**	electricity	**electricidad**
tor	***dor***	*ry*	***rio***
elevator	**elevador**	necessary	**necesario**
tion	***ción***	*ism*	***ismo***
construction	**construcción**	tourism	**turismo**

SOME KEY EXPRESSIONS
Algunas expresiones claves

People everywhere often converse in nothing more than short, friendly expressions. So why not do the same in Spanish?

Bless you!	**¡Salud!**
Congratulations!	**¡Felicitaciones!**
Enough!	**¡Basta!**
Give my regards to...	**Me saluda a...**
God bless you!	**¡Dios le bendiga!**
Good luck!	**¡Buena suerte!**
Happy New Year!	**¡Próspero año nuevo!**
Have a nice day!	**¡Qué le vaya bien!**
Have a nice trip!	**¡Buen viaje!**
Help!	**¡Socorro!**
Let's go!	**¡Vamos!**
Merry Christmas!	**¡Feliz navidad!**
Sure!	**¡Claro!**
Welcome!	**¡Bienvenidos!**
Wow!	**¡Caramba!**

Notice what's happening here. The word **qué** is all over the place!

Get well!	**¡Qué se mejore!**
Have a good time!	**¡Qué disfrute!**
How sad!	**¡Qué triste!**
So what!	**¡Qué importa!**
What a shame!	**¡Qué lástima!**

Hot Tips!

- Feel free to add these to your list of party expressions:

Happy anniversary!	**¡Feliz aniversario!**
Happy Easter!	**¡Felices pascuas!**
Happy holidays!	**¡Felices fiestas!**

- Notice how Spanish phrases often include references to God (**Dios**). Shout these phrases **con inspiración**:

  God willing! **¡Si Dios quiera!**
  Oh my God! **¡Dios mío!**
  Thank God! **¡Gracias a Dios!**

- Don't get nervous about all the different grammatical structures within these one-liners. We'll be discussing that stuff later!

- Throw in "and" (**y**), "or" (**o**), and "but" (**pero**) as often as possible:

  ¡Que le vaya bien *y* buena suerte!

AGAIN, PLEASE
Otra vez, por favor

Don't deny it. Often you get lost when someone is speaking Spanish to you. Well, just try to relax and do the best you can with the phrases below. They really help!

Do you understand?	**¿Entiende usted?**
I comprehend.	**Yo comprendo.**
I don't know.	**No sé.**
I don't understand.	**No entiendo.**
I speak a little Spanish.	**Hablo poquito español.**
I'm learning Spanish.	**Estoy aprendiendo español.**
More slowly.	**Más despacio.**
Thanks for your patience	**Gracias por su paciencia.**
What does it mean?	**¿Qué significa?**
Letter by letter.	**Letra por letra.**
Number by number.	**Número por número.**
Word for word.	**Palabra por palabra.**

MORE FANTASTIC PHRASES
Más frases fantásticas

En tonces...
Aunque...
Todavía...
Además...
Por fin...
O sea...

Open up with these words and phrases, and the rest is easy!

Above all...	**Sobre todo...**
According to...	**Según...**
Although...	**Aunque...**
At first...	**Al principio...**
At last...	**Por fin...**
At least...	**Por lo menos...**
Besides...	**Además...**
By the way...	**A propósito...**
For example...	**Por ejemplo...**
However...	**Sin embargo...**
In general...	**En general...**
In other words...	**O sea...**
In spite of...	**A pesar de...**
Little by little...	**Poco a poco...**
On the contrary...	**Por lo contrario...**
So...	**Así que...**
Still...	**Aún...**
Then...	**Entonces...**
Therefore...	**Por eso...**
Without a doubt...	**Sin duda...**
Yet...	**Todavía...**

Hot Tips!

- Another word for "but" is **sino**, which is used to contrast a negative statement with an affirmative one. Don't confuse it with **pero**. Watch this:

  I'm sorry, but I don't have any money.
  Lo siento, pero no tengo dinero.
  I don't have money, but I do have love.
  No tengo dinero, sino tengo amor.

- Collect your own set of three or four favorite expressions, and use them all the time. Once they are mastered, start all over again with a different set.

  backwards **al revés**
  upside down **boca abajo**
  the other side **el otro lado**

- Look for patterns in the language! Here's an example:

  Face to face **Cara a cara**
  Hand to hand **Mano a mano**
  Step by step **Paso a paso**

¡Yo recuerdo!

Bad news! There will be *no answers* provided in these review segments, so you'll have to look up the correct responses all by yourself!

Match each Spanish expression with the best response:

¿Qué pasa? **Creo que sí.**
¿Puedo ayudarle? **Muy amable.**
¡Felicitaciones! **Sin novedad.**

Look at the final letters of these words as you translate:

el público ____________________
conveniente ____________________
humanidad ____________________

SURVIVAL SPANISH
Español para sobrevivir

So you speak a little Spanish? Prove it by naming these items without looking at the translations. And watch your pronunciation!

Everyday Things
Las cosas diarias

book	**el libro**	money	**el dinero**
car	**el carro**	paper	**el papel**
chair	**la silla**	pen	**el lapicero**
clothing	**la ropa**	pencil	**el lápiz**
door	**la puerta**	room	**el cuarto**
floor	**el piso**	table	**la mesa**
food	**la comida**	telephone	**el teléfono**
house	**la casa**	water	**el agua**
light	**la luz**	work	**el trabajo**

People
La gente

baby	**el bebé**	person	**la persona**
child	**el niño**	relative	**el pariente**
friend	**el amigo**	woman	**la mujer**
man	**el hombre**	young person	**el muchacho**

Descriptions
Las descripciones

bad	**malo**	pretty	**bonito**
big	**grande**	short (in height)	**bajo**
good	**bueno**	short (in length)	**corto**
handsome	**guapo**	small	**chico**
long	**largo**	tall	**alto**
new	**nuevo**	ugly	**feo**
old	**viejo**	young	**joven**

Hot Tips!

- Add these words to elaborate:

más grande	bigger
lo más grande	biggest
tan grande como	as big as
un poco grande	a little big
muy grande	very big
demasiado grande	too big
tan grande	so big

- Here are more descriptions every Spanish student should know. Simplify the process by breaking them into opposites:

fat	**gordo**	easy	**fácil**
thin	**delgado**	difficult	**difícil**
strong	**fuerte**	cold	**frío**
weak	**débil**	hot	**caliente**
dirty	**sucio**	rich	**rico**
clean	**limpio**	poor	**pobre**
slow	**lento**	inexpensive	**barato**
fast	**rápido**	expensive	**caro**

- If you've ever taken a Spanish class, then these classroom words should sound familiar:

blackboard	**el pizarrón**
chalk	**la tiza**
class	**la clase**
desk	**el escritorio**
eraser	**el borrador**
folder	**el cuaderno**
student	**el estudiante**
teacher	**el maestro**

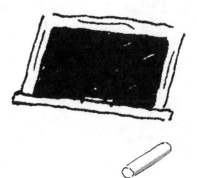

- One effective technique to remember the names for things is to write the name of an object in Spanish on a removable sticker, and place it on the item you are trying to learn.

- When referring to people, use these abbreviations:

Mr. or a man	**Señor (Sr.)**
Mrs. or a lady	**Señora (Sra.)**
Miss or a young lady	**Señorita (Srta.)**

- No list of people would be complete without the family members. Here are some of the basics:

brother	**el hermano**
daughter	**la hija**
father	**el padr**
husband	**el esposo**
mother	**la madre**
sister	**la hija**
son	**el hijo**
wife	**la esposa**

- It's common in Spanish to add on the **ito** or **ita** endings when you'd like to indicate smallness or affection:

  Mi abuelita está en su casita.
  My grandma is in her little house.

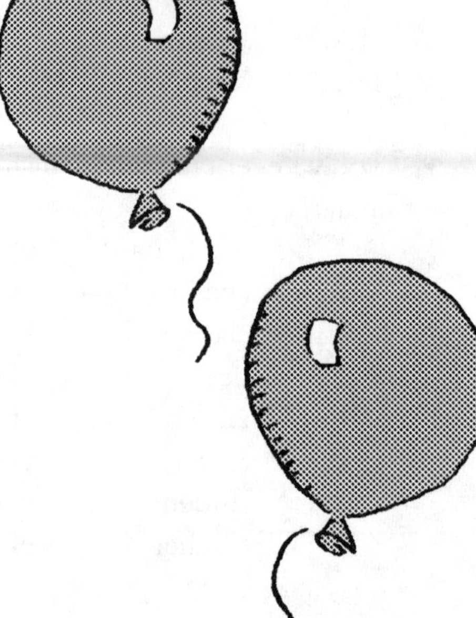

Pretty Colors
Los colores bonitos

black	**negro**	orange	**anaranjado**
blue	**azul**	purple	**morado**
brown	**café**	red	**rojo**
gray	**gris**	white	**blanco**
green	**verde**	yellow	**amarillo**

By the Numbers
Por números

0 **cero**	7 **siete**	14 **catorce**	30 **treinta**
1 **uno**	8 **ocho**	15 **quince**	40 **cuarenta**
2 **dos**	9 **nueve**	16 **dieciséis**	50 **cincuenta**
3 **tres**	10 **diez**	17 **diecisiete**	60 **sesenta**
4 **cuatro**	11 **once**	18 **dieciocho**	70 **setenta**
5 **cinco**	12 **doce**	19 **diecinueve**	80 **ochenta**
6 **seis**	13 **trece**	20 **veinte**	90 **noventa**

For all the numbers in-between, just add **y** (ee), which means "and":

21 **veinte y uno**	34 ________________
22 **veinte y dos**	55 ________________
23 **veinte y** _______	87 ________________

You'll also need to know how to say the larger numbers in Spanish. They aren't that difficult, so practice aloud:

100	**cien**	700	**setecientos**
200	**doscientos**	800	**ochocientos**
300	**trescientos**	900	**novecientos**
400	**cuatrocientos**	1000	**mil**
500	**quinientos**	million	**millón**
600	**seiscientos**		

Hot Tips!

- Advanced speakers know the names for lots of colors:

beige	**beige**	pink	**rosado**
fuchsia	**fucsia**	silver	**plata**
gold	**oro**	violet	**violeta**
magenta	**magenta**		

- Don't forget the ordinal numbers. Look up the rest on your own!

first	**primero**	seventh	**séptimo**
second	**segundo**	eighth	**octavo**
third	**tercero**	ninth	**noveno**
fourth	**cuarto**	tenth	**décimo**
fifth	**quinto**	eleventh	**undécimo**
sixth	**sexto**	twelfth	**duodécimo**

- And you'll always need words that describe "how much":

so much	**tanto**	none	**ninguno**
too much	**demasiado**	all	**todo**
almost	**casi**	both	**ambos**
the rest	**lo demás**	several	**varios**

¡Yo recuerdo!

Match these opposites:

viejo	**maestro**
limpio	**mujer**
padre	**sucio**
negro	**joven**
estudiante	**pobre**
rico	**blanco**
hombre	**madre**

Translate as fast as you can:

book ____

clothing ____

water ____

chair ____

food ____

Fill in the blanks:

tres, cuatro, cinco, ________________

primero, segundo, tercero, ________________

veinte, treinta, cuarenta, ________________

THE RULES
Las reglas

Here's a quick overview of some basic regulations in the world of Spanish grammar. Obey them, and your skills will improve!

First, there was the **el-la** matter:
Remember that the names for people, places, and things are either masculine or feminine, and so the article "the" in front may be either **el** (masculine) or **la** (feminine). Generally, if the word ends in the letter **o** there's **el** in front (e.g., **el cuarto**, **el niño**). Conversely, if the word ends in an **a** there's **la** in front (e.g., **la mesa**, **la persona**). There are some exceptions (e.g., **el agua**, **la mano**, **el sofá**).

Words not ending in either **o** or **a** need to be memorized (e.g., **el amor**, **la paz**). In the case of single objects, use **el** and **la** much like the word "the" in English: The house is big (**La casa es grande**).

Remember too, that **el** and **la** are used in Spanish to indicate a person's sex. **El doctor** is a male doctor, while **la doctora** is a female doctor. Here's how we change words to refer to the female gender:

el muchacho	**la muchacha**	**el bebé**	**la bebé**
el niño	**la niña**		

Next, you learned the "Reversal" Rule:

As you began to link your Spanish words together, you found that sometimes words were positioned in reverse order. This "Reversal" Rule is applied when you give a description. The descriptive word goes after the word being described. Study these examples:

the big house	**la casa grande**
the green chair	**la silla verde**
the important man	**el hombre importante**

And you also learned the "Once-and-for-all" Rule:

A few important steps must be taken when you refer to more than one item in Spanish. For example, when you talk in plurals, the words **el** and **la** become **los** and **las**, respectively:

el baño	**los baños**	**la mesa**	**las mesas**
el muchacho	**los muchachos**	**la niña**	**las niñas**

Then, not only do all the nouns and adjectives need to end in **s** or **es** to make the sentence plural, but when they are used together, the genders (the **o**'s and **a**'s), must match as well:

two white doors	**dos puertas blancas**
many red cars	**muchos carros rojos**
six little children	**seis niños pequeños**

By the way, to say "a" or "an" in Spanish, use **un** for masculine words or **una** for feminine words:

a floor	**un piso**	a bed	**una cama**
a blue floor	**un piso azul**	a big bed	**una cama grande**

And to say "some," use **unos** or **unas**, and don't forget the "Once-and-for-all" Rule:

some floors	**unos pisos**	some beds	**unas camas**
some blue floors	**unos pisos azules**	some big beds	**unas camas grandes**

Hot Tips!

- These words also mean "some":

some man	***algún*** **hombre**	some woman	***alguna*** **mujer**
some men	***algunos*** **hombres**	some women	***algunas*** **mujeres**

¿Cómo se escribe?

The final letters of Spanish nouns can signal whether it needs an **el** or a **la** in front. For example, nouns ending in **ma**, **pa**, or **ta** are generally masculine:

el programa **el mapa** **el planeta**

And nouns ending in **dad**, **tad**, **ión**, **umbre**, and **ie** are feminine:

la universidad **la misión** **la serie**
la libertad **la costumbre**

FORM A PHRASE!
¡Forme una frase!

In order to add detail, one clever technique in Spanish is to attach a few words to a simple preposition:

with	**con**	**con mis amigos**
without	**sin**	**sin el dinero**
to	**a**	**a mi casa**
from, of	**de**	**de la profesora**
in, on, at	**en**	**en Los Angeles**
for	**para**	**para su familia**
by	**por**	**por la silla**

HOT TIPS

Hot Tips!

- Here are a few unusual changes:

with me	**conmigo**
with you, him, her, them	**consigo**
with you (informally)	**contigo**

- Careful! These are the only two "contractions" in Spanish:

of, from, the	**del**	**Es del niño**
to the	**al**	**Vamos al restaurante**

- Almost everyone struggles with the differences between **por** and **para** in Spanish. Generally speaking, **para** means "to," "in order to," and "for the purpose of," while **por** means "by," "through," "because of," and "on account of." Listen to how each is used in conversations, and you'll get a feel for them in no time.

THIS AND THAT
Este y ese

Review these key words before you go any further. Notice the **el-la** situation:

that	**ese** or **esa**	**Ese amigo americano**
these	**estos** or **estas**	**Estos tacos chicos**
this	**este** or **esta**	**Este papel amarillo**
those	**esos** or **esas**	**Esos hombres buenos**

Hot Tips!

- When you don't care to be specific, use **esto** and **eso**:

  What's this? **¿Qué es esto?**
  What's that? **¿Qué es eso?**

- When the object of discussion is far away, try these:

  That book is mine. **Aquel libro es mío.**
  Those books are mine. **Aquellos libros son míos.**
  That pen is mine. **Aquella pluma es mía.**
  Those pens are mine. **Aquellas plumas son mías.**

¿Cómo se escribe?

Note the spelling when these words are stressed in the sentence:

I want *this one* and *that one*. **Quiero *éste* y *ése*.**

¡Yo recuerdo!

Change these phrases to the plural form:

La casa	*Las casas.*	**El baño**	________
Aquel carro	________	**Algún amigo**	________
Esta silla	________		

DO YOU HAVE A QUESTION?
¿Tiene una pregunta?

If you've studied any Spanish before, then these "question" words and phrases should be quite familiar to you. Go ahead and review:

How many?	**¿Cuántos?**
How old are you?	**¿Cuántos años tiene?**
How much?	**¿Cuánto?**
How much does it cost?	**¿Cuánto cuesta?**
How?	**¿Cómo?**
How are you?	**¿Cómo está?**
What?	**¿Qué?**
What's happening?	**¿Qué pasa?**
Where?	**¿Dónde?**
Where is it?	**¿Dónde está?**
Which?	**¿Cuál?**
Which is it?	**¿Cuál es?**
When?	**¿Cuándo?**
When is it?	**¿Cuándo es?**
Who?	**¿Quién?**
Who is it?	**¿Quién es?**
Whose?	**¿De quién?**
Whose is it?	**¿De quién es?**

Hot Tips!

- Bear in mind that not all "question" phrases can be translated literally. Here's an example:

  ¿Cuántos años tiene? How old are you?

- "Why?" is **¿Por qué?** To respond, simply reply with the word **porque** because it means "because":

  Why is he at home? **¿Por qué está en la casa?**
  Because he's sick. **Porque está enfermo.**

- Combine the words you know to create new question phrases:

  From where? **¿De dónde?**
  For when? **¿Para cuándo?**
  To whom? **¿A quién?**
  With what? **¿Con qué?**

- To ask in the plural, just add **-es** to the question word. Notice the difference:

  Which one is it? **¿Cuál es?**
  Which ones are they? **¿Cuáles son?**

  Whose is it? **¿De quién es?**
  Whose are they? **¿De quiénes son?**

- And always be aware of the **el-la** choice:

  How many boys? **¿Cuántos niños?**
  How many girls? **¿Cuántas niñas?**

- Follow the formula to conduct an interview:

What's your...?	**¿Cuál es su...?**
name	**nombre**
address	**dirección**
phone number	**número de teléfono**
date of birth	**fecha de nacimiento**
age	**edad**
place of birth	**lugar de nacimiento**
social security	**seguro social**
driver's license	**licencia de manejar**

TELL ME YOUR NAME!
¡Dígame su nombre!

When referring to others by name, it really helps if you're able to pronounce the names correctly, as it makes people feel much more at ease. Also, remember that it's not uncommon for someone in Spain or Latin America to have two last names. Don't get confused. Here's the order:

First name **primer nombre**	**María**
Father's last name **apellido paterno**	**García**
Mother's last name **apellido materno**	**Sánchez**

- The popular phrase **¿Cómo se llama?** is usually translated to mean, What's your name? However, you may also hear **¿Cuál es su nombre?,** which literally means *"Which* is your name?"

- Not all Hispanic people have two first names, and there is no middle name as we know it.

- When a woman marries, usually she follows one of three choices:
  She keeps her father's last name, drops her mother's last name, adds **de,** and follows it with her husband's last name
  (María López Ovalle becomes María López de Sepúlveda.)
  She drops both parents' last names and adds her husband's
  (Maria López Ovalle becomes María Sepúlveda.)
  She keeps her maiden name and her marriage has no effect in this matter.
  These choices depend on social status, culture, customs, and geographical location.

¿Cómo se escribe?

- When writing exclamations or questions in Spanish, you have to put an upside down exclamation or question mark at the beginning:
  ¿Cómo está?
  ¿Es usted estudiante de español?
  ¡Caramba!
  ¡Adiós!

¡Yo recuerdo!

Answer these questions aloud!

¿Cómo se llama usted?
¿Cuál es su dirección?
¿Cuántos años tiene usted?
¿Quién es su amigo favorito?
¿De quién es este libro?

THE ANSWERS
Las respuestas

When you are asked all these **preguntas** in Spanish, you should know how to respond. Here is what's usually heard out on the streets. Begin with those one-word replies about your health:

How are you? **¿Cómo está?**

angry	**enojado**	OK	**regular**
bored	**aburrido**	sad	**triste**
fine	**bien**	sick	**enfermo**
happy	**feliz**	tired	**cansado**
not bad	**así-así**	worried	**preocupado**
not well	**mal**		

Now review the basic location words, and don't be afraid to point:

Where is it? **¿Dónde está?**

above	**encima**	next to	**al lado**
at the bottom	**en el fondo**	outside	**afuera**
behind	**detrás**	straight ahead	**adelante**
down	**abajo**	there	**allí**
far	**lejos**	to the left	**a la izquierda**
here	**aquí**	to the right	**a la derecha**
in front	**enfrente**	under	**debajo**
inside	**adentro**	up	**arriba**
near	**cerca**	way over there	**allá**

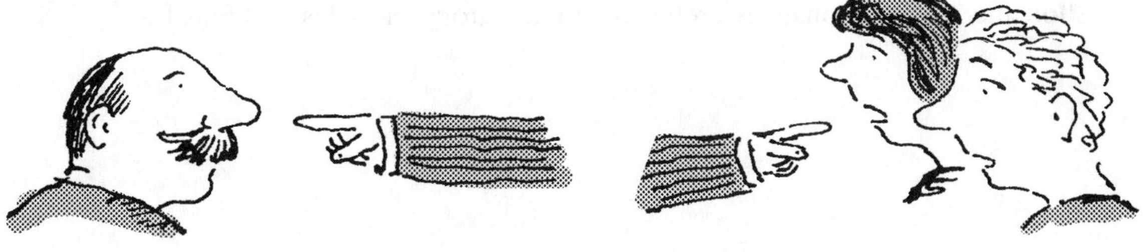

Everyone knows the people words! Are you still pointing?

Who is it?	**¿Quién es?**
I	**Yo**
You (formal)	**Usted**
He	**El**
She	**Ella**
They	**Ellos, Ellas (m, f)**
You guys	**Ustedes**
We	**Nosotros, Nosotras (m, f)**
You (informally)	**Tú**
Whose is it?	**¿De quién es?**
my	**mi**
your, his, her, their	**su**
our	**nuestro, nuestra (m, f)**
your (informally)	**tu**

Hot Tips!

- Add **de** to your location words:

  in front of **enfrente de** on top of **encima de**

- **Ellas** is "they," feminine, and **Nosotras** is "we," feminine.

- Just add **s** to both words (possessive adjective and noun) when talking about more than one person or thing:

  Son mis amigas **Son nuestros amigos**

- **él**, **ella**, **ellos** and **ellas** can refer to things as well as people:

  ¿Y los libros, dónde están ellos?
  And the books, where are they?

- **Ellos** and **Nosotros** may also refer to a mixed group of males and females.

- If someone or something belongs to someone else, use **de** to tell who the person is:

  It's Mary's house. **Es la casa de María.** It's hers. **Es de ella.**

- Look at all of the different ways that these pronouns are used in Spanish. We'll be practicing each of these forms a little later on:

  I want my book, so give it to me. It's mine.

  Yo quiero mi libro, así que démelo a mí. Es mío.

- Who knows? You may need a reflexive pronoun once in a while. Here's what they look like. Practice the pattern, without being concerned about grammar:

myself	**yo mismo**
yourself	**usted mismo, usted misma**
himself	**él mismo**
herself	**ella misma**
yourselves	**ustedes mismos, ustedes mismas**
themselves	**ellos mismos, ellas mismas**
ourselves	**nosotros mismos, nosotras mismas**

She did it herself.	**Lo hizo ella misma.**
I did it myself.	**Lo hice yo mismo.**
We did it ourselves.	**Lo hicimos nosotros mismos.**

- Now try these other possessive words. Do you know what they mean?

mine	**mío** or **mía**
	¿El dinero? Es mío.
yours, his, hers, theirs	**suyo** or **suya**
	¿La silla? Es suya.

¡Yo recuerdo!

Translate and practice:

¿Yo? Mi nombre es Susana. ______________________________

¿Ella? Su nombre es Cristina. ______________________________

¿Nosotras? ¡Nuestros nombres son Susana y Cristina! ____________________

____

THE *TÚ* FORM
Uso del tú

The word **tú** is the informal way of saying "you" in Spanish. This casual form is generally exchanged between family and friends.

Here are some examples.

You are my friend.	**Tú eres mi amigo.**
Do you speak Spanish?	**¿Tú hablas español?**
You don't have a car.	**Tú no tienes un carro.**

The word "your" is **tu**, which is the same as "you" but without the accent:

Where's your family?	**¿Dónde está tu familia?**

All informal verb forms require changes when you talk in casual settings. We'll learn more about this later. Most words can be recognized because they end in the letter **s**.

Do you have...?	**¿Tienes...?**
Do you want...?	**¿Quieres...?**
Do you need...?	**¿Necesitas...?**

Even Spanish command words take on a slightly different form when you speak informally. We'll look at all of the command forms soon:

Tell me.	**Dime.**
Come here.	**Ven aquí.**
Stand up.	**Levántate.**

You too will be able to establish informal relationships with Spanish-speaking people and, eventually, your new pals will be teaching you more about the **tú** form, along with lots of other useful tips. Throughout this guidebook, we'll be learning the formal **usted** form, because it's easier to remember and use. You'll find it is perfectly acceptable when speaking with anyone!

Hot Tips!

- Here's what some of the other **tú** forms look like:

Es para *ti*.	It's for you.
***Te* quiero mucho.**	I love you a lot.
¿Es la *tuya?*	Is it yours?

- If you ever come across **Ud.** or **Uds.** in your Spanish reading, don't fret! They're abbreviations for **Usted** and **Ustedes**.

- The plural form of **tú** is **vosotros**, and is used rarely outside of Spain. Listen for it, but don't panic if you can't respond. You'll figure out who they're talking to.

¿Cómo se escribe?

A number of Spanish words are marked with an accent only to distinguish it from another word that is spelled the same. Here are some examples:

dé	=	give	**de**	=	of, from
mí	=	me	**mi**	=	my
qué	=	what	**que**	=	that
si	=	if**s**	**í**	=	yes
tú	=	you	**tu**	=	your

Notice how all your questions words have accents. When it's used elsewhere, they don't:

¿Cuándo es la clase?	When's the class?
No sé cuando es la fiesta.	I don't know when the party is.

WHEN IS IT?
¿Cuándo es?

To truly communicate in a foreign language, you'll have to include some time-referenced vocabulary. These will do for now:

after	**después**	soon	**pronto**
always	**siempre**	then	**entonces**
before	**antes**	today	**hoy**
during	**durante**	tomorrow	**mañana**
early	**temprano**	until	**hasta**
late	**tarde**	while	**mientras**
later	**luego**	yesterday	**ayer**
never	**nunca**	yet	**todavía**
now	**ahora**	A.M.	**de la mañana**
since	**desde**	P.M.	**de la tarde**
sometimes	**a veces**		

WHAT TIME IS IT?
¿Qué hora es?

Why not take a few **minutos** to double-check your time-telling skills? To answer, simply give the hour, followed by the word **y** (and), and the minutes. For example, 6:15 is **seis y quince.**

Read aloud these other examples:

It's... **Son las...**
At... **A las...**

3:40	**tres y cuarenta**
10:30	**diez y treinta**
12:05	**doce y cinco**

WHAT'S THE DATE?
¿Cuál es la fecha?

And do you recall your calendar words? You should be saying them **todos los días**:

Days of the Week	**Los días de la semana**
Monday	**lunes**
Tuesday	**martes**
Wednesday	**miércoles**
Thursday	**jueves**
Friday	**viernes**
Saturday	**sábado**
Sunday	**domingo**

Months of the Year	**Los meses del año**
January	**enero**
February	**febrero**
March	**marzo**
April	**abril**
May	**mayo**
June	**junio**
July	**julio**
August	**agosto**
September	**septiembre**
October	**octubre**
November	**noviembre**
December	**diciembre**

Hot Tips!

- Weekend is **el fin de semana**.

- For 1:00–1:59, use **Es la...** (instead of **Son las...**)

  It's one o'clock. **Es la una.**
  It's one-thirty. **Es la una y treinta.**

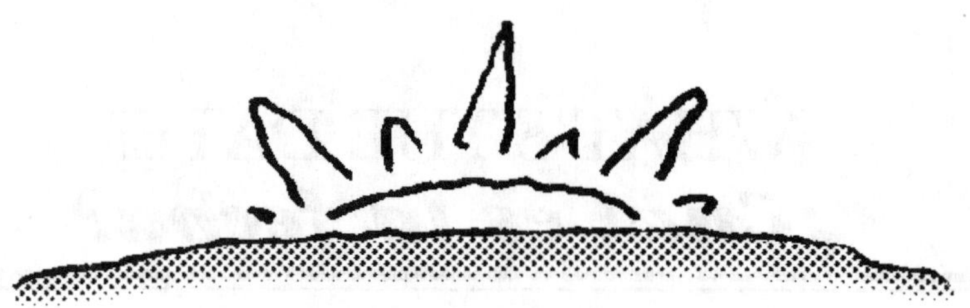

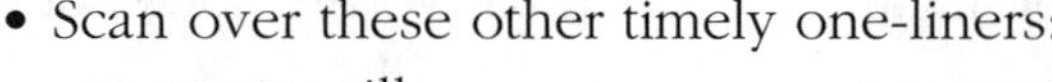

- Scan over these other timely one-liners:

a quarter till	**un cuarto para**
half past	**y media**
in the evening	**de la noche**
in the middle of	**a mediados de**
midnight	**medianoche**
noon	**mediodía**
on the dot	**en punto**
last night	**anoche**
next month	**el próximo mes**
last week	**la semana pasada**
an hour ago	**hace una hora**
the day after tomorrow	**pasado mañana**
the day before yesterday	**anteayer**

- Remember how to give the date in Spanish?

June 3rd	**el tres de junio**
February 15th	**el quince de febrero**

- The only one that's strange each month is the first:

  October 1 ***el primero de*** **octubre**

- Read the year as one large number:

  1999 **mil novecientos noventa y nueve**

- "On Monday" is **el lunes,** while "on Mondays" is **los lunes.**

¡Yo recuerdo!

Connect these opposites:

enfermo	**nunca**
mañana	**feliz**
triste	**después**
siempre	**hoy**
antes	**bien**

Say in Spanish:

11:45 P.M.
November 2, 1998
On Monday, at noon.

Fill in the missing words:

enero, febrero, ___________________, **abril, mayo,** ___________________
martes, miércoles, ___________________, **viernes, sábado** ___________________

¿Cómo se escribe?

Check out these tips on how to use capital letters (**las mayúsculas**) in Spanish:

- The first word of a sentence is always capitalized.
  ¿Cómo está?
- Proper names of people, places, and things are also capitalized.
  Carlos es de Cuba.
- Days of the week and months of the year are **not** capitalized.
  lunes y martes
- Religions, nationalities, and languages are **not** capitalized.
  español inglés y
- In titles of books or works of art, only the first word is capitalized.
  Español para gringos!

THE INTERVIEW
La entrevista

When it comes to questions and answers, what's the best way to practice? Why, the *interview method,* of course. The truth is, you can always learn how to communicate when you're forced to. Continue to interview folks that you meet, and you'll be fluent in no time. Here's what you should sound like:

Good morning, sir.	**Buenos días, señor.**
I'm a Spanish student.	**Soy estudiante de español.**
May I ask you some questions?	**¿Podría preguntarle unas preguntas?**

Translate as you review:

¿Dónde vive?	**Ahí, en aquella casa.**
¿Cómo se llama usted?	**Roberto García.**
¿Y cuántos años tiene?	**Tengo treinta años.**

Hot Tips!

During your flight through advanced Spanish, the interview will become part of your everyday experience. And obviously, the more you do it, the faster your Spanish will improve. To make sure you are prepared, let's add one more group of popular expressions before we move on to verbs and sentence structure:

something	**algo**	someone	**alguien**
anything	**cualquier cosa**	anyone	**cualquier persona**
nothing	**nada**	no one	**nadie**
everything	**todo**	everyone	**todo el mundo**

somewhere	**en alguna parte**
anywhere	**en cualquier parte**
nowhere	**en ninguna parte**
everywhere	**en todas partes**

HOW'S THE WEATHER?
¿Qué tiempo hace?

Can you make small talk in Spanish? At least make a comment about the weather outside:

This is my favorite season.	**Esta es mi estación favorita.**
I like...	**Me gusta...**
spring	**la primavera**
summer	**el verano**
fall	**el otoño**
winter	**el invierno**
It's...	**Hace...**
cold	**frío**
hot	**calor**
nice weather	**buen tiempo**
sunny	**sol**
windy	**viento**
It's...	**Está...**
clear	**despejado**
cloudy	**nublado**
drizzling	**lloviznando**
raining	**lloviendo**
snowing	**nevando**

Hot Tips!

- This is a great word to use in daily chitchat:

hace (ago):	**Hace dos días.**
hace (weather):	**Hace mucho frío.**
hace (does, makes):	**Hace tacos excelentes.**

TO BE AND TO BE
Estar and Ser

Now that we've reviewed the key phrases and vocabulary that are needed at *Level Two,* try to link them together with your beginning grammar skills. Let's practice the verb "to be" in Spanish, **estar** and **ser**.

First, focus on the difference between **está** and **es**. Both words mean "is," but don't really mean the same thing. The word **está** expresses a temporary state, condition, or location:

The girl is fine.	**La niña está bien.**
The girl is in the room.	**La niña está en el cuarto.**

However, the word **es** expresses an inherent characteristic or quality, including origin and ownership:

The girl is small.	**La niña es pequeña.**
The girl is American.	**La niña es americana.**
The girl is my friend.	**La niña es mi amiga.**

Can you see how helpful these two words can be? Countless comments can be made with only a minimum of vocabulary.

You'll also need to talk about more than one person, place, or thing. To do so, replace **está** with **están**, and **es** with **son**. And, don't forget that words must agree when you change to plurals:

The book is on the table.	**El libro está en la mesa.**
The books are on the table.	**Los libros están en la mesa.**

It's a man.	**Es un hombre.**
They are men.	**Son hombres.**

Check out these other examples and read them aloud as you focus on their structure and meaning:

Are the chairs black?	**¿Son negras las sillas?**
The papers are in the house.	**Los papeles están en la casa.**
They are not important.	**No son importantes.**
Are they good?	**¿Están buenos?**

Here I Am!
¡Aquí estoy!

To say "I am" and "we are" in Spanish, you must also learn the different forms. As with **está** and **están**, the words **estoy** and **estamos** refer to the location or condition of a person, place, or thing. And, just like **es** and **son**, the words **soy** and **somos** are used with everything else. Refresh your memory:

I am fine.	**Estoy bien.**
We are in the room.	**Estamos en el cuarto.**
I am Lupe.	**Soy Lupe.**
We are Cuban.	**Somos cubanos.**

Now, let's group all of these forms together. Look over the present tense forms of the verbs **estar** and **ser**.

To be	Estar	Ser
I am	**estoy**	**soy**
You are; He is, She is	**está**	**es**
You are (plural), They are	**están**	**son**
We are	**estamos**	**somos**

Hot Tips!

- As you've probably learned, sometimes it's OK to drop the subject pronoun since it's usually understood who is involved:

I am fine.	**(Yo) Estoy bien.**
They are not at home.	**(Ellos) No están en casa.**

- Two other words, **estás** and **eres** (from the **tú** form), may also be used to mean you are among family and small children.

- "There is" and "there are" are very simple. In both cases, you use the little word, **hay**:

There's one bathroom.	**Hay un baño.**
There are two bathrooms.	**Hay dos baños.**

I HAVE IT!
¡Lo tengo!

Tener (to have) is another common linking word in Spanish. No doubt you've already discovered its importance in everyday dialogs. Take just a moment to review:

To Have	Tener
I have	**tengo**
you have, he has, she has, it has	**tiene**
they have, you (plural) have	**tienen**
we have	**tenemos**

Read these sample sentences aloud:

I have a problem.	**Tengo un problema.**
She has a white car.	**Tiene un carro blanco.**
They have four children.	**Tienen cuatro niños.**
We have a big house.	**Tenemos una casa grande.**

Even though **tener** literally means "to have," sometimes it's used instead of the verb **estar** to express a temporary condition:

(I am) afraid	**(tengo) miedo**	(he is) sleepy	**(tiene) sueño**
(we are) at fault	**(tenemos) la culpa**	(we are) thirsty	**(tenemos) sed**
(they are) cold	**(tienen) frío**	(you are) right	**(tiene) razón**
(she is) 15 years old	**(tiene) quince años**	(I am) lucky	**(tengo) suerte**
(I am) hot	**(tengo) calor**	(they are) careful	**(tienen) cuidado**
(they are) hungry	**(tienen) hambre**		

Hot Tips!

- To say "not" in Spanish, put the word **no** in front of the verb.

José is not my friend.	**José no es mi amigo.**
I do not have the money.	**No tengo el dinero.**
There are no more.	**No hay más.**

- Spanish uses double negatives, so say **no** twice in your sentences:

No, no hay nada.	No, there is not nothing. (There isn't anything.)
No hay nadie aquí.	There is not no one here. (There isn't anyone.)

SPANISH IN ACTION!
¡Español en acción!

Putting a few words together in a new language is a thrilling experience, but real, meaningful communication begins once you start to use verbs (action words)! Although **estar**, **ser**, and **tener** are extremely useful, they do not express action. Learning how to use Spanish verbs will allow us to talk about what's going on in the world around us.

Notice that Spanish action words end in the letters **ar**, **er**, or **ir**, and they are not to be confused with the command forms you learned earlier:

to clean	**limpiar**	to read	**leer**	to wash	**lavar**
to drive	**manejar**	to run	**correr**	to work	**trabajar**
to eat	**comer**	to sleep	**dormir**	to write	**escribir**
to go	**ir**	to speak	**hablar**		

You can never learn enough action words in Spanish. Over one hundred verbs are listed in the specialized dictionary at the end of this book to be used as a reference tool. When you come across a verb as you study and practice, look it up in Spanish or English to learn its base form and meaning.

Hot Tips!

- You know that many Spanish words resemble their English equivalent. This is true when it comes to verbs. Look:

to absorb	**absorber**	to plant	**plantar**	to visit	**visitar**
to control	**controlar**	to refer		**referir**	

- Careful! False look-alikes are everywhere!

asistir	to attend, not to "assist"
contestar	to answer, not to "contest"
embarazar	to impregnate, not to "embarrass"

- Several Spanish verb infinitives have **se** attached. We'll talk more about this a little later on. Here are some familiar examples:

to stand up	**levantarse**
to sit down	**sentarse**
to lie down	**acostarse**

WHAT'S HAPPENING NOW? THE PRESENT PROGRESSIVE!
¿Qué está pasando ahora? ¡El presente progresivo!

Throughout this guidebook, you'll be introduced to a variety of conjugated verb forms. By practicing the patterns, you'll soon be able to discuss past, present, and future events.

In order to express your thoughts in Spanish, you'll need to learn as many verb tenses as possible. We'll start with the present progressive tense because it refers to what's happening *right now*. The present progressive is similar to our "-ing" form in English.

First, change all your verbs that end in **-AR** to **-ando** endings:

cantar **cantando**
robar **robando**

Second, change your verbs that end in **-ER** and **-IR** to **-iendo** endings:

correr	**corriendo**	**abrir**	**abriendo**
beber	**bebiendo**	**salir**	**saliendo**

Third, use the verb **estar** in the present tense:

estar **estoy, esá(n), estamos**

Now, put them together, and you have a wonderful new way to express complex situations:

I am walking.	**Yo estoy caminando.**
He is counting.	**El está contando.**
We are returning to our home.	**Estamos volviendo a nuestra casa.**
They are running fast.	**Están corriendo rápido.**
She is living in Akron.	**Ella está viviendo en Akron.**
Are we opeing the door?	**¿Estamos abriendo la puerta?**

Now, it's your turn. Follow the three steps with verbs of your own, put them together, and add as many nouns and adjectives as you can! Look at this example:

El está manejando mientras ella está mirando el mapa. Los dos están volviendo de unas hermosas vacaciones.

Hot Tips!

- Some verbs change in pronunciation when you add the **-ndo** ending. Practice:

follow	**seguir**	sleep	**dormir**
following	**siguiendo**	sleeping	**durmiendo**

- Words with the **-ndo** ending are often called gerunds in grammar class, and they have several uses. However, they aren't very common, so we'll just look at some examples:

  ***Estando* en mi casa, escribí muchas cartas.**
  While I was at home, I wrote many letters.

  ***Estudiando* un poco más, podré aprender español.**
  By studying a little more, I'll be able to learn Spanish.

  Miraba a mis hijos *jugando* béisbol en el parque.
  I watched my children playing baseball at the park.

- The present progressive tense was presented in detail in the first *Spanish for Gringos* guidebook. Go back and review those pages if you have to.

¡Yo recuerdo!

Use **tengo** (I have) to answer these questions:

¿Tiene usted un carro blanco? ______________________________

¿Cuántos amigos tiene usted? ______________________________

Tiene usted mucha hambre? ______________________________

Now change these base verbs to the present progressive tense:

caminar	***caminando***	**recibir**	______________
manejar	______________	**seguir**	______________
vender	______________		

Read the following story. How much can you understand?

Yo soy María. Estoy en mi cuarto.
Estoy escribiendo en el libro de inglés.
Hay una mesa y dos sillas en el cuarto.
El cuarto tiene una puerta y dos ventanas.
Mis amigos no están aquí porque están trabajando.

¿Cómo se escribe?

No language is without quirks. Now you must suffer and memorize these spelling changes:

to read	**leer**	reading	**leyendo**
to hear	**oír**	hearing	**oyendo**
to go	**ir**	going	**yendo**
to say	**decir**	saying	**diciendo**
to follow	**seguir**	following	**siguiendo**
to serve	**servir**	serving	**sirviendo**
to sleep	**dormir**	sleeping	**durmiendo**

By the way, most verb infinitives end in **-ar**, so you'll be using a lot of **-andos:**

to study	**estudiar**	studying	**estudiando**
to practice	**practicar**	practicing	**practicando**

Can you add any others?

______________________________ ______________________________

______________________________ ______________________________

______________________________ ______________________________

Verbal Advice
Consejos verbales

One of the most effective ways to put your verbs into action is to combine them with simple phrases that create complete commands. For example, look what happens when you add these verb infinitives to **Favor de...**, which implies, Would you please...:

Please...	**Favor de...**
write the number	**escribir el número**
go to the party	**ir a la fiesta**
speak in English	**hablar en inglés**

Here's another tip. By adding the word **no** in front of the verb, you communicate the command don't:

Please don't eat the food. **Favor de *no* comer la comida.**

Favor de is one of several key expressions that can be found in chapter segments entitled *Verbal Advice*. These phrases are combined with basic verb forms in order to raise your language skills to a higher, more productive level.

Demand It!
¡Ordénelo!

One incredible way to plant basic verbs into the memory is through the use of commands. The command form of verbs can be practiced all day, since all you're doing is telling others what to do. (Respectfully, of course!)

These commands are actually unique forms of Spanish verb infinitives. See the pattern for **-ar** verbs? The ending is **e**:

to speak	**hablar**	to walk	**caminar**
Speak!	**¡Hable!**	Walk!	**¡Camine!**

Now observe what happens to most **-er** and **-ir** verbs. Conversely, they end in **-a**:

to write	**escribir**	to open	**abrir**
Write!	**¡Escriba!**	Open!	**¡Abra!**
to run	**correr**	to read	**leer**
Run!	**¡Corra!**	Read!	**¡Lea!**

Try some:

to point	**señalar**	Point!	____________
to eat	**comer**	Eat!	____________
to look	**mirar**	Look!	____________

The commands above are only exchanged in formal settings. The informal **tú** commands are a little different, and will be discussed later in another **¡Ordénelo!** segment. Watch for the signposts!

Hot Tips!

- Don't be fooled! Spanish has a variety of irregular command forms that have to be memorized. We'll explain more about these changes in the pages ahead:

to go	**ir**	to come	**venir**
Go!	**¡Vaya!**	Come!	**¡Venga!**
to move	**mover**	to bring	**traer**
Move!	**¡Mueva!**	Bring!	**¡Traiga!**
to sit down	**sentarse**	to stand	**levantarse**
Sit down!	**¡Siéntese!**	Stand!	**¡Levántese!**

- To give a command to more than one person, add the letter **n**:

¡Hablen!	Speak, you guys!
¡Corran!	Run, you guys!

- Any vocabulary item can be learned quickly if it's practiced in conjunction with a command word. For example, to pick up the names for furniture, have a native Spanish speaker command you to touch, look at, or point to things throughout the house. This exercise really works, and more importantly, it can be lots of fun:

Touch...	**Toque**	**Toque la mesa.**
Look at...	**Mire**	**Mire la muchacha.**
Point to...	**Señale**	**Señale la casa.**

¿Cómo se escribe?

When it comes to commands, some changes occur in spelling so that the forms can be pronounced correctly. In other words, beware!

to pick up	**recoger**	to touch	**tocar**	to give	**dar**
Pick up...	**Recoja...**	Touch...	**Toque...**	Give...	**Dé...**

EVERY GRINGO SHOULD KNOW: *Cada gringo debe saber:*

Here's one more set of verbs. They could be the most valuable words in the entire book! And, don't forget to read everything out loud!

-AR Verbs

caminar	to walk
cerrar	to close
cocinar	to cook
comprar	to buy
contestar	to answer
dar	to give
empezar	to begin
escuchar	to listen
estudiar	to study
hablar	to speak
jugar	to play
lavar	to wash
limpiar	to clean
llamar	to call
llegar	to arrive
llevar	to carry
manejar	to drive
mirar	to look
pagar	to pay
parar	to stop
pasar	to happen
preguntar	to ask
terminar	to end
tomar	to take
trabajar	to work
usar	to use

-ER Verbs

aprender	to learn
beber	to drink
comer	to eat
correr	to run
entender	to understand
ir	to go
poner	to put
vender	to sell
ver	to see
volver	to return

-IR Verbs

abrir	to open
decir	to say
dormir	to sleep
escribir	to write
leer	to read
morir	to die
recibir	to receive
salir	to leave
venir	to come
vivir	to live

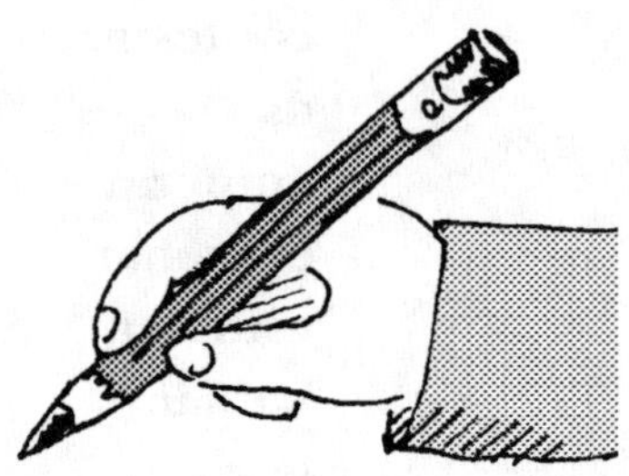

Hot Tips!

- Don't get excited. This brief list covers only a fraction of all the action words you'll need to learn. Dozens more can be found in the back of this guidebook.

- Can you change all these verbs to **-ando** or **-iendo** endings? Look at the previous list, and give it a try!

- Tons of Spanish verbs have more than one meaning in English. Study these examples:

cambiar	to change, to exchange
ganar	to win, to earn
llevar	to carry, to wear
pasar	to pass, to happen
pegar	to hit, to stick
tomar	to take, to drink
probar	to prove, to try

- And many English words have more than one translation in Spanish:

to play (games)	**jugar**
to play (music)	**tocar**
to leave (depart)	**salir**
to leave (behind)	**dejar**
to save (things)	**ahorrar**
to save (life)	**salvar**

- And don't forget those synonyms:

to drink	**tomar, beber**
to walk	**caminar, andar**
to finish	**acabar, terminar**

- Be careful! Sometimes, it pays to be very specific:

to return	**regresar**
to return (something)	**devolver**
to know	**saber**
to know (someone)	**conocer**

¡Yo recuerdo!

Put all your Spanish together as you practice these action words:

aprender (to learn):
Estamos aprendiendo mucho español con este libro excelente.

usar (to use):

____

trabajar (to work):

____

beber (to drink):

____

2

CHAPTER *DOS*
Siempre practico español

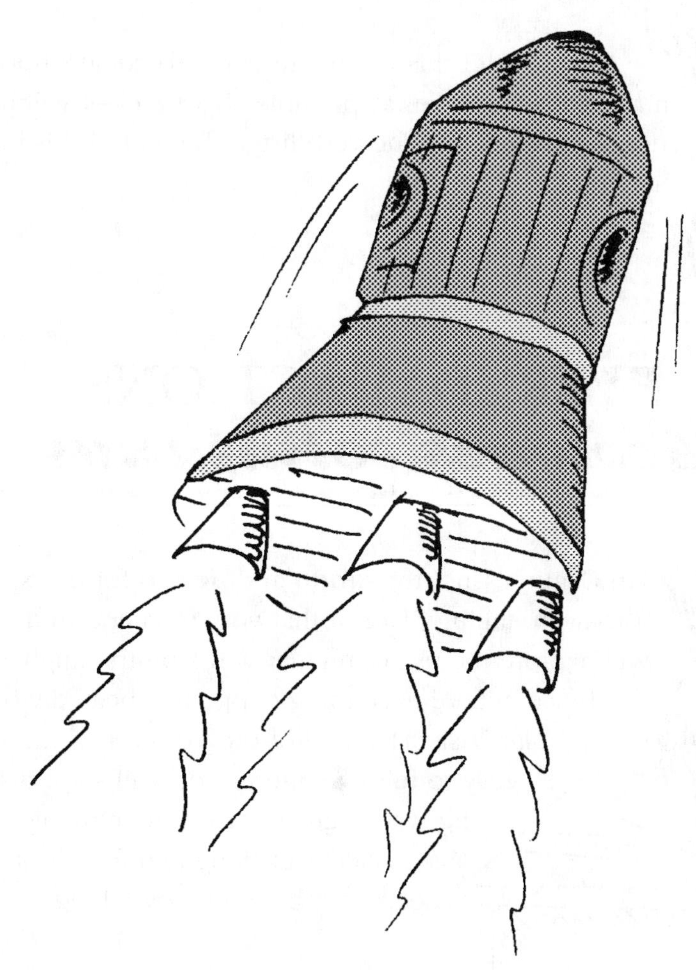

WELCOME TO *PLANET PRESENT TENSE*
Bienvenidos al planeta del tiempo presente

We've fueled up with the basics, and lifted off with a quick review of verb usage. Our flight into advanced Spanish has begun!

Just ahead looms the world of action verbs in the present indicative tense. It's a place that is visited quite frequently, and is best known for its abundance of *regular* and *irregular* inhabitants. Do not fear, however, for Planet Present Tense can be conquered quite easily. All we need are a few shortcuts to successful communication.

As you enter this useful area of verb conjugations, grab onto as many verb infinitives as possible. Trust me—it will make a difference. As always, use the verb list at the end of this book as a reference tool.

EVERYDAY ACTIONS
Acciones cotidianas

In Chapter Uno, the **-ando** and **-iendo** forms expressed actions that were taking place at that very moment. In this chapter, we will explore the use of regular verbs on the mighty Planet Present Tense, where everything happens repeatedly on a pretty regular basis. Here, all of our verb forms follow a consistent, easy-to-follow pattern. You will soon discover that working with regular verbs to communicate everyday activities is exciting and fun. So just relax, take a deep breath, and follow along.

We learned earlier that in order to talk about current action, we alter our endings slightly, much like we do in English:

to speak	**hablar**	to eat	**comer**
I'm speaking.	**Estoy hablando.**	We're eating.	**Estamos comiendo.**

A similar thing happens when we refer to everyday actions in the present tense. However, this time the verbs shift to *the one who completes the action.* More importantly, the forms of **estar** are dropped. This next pattern is the same for most verbs in Spanish.

To Speak	**Hablar**
I speak	**hablo**
You speak; He, She speaks	**habla**
You (plural), They speak	**hablan**
We speak	**hablamos**

To Eat	**Comer**
I eat	**como**
You eat; He, She eats	**come**
You (plural), They eat	**comen**
We eat	**comemos**

To Write	**Escribir**
I write	**escribo**
You write; He, She writes	**escribe**
You (plural), They write	**escriben**
We write	**escribimos**

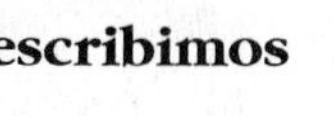

Hot Tips!

- On Planet Present Tense, these three letters send a signal as to who's involved in the action:

Yo	____**o**
Ellos, Ellas, Ustedes	____**n**
Nosotros	____**mos**

- Notice how the **-ar** endings differ from those in the **-er** and **-ir** verbs, yet all the forms seem to follow a similar pattern. This information will be helpful as you pick up more action forms later on.

- Again, there's no need to put the subject pronouns in front of these verb forms since most of the endings tell the listener who is doing the action.

- Look at what happens to the **nosotros** form of **-ir** verbs. It keeps the **i** to make **-imos**. Here's a little jingle to help you recall present tense **ir** verb conjugations:

  IT'S JUST LIKE THE **-ER**, BUT WITH **-IMOS** AT THE END

- If you make the wrong sound in the middle of a verb form—don't stress. As long as your ending is loud and clear, most people can figure out what it is you're trying to say.

- As we mentioned earlier, the **tú** forms of verb conjugations can be acquired at a later time. Learning these four forms is really all you need, and will make memorization a whole lot easier!

- The third person singular form can also refer to "it":

  It eats a lot! **¡Come mucho!**

- Here's how the negative and question forms are put together:

Does he live in the house?	**¿Vive en la casa?**
No, he doesn't live in the house.	**No, no vive en la casa.**

- Sometimes this present indicative tense can be translated differently into English. For example:

Siempre hablo español.	I always speak Spanish.
	I always do speak Spanish.
	I'm always speaking Spanish.

- A great way to remember verb patterns is to write down all four forms on one side of a 3x5 card, and then put the verb infinitive in large letters on the other side. Separate by color if you feel inclined, and then use them as flashcards! Simply look at the infinitive and try to recall each of its conjugated forms without turning the card over. Develop ways to keep things simple:

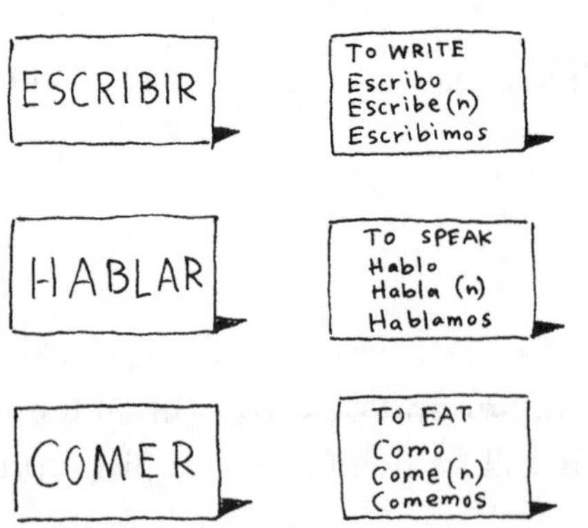

hablo	**como**	**escribo**
habla (n)	**come (n)**	**escribe (n)**
hablamos	**comemos**	**escribimos**

¡Yo recuerdo!

Regular verbs are in demand every day since most conversations center around routine activities. To get a handle on them, it'll take some practice, so spend plenty of time with these next examples. Read each Spanish sentence aloud, and try to translate without looking. Remember, the key lies in the word endings:

Trabajo en el restaurante. I work in the restaurant.
No estudiamos italiano. We don't study Italian.
¿Habla usted español? Do you speak Spanish?
Ella compra muchos libros. She buys a lot of books.
Los niños toman leche. The children drink milk.

Comemos mucha fruta. We eat a lot of fruit.
Carlos vende carros. Carlos sells cars.
¿Lee usted novelas románticas? Do you read romantic novels?
No corro en el parque. I don't run in the park.
¡Aprendemos español! We learn Spanish!

¿Dónde vive usted? Where do you live?
Abro las puertas a las nueve. I open the doors at nine.
No recibimos nada. We don't receive anything.
Escriben en inglés. They write in English.
No permiten perros. They don't allow dogs.

Consejos verbales

Infinitives are picked up best when they're learned as part of a complete phrase or expression:

to call by phone **llamar por teléfono**
to dial the number **marcar el número**
to knock at the door **tocar la puerta**
to watch TV **mirar televisión**

NOTHING LIKE THE PRESENT
Como el presente no hay

On Planet Present Tense, everything you hear refers to regular, repeated activities. So why not add a time-related expression that tells *when* the action takes place? Choose one of these phrases that often accompany comments made in the present indicative tense.

all the time	**todo el tiempo**
always	**siempre**
daily	**a diario**
each week	**cada semana**
every day	**todos los días**
frequently	**con frecuencia**
never	**nunca**
often	**a menudo**
seldom	**casi nunca**
sometimes	**a veces**

Now make sense of these examples!

Siempre maneja muy rápido.
A veces duermen en la sala.
Miramos televisión todos los días.

Hot Tips!

- Remember this page number. The time words above can be used with present tense actions throughout the following chapter, too!

WE PRACTICE AT HOME
Practicamos en casa

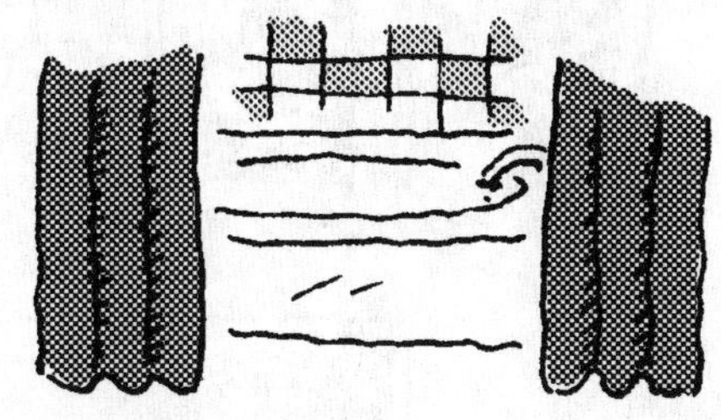

Since many of our daily experiences relate to life around the home, you should expand your household vocabulary in Spanish. Most Spanish students know what all of the rooms are called. Practice your new verb form with the words below:

bathroom	**el baño**	**Limpiamos en el baño.**
bedroom	**el dormitorio**	**Estudiamos en el dormitorio.**
garage	**el garaje**	**Trabajamos en el garaje.**
kitchen	**la cocina**	**Comemos en la cocina.**
living room	**la sala**	**Hablamos en la sala.**

Keep going, but this time, come up with sentences of your own:

attic	**el desván**	________________
basement	**el sótano**	________________
den	**la sala de familia**	________________
dining room	**el comedor**	________________
dressing room	**el vestidor**	________________
guest room	**el cuarto de visitas**	________________
hallway	**el pasillo**	________________
library	**la biblioteca**	________________
playroom	**la sala de juegos**	________________
storeroom	**el depósito**	________________

Now, look over these other parts of **la casa**. Which are easy to recognize and which are not?

balcony	**el balcón**
bar	**el bar**
cabinet	**el gabinete**
ceiling	**el techo**
chimney	**la chimenea**
closet	**el ropero**
door	**la puerta**
driveway	**la entrada para carros**
fence	**la cerca**
floor	**el piso**
fireplace	**el fogón**
gate	**el portón**
pool	**la piscina**
porch	**el pórtico**
roof	**el tejado**
terrace	**la terraza**
wall	**la pared**
window	**la ventana**
yard	**el patio**

Hot Tips!

- Jot down the forms of this popular verb. It's ideal for daily household chitchat:

To Need	**Necesitar**
I need	**necesito** **Necesito una cerca.**
You need; He, She needs	**necesita** **No necesita la piscina.**
You (plural), They need	**necesitan** **¿Necesitan usar el baño?**
We need	**necesitamos** **Necesitamos más ventanas.**

Furniture and Fixtures
Los muebles y las instalaciones

More than likely, you can already name several furnishings all by yourself. Try to translate these Spanish words without looking at the English:

el armario ________________ armoire
el banquillo ________________ stool
el baúl ________________ chest
la cama ________________ bed
la ducha ________________ shower
el escritorio ________________ desk
el estéreo ________________ stereo
la estufa ________________ stove
el excusado ________________ toilet
el fregadero ________________ kitchen sink
la lámpara ________________ lamp
el lavabo ________________ bathroom sink
el librero ________________ bookshelf
la mesa ________________ table
la mesita de noche ________________ nightstand
la pintura ________________ painting
el refrigerador ________________ refrigerator
el reloj ________________ clock
la silla ________________ chair
el sillón ________________ armchair
el sofá ________________ sofa
el teléfono ________________ telephone
el televisor ________________ television
la tina ________________ bathtub
el tocador ________________ dresser

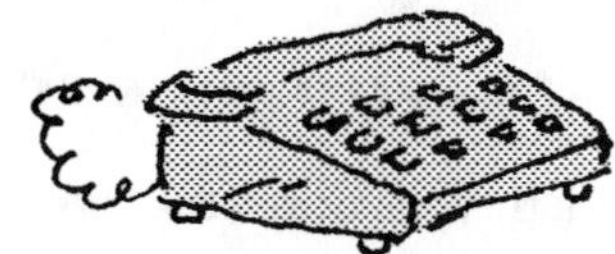

¡Ordénelo!

How are you at giving household commands? Translate the words in parentheses and create a command sentence with the words on their right:

(cortar) corte ______________________________

(quitar) quite ______________________________

(meter) meta ______________________________

(cubrir) cubra ______________________________

(preparar) prepare ______________________________

(cocinar) cocine ______________________________

(mezclar) mezcle ______________________________

¡Yo recuerdo!

Go ahead and read these sample sentences. You know what all the words mean:

¡Mueva las sillas grandes!
Estamos cerrando la puerta.
No tengo muchas pinturas.
¿Dónde está el baño?
El librero es blanco y negro.

And, here's how they talk on Planet Present Tense:

Estudio con mi amiga en el sofá.
Ella siempre habla por teléfono.
Comemos en la mesa cada noche.
Alfredo abre las ventanas todos los días.
Limpiamos las tinas y los excusados.

¿Cómo se escribe?

In Spanish, you don't use a comma between the last two words of a series:

I study, read, and write every day! **¡Estudio, leo y escribo todos los días!**

IT PLEASES ME!
¡Me gusta!

Careful what you say around the house—some words aren't what they seem! Contrary to popular belief, **gustar** doesn't mean "to like" in English. It means "to be pleasing to," and so the word order is reversed. The subject goes after the verb, and whoever receives the action is put in front. These are the words you use:

me	**me**	us	**nos**
you, him, her	**le**	you (plural), they	**les**

Think "backwards!" Check it out:

The car is pleasing to me. (I like it!) **Me gusta el carro.**

The cars are pleasing to her. (She likes them!) **Le gustan los carros.**

The car is not pleasing to us. (We don't like it!) **No nos gusta el carro.**

Are they pleasing to them? (Do they like them?) **¿Les gustan?**

You try it. Use either **gusta** or **gustan**:

We like it.	He likes them.	I don't like them.	Do you like it?
Nos gusta.	**Le gustan.**	___________________	___________________

Hot Tips!

- **Parecer** (to seem) is another unique verb, a lot like **gustar**. Read on:

It seems pretty to me.	Does it seem OK?	They don't seem tall.
Me parece bonito.	**¿Le parece bueno?**	**No nos parecen altos.**

More Household Things
Más cosas caseras

Continue to wander around the house, pointing out things in Spanish. Get as detailed as you like!

bannisters	**las barandas**
curtains	**las cortinas**
draperies	**las colgaduras**
drawers	**los cajones**
faucets	**los grifos**
lamps	**las lámparas**
lampshades	**las pantallas**
rugs	**las alfombras**
screens	**los mosquiteros**
shelves	**las repisas**
shutters	**los postigos**
stairs	**las escaleras**
steps	**los escalones**
windowsills	**los antepechos**

Patio Stuff
Las cosas del patio

Are you still placing removable labels on everything? Keep it up as you head for the yard.

barbeque grill	**la parrilla**
beach chair	**la silla de playa**
hammock	**la hamaca**
lawn chair	**la silla de patio**
trash can	**el bote de basura**
umbrella	**la sombrilla**

The Appliances
Los electrodomésticos

Here's a fun way to practice or review the names for household appliances. Just add a command and start training your friends and family!

Turn on...	**Prenda...**	Move...	**Mueva...**
Turn off...	**Apague...**	Touch...	**Toque...**
Bring...	**Traiga...**	Point to...	**Señale...**
Carry...	**Lleve...**	Plug in...	**Enchufe...**
Look at...	**Mire...**	Unplug...	**Desenchufe...**
Pick up...	**Recoja...**	Clean...	**Limpie...**

air conditioner	**el acondicionador de aire**
answering machine	**el contestador telefónico**
cassette player	**el tocador de casetes**
computer	**la computadora**
dishwasher	**el lavaplatos**
dryer	**la secadora**
fan	**el ventilador**
freezer	**el congelador**
garage door opener	**el abridor de garajes**
hair dryer	**el secador de pelo**
heater	**el calentador**
hot water heater	**el calentador de agua**
microwave	**el horno de microonda**
oven	**el horno**
radio	**el radio**
scale	**la báscula**
sewing machine	**la máquina de coser**
smoke detector	**el detector de humo**
toaster	**la tostadora**
VCR	**la videocasetera**
washer	**la lavadora**

Hot Tips!

- Not everything can be touched or labeled:

plumbing	**la tubería**	electricity	**la electricidad**
heating	**la calefacción**		

- These popular items should be learned in case of emergency:

alarm	**la alarma**
electrical outlet	**el enchufe**
fire extinguisher	**el extintor**
first aid kit	**la caja de primeros auxilios**
fusebox	**la caja de fusibles**
gas meter	**el medidor de gas**
light switch	**el interruptor**
medicine chest	**el botiquín**
security system	**el sistema de seguridad**
thermostat	**el termostato**
water valve	**la válvula de agua**

- How detailed do you want to get?

doorbell	**el timbre**	lock	**la cerradura**
doorknob	**la perilla**	mailbox	**el buzón**

And for Decoration?
¿Y para decoración?

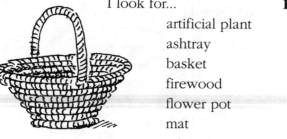

I need...	**Necesito...**
I sell...	**Vendo...**
I look for...	**Busco...**

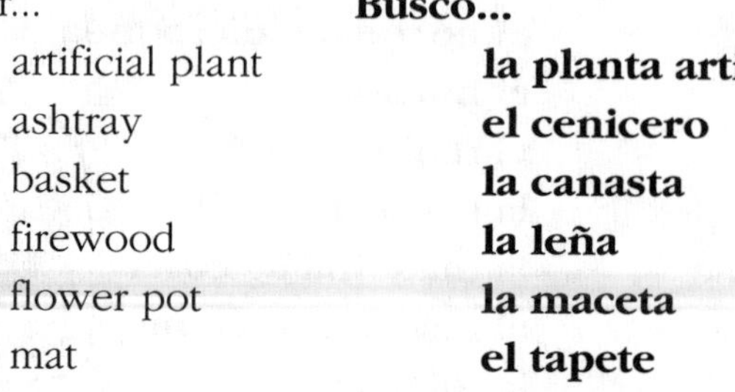

artificial plant	**la planta artificial**
ashtray	**el cenicero**
basket	**la canasta**
firewood	**la leña**
flower pot	**la maceta**
mat	**el tapete**
mirror	**el espejo**
ornament	**el ornamento**
pedestal	**el pedestal**
picture frame	**el marco**
portrait	**el retrato**
pottery	**la loza**
rug	**la alfombra**
statue	**la estatua**
tapestry	**el tapiz**
vase	**el florero**

In the Kitchen
En la cocina

Take a stab at naming all your kitchen wares, utensils, and appliances in Spanish. Say a few things about life around the kitchen, using present tense forms of the regular verbs below:

to cook	**cocinar**
to drink	**beber**
to eat	**comer**
to empty	**vaciar**
to fill	**llenar**
to prepare	**preparar**
to put inside	**meter**
to take out	**sacar**
to use	**usar**
to wash	**lavar**

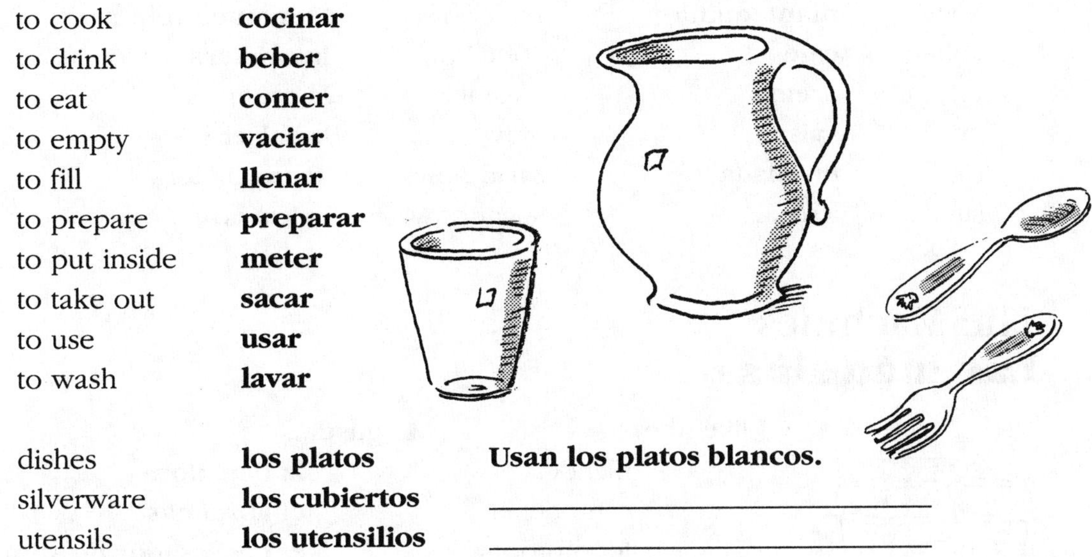

dishes	**los platos**	**Usan los platos blancos.**
silverware	**los cubiertos**	______________________
utensils	**los utensilios**	______________________

Don't stop now!

bowl	**el plato hondo**	plate	**el plato**
china	**la loza de porcelana**	platter	**la fuente**
cup	**la taza**	pot	**la olla**
fork	**el tenedor**	rack	**la rejilla**
fruit dish	**el frutero**	roasting pan	**el asador**
funnel	**el embudo**	rolling pin	**el rodillo**
glass	**el vaso**	salt shaker	**el salero**
griddle	**el comal**	saucepan	**la cacerola**
knife	**el cuchillo**	saucer	**el platillo**
ladle	**el cucharón**	spatula	**la espátula**
mold	**el molde**	spoon	**la cuchara**
napkin	**la servilleta**	strainer	**el colador**
pan	**el sartén**	tea kettle	**la tetera**
peeler	**el pelador**	thermos	**el termo**
pepper shaker	**el pimentero**	tongs	**las tenazas**
pitcher	**el cántaro**	tray	**la bandeja**
placemat	**el tapete individual**		

Hot Tips!

- Note the pattern. The **-era** ending is often added to a food item to make it a container. Observe:

butter	**mantequilla**	butter dish	**la mantequillera**
coffee	**café**	coffee pot	**la cafetera**
cream	**crema**	creamer	**la cremera**
gravy	**salsa**	gravy boat	**la salsera**
salad	**ensalada**	salad bowl	**la ensaladera**
sugar	**azúcar**	sugar bowl	**la azucarera**

The Machines
Las máquinas

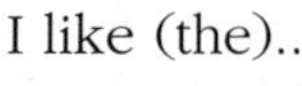

I like (the)...	**Me gusta...**
blender	**la licuadora**
can opener	**el abrelatas**
food processor	**el procesador de alimentos**
garbage disposal	**el desechador**
ice maker	**la hielera**
microwave	**el horno de microonda**
mixer	**la batidora**
popcorn popper	**la máquina de palomitas**
toaster	**el tostador**
trash compacter	**el comprimidor de basura**

¡Yo recuerdo!

Connect the words that belong in the same category:

la azucarera	**la olla**
la lavadora	**el pimentero**
el sartén	**la cremera**
el tenedor	**la secadora**
el salero	**la cuchara**

Check out this sample phrase. How creative can you be?

Usamos ____________________ para ____________________.

Usamos *la licuadora* para *mezclar la leche y el chocolate.*

Usamos *el abrelatas* para *abrir latas.*

Usamos ____________________ para ____________________.

Usamos ____________________ para ____________________.

Usamos ____________________ para ____________________.

Hot Tips!

- Tired? You should be. Hopefully, you've been holding onto or pointing to each of these items as you were saying its Spanish name aloud!

- Don't complain about some of these words being "different" from what you have heard. Vocabulary varies depending on the region the Spanish speaker is from.

- In some parts, Spanglish replaces the proper Spanish word. Listen for items such as **el CD**, **el closet**, **el switch**, **el beeper**, and countless others.

- Homes come in all shapes and sizes. Practice:

He lives in (the)...	**Vive en...**
apartment	**el apartamento**
condominium	**el condominio**
mobile home	**la casa rodante**
cabin	**la cabaña**
tent	**la tienda**

- **La televisión** is TV programming. Don't confuse it with the object itself, **el televisor**.

- Learn how to expand on a simple theme:

painting	**la pintura**
drawing	**el dibujo**
photograph	**la fotografía**
picture	**el cuadro**
portrait	**el retrato**

Consejos verbales

A handful of regular verbs can be combined with various infinitive forms to express meaningful, complete messages. Here are some of the best. Pay special attention to the sample sentences:

To Finish (Doing Something)	**Acabar de**
I finished...	**Acabo de...**
You finished; He, She finished...	**Acaba de...**
You (plural), They finished...	**Acaban de...**
We finished...	**Acabamos de...**
I finished cleaning.	**Acabo de limpiar.**
Did you finish playing?	**¿Acaba de jugar?**
They finished cooking.	**Acaban de cocinar.**

To Must	**Deber**
I must...	**Debo...**
You must; He, She must...	**Debe...**
You (plural), They must...	**Deben...**
We must...	**Debemos...**
We must walk.	**Debemos caminar.**
She must not speak.	**No debe hablar.**
I must read and write.	**Debo leer y escribir.**

To Wish	**Desear**
I wish...	**Deseo...**
You wish; He, She wishes...	**Desea...**
You (plural), They wish...	**Desean...**
We wish...	**Deseamos...**
Do you guys really want to go?	**¿Desean ir ustedes?**
He really wants to paint.	**Desea pintar.**
I really want to study.	**Deseo estudiar.**

Hot Tips!

- To clarify whom you are referring to, state the subject pronoun after the verb form when you ask a question:

  ¿Desea *usted* mover la silla? Do *you* wish to move the chair?

- Make sure you learn all the meanings for the words you use:

  acabar to finish, to end **desear** to wish, to desire, to really want
  deber to must, to owe

¿Cómo se escribe?

Although they may sound normal in conversation, some regular verbs should be labeled as "different" because they require unusual spelling changes. Notice the pattern with these action words. Fill in the translations as you practice:

to catch	**coger:**	**cojo** I catch
		coge You catch; He, She catches
		cogen You (plural), They catch
		cogemos We catch
to choose	**escoger:**	**escojo** ________________
		escoge ________________
		escogen ________________
		escogemos ________________
to protect	**proteger:**	**protejo** ________________
		protege ________________
		protegen ________________
		protegemos ________________
to direct	**dirigir:**	**dirijo** ________________
		dirige ________________
		dirigen ________________
		dirigimos ________________
to pick up	**recoger:**	**recojo** ________________
		recoge ________________
		recogen ________________
		recogemos ________________

USE OF *SE*
Uso del se

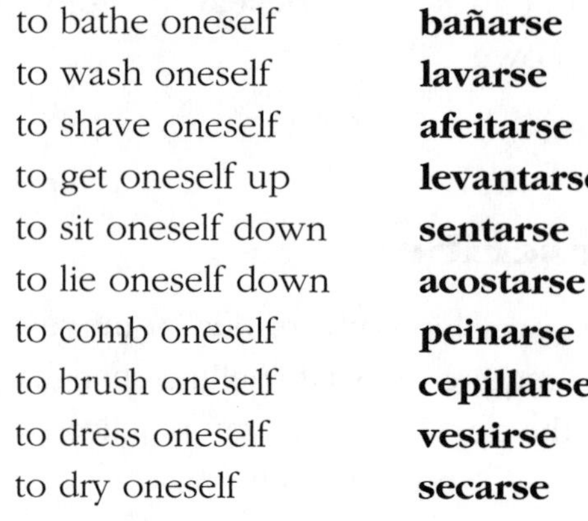

When a verb infinitive has **-se** attached, it usually means that the action is reflexive. Reflexives are actions that we do to ourselves—like shaving, bathing, and lying down. Check out this group of examples:

to bathe oneself	**bañarse**
to wash oneself	**lavarse**
to shave oneself	**afeitarse**
to get oneself up	**levantarse**
to sit oneself down	**sentarse**
to lie oneself down	**acostarse**
to comb oneself	**peinarse**
to brush oneself	**cepillarse**
to dress oneself	**vestirse**
to dry oneself	**secarse**

Here's how they work. The **-se** ending is changed depending upon *who* is involved in the action. If "I" do the action, it changes to **me**, and if "we" do the action, it changes to **nos**. As you study the following sentences, notice the position of each word. Also, see how the base verb form stays with its normal pattern:

I bathe at night.	**Yo me baño en la noche.**
She bathes at night.	**Ella se baña en la noche.**
They bathe at night.	**Ellos se bañan en la noche.**
We bathe at night.	**Nosotros nos bañamos en la noche.**

Now, you explain what's happening here:

María se está cepillando ahora, y yo me estoy peinando.
José se baña todos los días, pero no se afeita.
Mi hermano y yo nos levantamos a las seis.

Hot Tips!

- Note the basic difference:

to wash	**lavar**	to wash oneself	**lavarse**
I wash the car	**Lavo el carro.**	I wash my hands.	**Me lavo las manos.**

- And sometimes **se** changes the meaning of a word:

to go	**ir**
to leave	**irse**
to do	**hacer**
to become	**hacerse**
to lift	**levantar**
to get up	**levantarse**

- **Se** can also be part of a common expression:

to forget about	**olvidarse de**	**Siempre se olvida de su dinero.**
to make fun of	**burlarse de**	**A veces se burlan de mi amiga.**
to realize	**darse cuenta de**	**Nunca se da cuenta del problema.**
to get tired of	**cansarse de**	**Me canso de mi trabajo.**
to complain	**quejarse de**	**Nos quejamos de ella todo el tiempo.**
to hurry up	**darse prisa**	**No me doy prisa en la mañana.**
to fall down	**caerse**	**Los bebés siempre se caen.**
to fall asleep	**dormirse**	**Sandra se duerme temprano.**
to worry about	**preocuparse**	**Me peocupo mucho.**
to behave	**portarse**	**Jaime no se porta bien.**

- Be on the lookout for irregular verbs whose letters change in the middle! All of this will be discussed in the next chapter:

to sit oneself down	**sentarse**	**Se sienta aquí.**
to lie oneself down	**acostarse**	**Se acuesta ahí.**
to dress oneself	**vestirse**	**Se viste allá.**

- If you want, use **se** to indicate "each other":

They write to each other.	**Se escriben.**
They visit each other.	**Se visitan.**
They understand each other.	**Se entienden.**

- Sometimes **se** refers to announcements and general directions:

Clothes are sold here.	**Se vende ropa aquí.**
Spanish is spoken there.	**Se habla español ahí.**
They say the food is good.	**Se dice que la comida es buena.**

- And among friends and family members, continue using the **tú** form. Study the pattern below:

Do you get up early?	**¿Te levantas temprano?**
You bathe a lot.	**Te bañas mucho.**
You don't shave.	**No te afeitas.**

- Many **se** words refer to "get" in English:

to get ready	**arreglarse**
to get ill	**enfermarse**
to get married	**casarse**

- Put the **se** at the end of your **-ndo** verb form if you feel like it:

Está arreglándose.	She's getting ready.
Están vistiéndose.	They're getting dressed.

- Command words are often reflexive, too. The **se** goes *at the end* of these actions, which are directed at one or more people:

You stand up!	**¡Levántese!**
You guys stand up!	**¡Levántense!**

¡Ordénelo!

Negative formal commands are easy. Just say **No**:

Come!	**¡Venga!**	Write, you guys!	**¡Escriban!**
Don't come!	**¡No venga!**	Don't write, you guys!	**¡No escriban!**

But what about the **se** words? Pay attention to the word order:

(levantarse) Don't get up!	**¡No se levante!**
(lavarse) Don't wash, you guys!	**¡No se laven!**
(cepillarse) Don't brush yourself!	**¡No se cepille!**

ALL TOGETHER!
¡Todos juntos!

Beginners in a new language tend to speak in brief, one- or two-word sentences. Conversations generally consist of greetings, expressions, and isolated phrases. Now that you know at least two common verb tenses, why not take a shot at saying longer strings of words. And when you speak, think about sharing separate bits of information, instead of struggling to express too many different ideas at once.
Power through these examples:

I'm driving to the office now with two of my friends.
Estoy manejando a la oficina ahora con dos de mis amigos.

Are they selling the black chairs at the store this week?
¿Están vendiendo las sillas negras en la tienda esta semana?

Raul is writing many things in English and Spanish.
Raúl está escribiendo muchas cosas en inglés y español.

We don't work in the garden today because Bob isn't here.
No trabajamos en el jardín hoy porque Roberto no está aquí.

John eats his dinner in front of the TV every night.
Juan come su cena en frente del televisor todas las noches.

I get up early every morning because I clean the house.
Me levanto temprano cada mañana porque yo limpio la casa.

Hot Tips!

- You don't always have to put your ideas together the same way. In Spanish, as well as in English, emotions and meanings may change according to the way you arrange the words. All you need are the pieces.

Mi padre siempre trabaja en la oficina.	My father always works at the office.
Siempre trabaja en la oficina mi padre.	Always works at the office, my father.
En la oficina mi padre siempre trabaja.	At the office, my father always works.

- Describe your activities by adding a few **-mente** words. They are the **-ly** adverbs in English. To learn more, please observe:

quick	**rápido**	quickly	**rápidamente**
slow	**lento**	slowly	**lentamente**
clear	**claro**	clearly	**claramente**
easy	**fácil**	easily	**fácilmente**
brave	**valiente**	bravely	**valientemente**
sad	**triste**	sadly	**tristemente**

Yo trabajo lentamente y José trabaja rápidamente.

3

CHAPTER *TRES*
Quiero practicar el español

LIFE ON THE DARK SIDE
La vida en el lado oscuro

In the previous chapter, we had the pleasurable experience of playing around with regular verbs on the brighter side of Planet Present Tense.

Gear up, fellow travelers, for now we're headed into much more dangerous territory—the dark land of irregular verbs, where strange and unusual verb forms abound. Our goal will be to capture and categorize as many verbs as we can, and then study their unique characteristics. This mission is so important! For once under our control, these irregular beasts will allow us to sound like we really know what we're talking about!

THEY'RE RADICAL!
¡Son radicales!

In the present tense, regular verbs were easy to work with because they all followed very simple patterns. Irregular verbs differ however, and must be divided into groups that share similar characteristics. One of the largest groups of irregular verbs are called the radical stem-changers. Here are two of its largest families:

The **ie** Family

In one family of verbs, the letter **e** (stem) inside the word changes to **ie**. As you read through these next irregular forms, put emphasis on the **ie** sound. Fortunately, the rest of the letters are the same as regular verbs in the present tense. And look at the **nosotros** form: it doesn't change at all.

To Understand	**Entender**
I understand	**entiendo**
You understand; He, She understands	**entiende**
You (plural), They understand	**entienden**
We understand	**entendemos**

To Want	**Querer**
I want	**quiero**
You want; He, She wants	**quiere**
You (plural), They want	**quieren**
We want	**queremos**

To Lose	**Perder**
I Lose	**pierdo**
You lose; He, She loses	**pierde**
You (plural), They lose	**pierden**
We lose	**perdemos**

Now read a few examples:

I understand a lot of Spanish.	**Entiendo mucho español.**
John wants more money.	**Juan quiere más dinero.**
They always lose their books.	**Siempre pierden sus libros.**

More members:

to advise	**advertir**
to begin	**comenzar**
to boil	**hervir**
to close	**cerrar**
to feel	**sentir**
to lie	**mentir**
to prefer	**preferir**
to refer	**referir**
to think	**pensar**

Hot Tips!

- Notice how irregular verbs end in **-ar**, **-er**, or **-ir**, just like regular verbs do.

- Take what you want from these other **ie** relatives. Most are easy to remember:

to adhere	**adherir**	to convert	**convertir**
to ascend	**ascender**	to defend	**defender**
to attend to	**atender**	to injure	**herir**
to consent	**consentir**	to repent	**arrepentir**

- **Nevar** (to snow), is also a member:
  It snows a lot! **¡Nieva mucho!**

- Note the same kind of shift in these **se** verbs:

to have fun	**divertirse**
She has fun.	**Se divierte.**
to wake up	**despertarse**
He wakes up late.	**Se despierta tarde.**
to sit down	**sentarse**
Where do you sit?	**¿Dónde se sienta usted?**

- Both these verbs mean "to begin":
  empezar **Empieza a las cinco.**
  comenzar **Comienza a las cinco.**

- Learn the **tú** form! Just add an **s:**
  ¿Entiendes? Do you (informal) understand?

Irregularities in verb forms scare the life out of Spanish students, so it's normal if you're feeling a bit uneasy. Just remember—*everything can be memorized* if you file each new verb into a group or family. If you're using the 3x5 system, try dividing the verb groups into different colored cards. And, as always, try them out whenever you get the chance. It may not be easy at first, but over time your brain will begin to do the filing all by itself!

The **ue** Family

Just down the road from the **ie** family is a similar group of Spanish verbs that also have a stem change in the middle. They are the **ue** family and must be memorized, just like their cousins up the street.

The forms below hold true for most **ue** verbs in the present tense, so pay special attention to what's going on. This time, the **o** changes to **ue**. And again, the **nosotros** form is regular:

To Count	**Contar**
I count	**cuento**
You count; He, She counts	**cuenta**
You (plural), They count	**cuentan**
We count	**contamos**

To Be Able To	**Poder**
I can	**puedo**
You, He, She can	**puede**
You (plural), They can	**pueden**
We can	**podemos**

To Sleep	**Dormir**
I sleep	**duermo**
You sleep; He, She sleeps	**duerme**
You (plural), They sleep	**duermen**
We sleep	**dormimos**

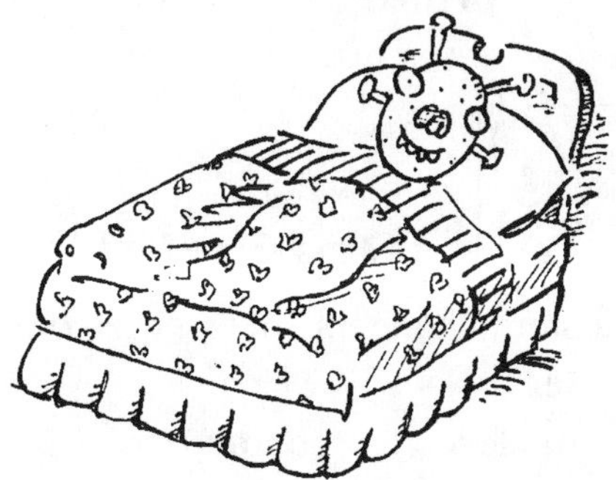

Examples:

We count the books every day.	**Contamos los libros cada día.**
I can write in Spanish.	**Puedo escribir en español.**
She sleeps in her bed.	**Ella duerme en su cama.**

Meet these other important members:

to bite	**morder**	to hang	**colgar**
to die	**morir**	to move	**mover**
to dream	**soñar**	to remember	**recordar**
to find	**encontrar**	to return	**volver**
to fly	**volar**		

Hot Tips!

- Still more **ue** relations:

to bet	**apostar**	to loosen	**soltar**
to cost	**costar**	to prove	**probar**
to dissolve	**disolver**	to remember	**acordarse**
to have lunch	**almorzar**	to renovate	**renovar**
to hurt	**doler**	to show	**mostrar**
to involve	**envolver**	to stir	**revolver**
to lie down	**acostarse**		

- Bear in mind that many Spanish words carry more than one meaning:

acostarse	to lie down, to go to bed
contar	to count, to tell
probar	to prove, to try

¡Ordénelo!

All stem-changers shift in the command words, too:

ie

to close	**cerrar**	Close...	**Cierre...**
to begin	**empezar**	Begin...	**Empiece...**
to think	**pensar**	Think...	**Piense...**

ue

to sleep	**dormir**	Sleep...	**Duerma...**
to move	**mover**	Move...	**Mueva...**
to show	**mostrar**	Show...	**Muestre...**

¡Cierre la puerta y mueva el sofá! Close the door and move the sofa!

¡Yo recuerdo!

Change these irregular verbs from the present progressive tense to the present indicative. In other words, follow the examples given:

I'm thinking.	**Estoy pensando.**
I think.	**Pienso.**
It's moving.	**Está moviendo.**
It moves.	**Mueve.**
They're counting.	**Están contando.**
They count.	________________.
We're losing.	**Estamos perdiendo.**
________________.	________________.
She's sleeping.	**Está durmiendo.**
________________.	________________.
I'm remembering.	**Estoy recordando.**
________________.	________________.
They're closing.	**Están cerrando.**
________________.	________________.

Hot Tips!

- The power of **querer** and **poder** is obvious. Learn their forms before any of the others!

  ¿Puede usted hablar español? **Sí, puedo hablar un poquito.**
  ¡Pero quiero hablar mucho más!

- **Llover** (to rain) is another common **ue** verb:

  It rains a little. **Llueve un poquito.**

- Here's one that actually shifts from a **u** to **ue** in the present tense. Perhaps you can make a special card for it:

  jugar (to play): **juego**, **juega(n)**, **jugamos**

¿Cómo se escribe?

These commands sound normal, but watch the spelling!

to turn off	**apagar**	Turn off...	**Apague...**
to pay	**pagar**	Pay...	**Pague...**
to touch	**tocar**	Touch...	**Toque...**
to take out	**sacar**	Take out...	**Saque...**
to give	**dar**	Give...	**Dé...**

All those abnormal changes in irregular verbs apply also to the **se** series. And don't forget those accent marks!

to sit down	**sentarse**	Sit down	**Siéntese**
to lie down	**acostarse**	Lie down	**Acuéstese**

The **e** to **i** Bunch

Watch out! Another clan of irregulars can be seen roaming around this land of troublesome inhabitants. They're slightly different because their stem shifts from an **e** to an **i**. Here's a typical example. You should know by now what these four conjugations mean:

Pedir — To Ask For

pido	**Pido más dinero.**	I ask for more money.
pide	**No pide nada.**	She doesn't ask for anything.
piden	**Piden muchas cosas.**	They ask for lots of things.
pedimos	**Pedimos un taxi.**	We ask for a taxi.

Now it's your turn. Review the above examples as you write your own sentences below. Keep in mind that each action takes place in the present tense:

Medir — To Measure

mido	**Siempre mido el agua.**	I always meaure the water.
mide	____________	____________
miden	____________	____________
medimos	____________	____________

Servir — To Serve

sirvo	**Siempre sirvo la comida.**	I always serve the food.
sirve	____________	____________
sirven	____________	____________
servimos	____________	____________

Hot Tips!

- Notice how these **e** to **i** verbs all end in **-ir**. There aren't that many to remember, so why not list these words separately on a piece of paper and practice their forms when you have the time. Here are a few more:

to block	**impedir**	to invest	**invertir**
to compete	**competir**	to melt	**derretir**
to conceive	**concebir**	to repeat	**repetir**
to expedite	**expedir**	to surrender	**rendir**

- Add these **se** verbs to the list:

despedirse	to say goodbye	**Se despide cada mañana.**
reirse	to laugh	**Se ríe mucho.**
vestirse	to get dressed	**Se viste muy rápido.**

- Caution! Don't confuse **pedir** (to ask for) with **preguntar** (to ask)!

- Are you adding these phrases to each of your sentences? Remember—we're still on Planet Present Tense!:

todos los días	**Consiguen muchos papeles todos los días.**
cada semana	**Cada semana ella sirve buena comida.**
siempre	**Siempre pedimos más trabajo.**
nunca	**Nunca me visto en el baño.**
a veces	**Los niños compiten a veces.**

¿Cómo se escribe?

Check over the spelling changes in the following verb forms. Fill in the blanks with their translations:

Seguir — To Follow

sigo I follow
sigue ________________
siguen ________________
seguimos ________________

This pattern also applies to these other **e** to **i** words:
conseguir (to get)
perseguir (to pursue)
extinguir (to extinguish)
distinguir (to distinguish)

¡Ordénelo!

The **e** to **i** commands change in a similar way:

to repeat	**repetir**	Repeat...	**Repita...**
to serve	**servir**	Serve...	**Sirva...**
to follow	**seguir**	Follow...	**Siga...**
to get dressed	**vestirse**	Get dressed...	**Vístase...**

EVIL VERBS
Los verbos malvados

Until now, our trip to the dark side of Planet Present Tense has included visits to three verb families that require some kind of change within their conjugated forms.

Guess what? These beings are *not* the only inhabitants here. A closer look around reveals numerous other misfits who seem to follow no rules at all. As a result, each of the following troublemakers should be studied separately. Here are a few that you already know:

Ir To Go

voy I go
va You go; He, She goes
van You (plural), They go
vamos We go

Take a minute to fill in these translations:

Tener To Have

tengo ________________
tiene ________________
tienen ________________
tenemos ________________

Estar To Be

estoy ________________
está ________________
están ________________
estamos ________________

Ser To Be

soy ________________
es ________________
son ________________
somos ________________

Try these! You are taking notes, aren't you?

Venir To Come

vengo ________________
viene ________________
vienen ________________
venimos ________________

Decir To Say

digo ________________
dice ________________
dicen ________________
decimos ________________

Oír To Hear

oigo ________________
oye ________________
oyen ________________
oímos ________________

Practice reading aloud:

¿Cuándo vienen los doctores?
¿Qué dice usted?
¿Quién oye la música?

This next set is only weird in the **yo** form. Remember the shortcut to memorization—add an **n** to indicate the plural, and a **mos** to refer to we:

Caer	To Fall	**Dar**	To Give
caigo	______	***doy***	______
cae (n)	______	**da (n)**	______
caemos	______	**damos**	______

Hacer	To Do, Make	**Poner**	To Put
hago	______	***pongo***	______
hace (n)	______	**pone (n)**	______
hacemos	______	**ponemos**	______

Salir	To Leave	**Traer**	To Bring
salgo	______	***traigo***	______
sale (n)	______	**trae (n)**	______
salimos	______	**traemos**	______

Traigo **mi libro,** ***hago*** **mucho trabajo y** ***salgo*** **a las cinco.**

Keep going:

Caber	To Fit	**Valer**	To Be Worth	**Ver**	To See
quepo	______	**valgo**	______	**veo**	______
cabe (n)	______	**vale (n)**	______	**ve (n)**	______
cabemos	______	**valemos**	______	**vemos**	______

Now, study and translate:

El piano no cabe en la casa.
Los carros valen mucho.
Siempre vemos nuestros amigos.

To know or To know?
¿Saber o conocer?

Keep your eyes on this dynamic duo. The verbs **saber** and **conocer** both mean "to know," but here's how they differ. **Saber** means "to know something," while **conocer** means "to know someone":

sé	**No sé el número.**	I don't know the number.
sabe	**Sabe la información.**	He knows the information.
saben	**¿Saben mucho?**	Do you know a lot?
sabemos	**Sabemos cocinar.**	We know how to cook.
conozco	**Le conozco a su tío.**	I know your uncle.
conoce	**¿Le conoce a usted?**	Does he know you?
conocen	**No le conocen a Luz.**	They know Luz.
conocemos	**Le conocemos a él.**	We know him.

Hot Tips!

- Don't look at me! You are responsible for finding out the informal **tú** forms for each of the verbs mentioned.

- In Spanish, the little word **a** must be used when an action is directed toward people. It's called the personal **a**. Notice its position:

We always visit Mary.	**Siempre visitamos *a* María.**
I don't understand the teacher.	**No entiendo *a* la profesora.**
Can you call your friend?	**¿Puede usted llamar *a* su amigo?**

And don't confuse the personal **a** with the word **a** (to) in Spanish:

He knows Cecilia.	**El conoce *a* Cecilia.**
He goes to Cecilia.	**El va *a* Cecilia.**

- We'll learn about the word **le** just ahead!

LE, LO, AND LA

It's not the big words that create turmoil when learning Spanish. It's usually the little ones like **le**, **lo**, and **la**. The simplest way to explain them is to define their general usage. In most Spanish-speaking countries, **le** and its plural form **les** are object pronouns that refer to people:

le	you, to you, for you, him, to him, for him, her, to her, for her
les	you, to you, for you (plural), them, to them, for them

In most sentences, **le** and **les** go in front of the verb:

***Le* mando mucho dinero.**	I send lots of money to him.
***Les* compramos la comida.**	We buy the food for them.
***Le* entiendo.**	I understand you.

The words **lo** and **la**, along with their plural forms, **los** and **las**, are a little different. Although in some dialects they can refer to people, you'll be fine if you use them with things instead:

lo, los	it, them (masculine)
la, las	it, them (feminine)

Again, put them in front of the verbs:

***Lo* tengo.**	I have it.
***La* quieren comer.**	They want to eat it.
No *los* encuentro.	I can't find them.
***Las* estamos abriendo.**	We're opening them.

Hot Tips!

- **Le** goes with these other people words. Feel free to use them all the time. Notice their positions as pronouns:

***Le* habla.**	He talks to her.
***Les* habla.**	He talks to them.
***Me* habla.**	He talks to me.
***Nos* habla.**	He talks to us.

- **Lo** is also part of a common expression. Figure out how you can use it, too.

  The good thing is... **Lo bueno es...**
  The bad thing is... **Lo malo es...**
  The important thing is... **Lo importante es...**

- And some **lo** phrases are real popular:

  I know **Lo sé**
  The best **Lo mejor**
  I'm sorry **Lo siento**

- **La** and **las** are also definite articles:

  La casa (the house) **Las casas** (the houses)

- The informal form of "you" in this case is **te**:

  I want to write you. **Te quiero escribir.**

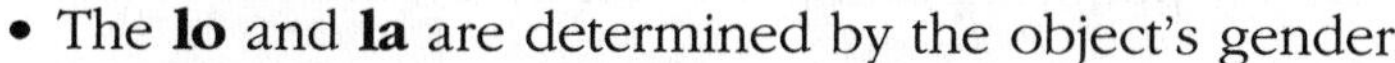

- The **lo** and **la** are determined by the object's gender:

  ¿El libro? **Lo uso.**
  ¿La pluma? **La uso.**

- Most object pronouns can be placed at the end of these important base verb forms:

  I want to tell you. **Quiero decirle.**
  You need to eat them. **Necesita comerlos.**
  They can see me. **Pueden verme.**

- The toughest part of pronoun usage is when they all are used together. Just remember that the people pronouns go first, followed by the "object" ones:

  Me lo prepara. He prepares it for me.
  Nos la cantan. They sing it to us.

Now, if **le** or **les** are involved, they are changed to the word **se**.

(Le) Se lo prepara. He prepares it for her.
(Les) Se la cantan. They sing it to them.

This is important! **Le** and **les** are never found in the same structure with **lo** or **la**!

- Have you noticed? Using object pronouns is another example of the reversal rule in Spanish, since the order is backwards.

Ordénelo!

Whether it's **le**, **lo**, or **la**, it always goes at the tail end of an affirmative command. By the way, notice the accent marks:

Háblele en español.	Talk to him in Spanish.
Tráigala mañana.	Bring it tomorrow.
¡Préndalas!	Turn them on!
Míreles.	Look at them.
¡Ordénelo!	Demand it!

And do the same with **me** and **nos:**

Escríbame, por favor.	Write me, please.
Díganos todo.	Tell us everything.

Now put them all together! Insert the "people" pronouns before the others. Again, the **le** and **les** must change to **se**:

Hágamelo.	Do it for me.
Tráigasela.	Bring it to her.

¡Yo recuerdo!

Translate into Spanish:

I never ask for money. ______________________________

Repeat in Spanish, please. ______________________________

Sometimes we go to his house. ______________________________

They hear music. ______________________________

She puts the books on the table. ______________________________

I leave at three. ______________________________

Do you know his name? ______________________________

We don't know Ricardo. ______________________________

Fill in the blank with **le**, **lo**, or **la**:

¿El libro? _____ leo en la noche.
¿Tony? _____ llama por teléfono.
¿Su amigo? _____ da mucho trabajo.
¿La casa? _____ estamos pintando.
¿Mi carro? _____ pueden llevar.

Consejos verbales

The infinitive sometimes functions as a concept or thing:

the dawn	**el amanecer**
a duty	**un deber**
the power	**el poder**

Now look at these:

Reading is fantastic.	**Leer es fantástico.**
Eating fruit is important.	**Comer fruta es importante.**
Smoking is bad.	**Fumar es malo.**

FAMILY PROBLEMS
Problemas en la familia

Stay on your toes! A few gangs of verb forms seem to be causing trouble on the Dark Side. Just follow along, and don't allow them to bother you.

-Uir and Company

Verbs ending in the letters **-uir** are a lot alike. Check out the **y** sound as you translate:

incluir (to include)
incluyo, incluye (n), incluimos

construir (to construct)
construyo, construye (n), construimos

contribuir (to contribute)
contribuyo, contribuye (n), contribuimos

huir (to escape)
huyo, huye (n), huimos

destruir (to destroy)
destruyo, destruye (n), destruimos

We build houses.	**Construimos casas.**
She contributes a lot.	**Contribuye mucho.**
They destroy everything.	**Destruyen todo.**

The **-cer** and **-cir** Clan

Verbs ending in either **-cer** or **-cir** are pretty harmless in the Present Tense. Only the **yo** form is strange. Watch, and keep translating:

ofrecer (to offer)
ofrezco, ofrece (n), ofrecemos

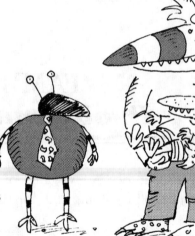

obedecer (to obey)
obedezco, obedece (n), obedecemos

agradecer (to thank)
agradezco, agradece (n), agradecemos

Take on these other members of the **-cer** tribe, who follow the formula above:

aparecer (to appear)
conocer (to know someone)
nacer (to be born)
parecer (to seem)
pertenecer (to belong)

The **-cir** group is the same, but keeps **-imos** at the end:

conducir (to conduct)
conduzco, conduce (n), conducimos

producir (to produce)
produzco, produce (n), producimos

reducir (to reduce)
reduzco, reduce (n), reducimos

traducir (to translate)
traduzco, traduce (n), traducimos

Hot Tips!

- Obviously, you don't have to learn every one of these present tense forms right now. Only focus on those verbs that will meet your immediate needs.
- If you use cards to practice the present tense, make a brightly colored card for each of the really bizarre verbs!
- Remember that the **uir** group doesn't include verbs ending in **guir**.
- The forms of the verb **haber** (to have) are popular when you form the perfect tenses, which will be covered in a chapter up ahead. Don't confuse **haber** with **tener**. Watch:

I have eaten.	***He* comido.**	They have worked.	***Han* trabajado.**
He has gone.	***Ha* ido.**	We have played.	***Hemos* jugado.**

I have a problem. ***Tengo* un problema.**

¡Yo recuerdo!

Without looking back, write in the four present tense forms of these irregular verbs:

construir ________________ ________________ ________________ ________________
obedecer ________________ ________________ ________________ ________________
reducir ________________ ________________ ________________ ________________

LOTS OF PEOPLE
Muchas personas

Let's now explore the world of Spanish vocabulary words. In Chapter Dos, we learned the names of items in and around the home. This time, let's gather words that relate to people, or **la gente.**

There's a good chance you already know some of the following names. These words are very basic, so pay close attention. To refer to females, change **el** to **la** and, in most cases, change the last letter of the person to **a:**

adult	**el adulto**	**la adulta**
teenager	**el adolescente**	**la adolescente**
partner	**el socio**	**la socia**
elderly person	**el anciano**	____________
buddy	**el compañero**	____________
gentleman	**el caballero**	____________

It's (the)...	**Es...**
girlfriend, bride	**la novia**
boyfriend, groom	**el novio**
lady	**la dama**
enemy	**el enemigo**
youth	**el joven**
roommate	**el compañero de cuarto**
lover	**el amante**

A LOT OF FAMILY
Mucha familia

La familia is a big deal in Spanish-speaking countries, so go as far as you can with this list below. If you feel brave enough, make a remark in the present tense, using the base verb provided. But beware! Most of these action words are irregular!

aunt	**la tía**	**(trabajar)**	***Mi tía trabaja mucho.***
brother-in-law	**el cuñado**	**(vivir)**	***Su cuñado vive en México.***
cousin	**el primo**	**(saber)**	***Nuestro primo sabe cocinar.***
daughter-in-law	**la nuera**	**(hablar)**	______________
father-in-law	**el suegro**	**(querer)**	______________
granddaughter	**la nieta**	**(bañarse)**	______________
grandfather	**el abuelo**	**(entender)**	______________
grandmother	**la abuela**	**(comer)**	______________
grandson	**el nieto**	**(jugar)**	______________
mother-in-law	**la suegra**	**(dormir)**	______________
nephew	**el sobrino**	**(construir)**	______________
niece	**la sobrina**	**(pedir)**	______________
sister-in-law	**la cuñada**	**(seguir)**	______________
son-in-law	**el yerno**	**(ir)**	______________
uncle	**el tío**	**(poder)**	______________

More family fun:

parents	**los padres**
grandparents	**los abuelos**
great grandparents	**los bisabuelos**
great grandchildren	**los bisnietos**
great-great grandparents	**los tatarabuelos**
great-great grandchildren	**los tataranietos**

Hot Tips!

- Everyone around us can be identified. Acquire the names for each individual:

citizen	**el ciudadano**	immigrant	**el inmigrante**
disabled	**el incapacitado**	neighbor	**el vecino**
foreigner	**el extranjero**	resident	**el residente**
homeless	**el desamparado**	visitor	**el visitante**

- Talk about our physical differences. Again, females would end in **a**:

twin	**gemelo**	left-handed	**zurdo**
blind	**ciego**	mute	**mudo**
cross-eyed	**bizco**	near-sighted	**miope**
deaf	**sordo**	one-eyed	**tuerto**
dwarf	**enano**	right-handed	**diestro**
far-sighted	**présbita**	handicapped	**minusválido**
giant	**gigante**	male	**masculino**
lame	**cojo**	female	**femenino**

- Most of these terms can be found on application forms. They refer to marital status:

divorced	**divorciado**
married	**casado**
separated	**separado**
single	**soltero**
widowed	**viudo**

- Conduct a brief family interview in Spanish, or whip out the old picture albums and start pointing. Can you recognize any of these people?

Godmother	**la madrina**	stepmother	**la madrastra**
Godfather	**el padrino**	stepfather	**el padrastro**
Godson	**el ahijado**	stepson	**el hijastro**
Goddaughter	**la ahijada**	stepdaughter	**la hijastra**

RACE AND NATIONALITY
Raza y nacionalidad

Identify the folks around you by race and nationality. Use these Spanish words to describe:

She's...	**Ella es...**
Asian	**asiática**
black	**negra**
Hispanic	**hispana**
Latin	**latina**
Middle Eastern	**medio-oriental**
Native American	**amerindia**
Polynesian	**polinesia**
white	**blanca**

He's...	**Él es...**
African-American	**afroamericano**
Anglo-Saxon	**anglosajón**
Asian-American	**asiáticoamericano**
Latin-American	**latinoamericano**

Here's another pattern. Just stick in the appropriate word:

The money is...	**El dinero es...**
African	**africano**
Arab	**árabe**
Australian	**australiano**
Canadian	**canadiense**
Chinese	**chino**
Dutch	**holandés**
English	**inglés**
French	**francés**
German	**alemán**
Greek	**griego**
Irish	**irlandés**
Italian	**italiano**
Japanese	**japonés**
Portuguese	**portugués**

Russian	**ruso**
Scottish	**escocés**
Spanish	**español**
Swedish	**sueco**
Swiss	**suizo**
U.S.	**norteamericano**
Vietnamese	**vietnamita**

And how about south of the border?

I'm ________	**Soy ________**
Argentinian	**argentino**
Bolivian	**boliviano**
Brazilian	**brasileño**
Chilean	**chileno**
Costa Rican	**costarricense**
Cuban	**cubano**
Dominican	**dominicano**
Ecuadorean	**ecuatoriano**
Guatemalan	**guatemalteco**
Haitian	**haitiano**
Honduran	**hondureño**
Mexican	**mexicano**
Nicaraguan	**nicaragüense**
Panamanian	**panameño**
Paraguayan	**paraguayo**
Peruvian	**peruano**
Puerto Rican	**puertorriqueño**
Salvadorean	**salvadoreño**
Uruguayan	**uruguayo**
Venezuelan	**venezolano**

¿Cómo se escribe?

- Check out this new vocabulary. Notice what *is not capitalized* in Spanish!

You are...	**Usted es...**
Buddhist	**budista**
Catholic	**católico**
Christian	**cristiano**
Jewish	**judío**
Muslim	**musulmán**
Protestant	**protestante**

It's...	**Es...**
European	**europeo**
U.S.	**estadounidense**
Indian	**indio**

- Did you catch the unique letter **ü** in **nicaragüense**? It's pronounced "gw," as in Gwendolyn.

¡Yo recuerdo!

Connect the opposites:

yerno	**diestro**
zurdo	**nuera**
joven	**miope**
amigo	**enemigo**
présbita	**adulto**

Finish this list:

España	***español*** ________
Portugal	________________
Grecia	________________
Francia	________________
Inglaterra	________________
Canadá	________________

WHAT'S YOUR PROFESSION?
¿Cuál es su profesión?

Big-time conversations in Spanish often include phrases about people at work. Do you know what your job title is **en español**? As long as we're chatting about occupations, why not take on this next list of vocabulary words. How would you alter these terms if they referred to females?

architect	**el arquitecto**
carpenter	**el carpintero**
cashier	**el cajero**
clerk	**el dependiente**
consultant	**el consultor**
cook	**el cocinero**
data processor	**el procesador de datos**
dentist	**el dentista**
doctor	**el doctor**
engineer	**el ingeniero**
farmer	**el campesino**
firefighter	**el bombero**
lawyer	**el abogado**
mail carrier	**el cartero**
mechanic	**el mecánico**
nurse	**el enfermero**
plumber	**el plomero**
police officer	**el policía**
salesman	**el vendedor**
secretary	**el secretario**
teacher	**el maestro**
waiter	**el mesonero**

MORE WORKERS!
¡Más trabajadores!

Continue practicing your present tense verb forms with this next series of job-related terminology. These titles are a little more career-specific, so find a special verb to fit the pattern.

artist	**el artista**	***El artista pinta mucho.***
janitor	**el conserje**	***El conserje limpia todo.***
babysitter	**el niñero**	__________
bartender	**el cantinero**	__________
bellhop	**el botones**	__________
chauffeur	**el chofer**	__________
contractor	**el contratista**	__________
dishwasher	**el lavaplatos**	__________
gardener	**el jardinero**	__________
laborer	**el obrero**	__________
librarian	**el bibliotecario**	__________
maid	**el criado**	__________
painter	**el pintor**	__________
surgeon	**el cirujano**	__________
truck driver	**el camionero**	__________
typist	**el mecanógrafo**	__________
writer	**el escritor**	__________

It's always good to know what to call folks in the business world. Work on these for awhile. Are you still making changes according to everyone's sex? Follow along:

owner	**el dueño**	***la dueña***
president	**el presidente**	***la presidente***
assistant	**el asistente**	__________
boss	**el jefe**	__________
client	**el cliente**	__________
employee	**el empleado**	__________
employer	**el empresario**	__________
manager	**el gerente**	__________
supervisor	**el supervisor**	__________

- Some job titles are more unique than others. Do you know anyone involved in these professions?

actor	**el actor**	judge	**el juez**
actress	**la actriz**	minister	**el pastor**
astronaut	**el astronauta**	musician	**el músico**
athlete	**el atleta**	pilot	**el piloto**
clown	**el payaso**	priest	**el sacerdote**
comedian	**el comediante**	soldier	**el soldado**
guide	**el guía**	thief	**el ladrón**

- Have you noticed how some of these titles break the rules about **el** and **la**?

el atleta
el dentista
el astronauta

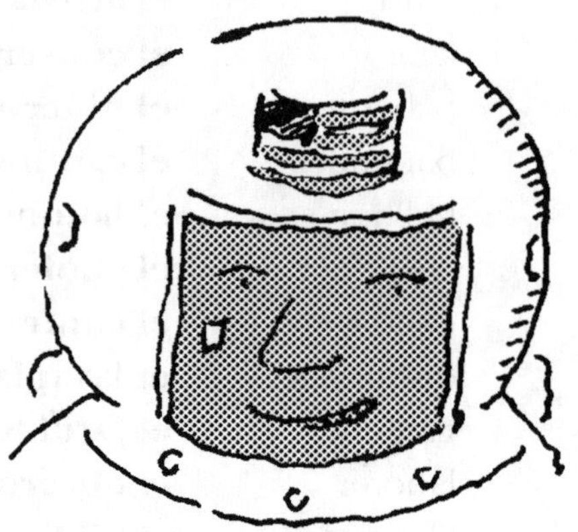

Consejos verbales

Use any form from these verbs, along with an infinitive, to express complete meaningful messages:

Tener que to have to
Tengo que trabajar I have to work

Deber should
Debemos trabajar We should work

Acabar de to have just finished
Acabo de trabajar I just finished working

Volver a to do it again
Vuelve a trabajar She's working again

Necesitar to need
Necesito trabajar I need to work

Poder to be able
Pueden trabajar They are able to work

Querer to want
Queremos trabajar We want to work

PLEASE DESCRIBE
Favor de describir

Strengthen your supply of vocabulary with these helpful words below. Use the sample sentences to practice your grammar:

Carlos es __________ y __________.
Es un muchacho __________.
María es __________ y __________.
Es una muchacha __________.

bald	**calvo**
beautiful	**bello**
blonde	**rubio**
brave	**valiente**
brunette	**moreno**
cowardly	**cobarde**
crazy	**loco**
curious	**curioso**
dark-skinned	**moreno**
dumb	**tonto**
healthy	**saludable**
industrious	**trabajador**
interesting	**interesante**
lazy	**perezoso**
mature	**maduro**
middle-aged	**de edad mediana**
nice	**simpático**
older	**mayor**
pale	**pálido**
patient	**paciente**
polite	**cortés**
prompt	**puntual**
quiet	**quieto**
red-headed	**pelirrojo**
rough	**tosco**
rude	**rudo**
sane	**cuerdo**
shy	**tímido**
smart	**inteligente**
strange	**extraño**
sure	**seguro**
wise	**sabio**
younger	**menor**

Bear in mind that dozens of descriptive words end in the letters **oso**. Notice how each evolves from an important root word:

ambitious	**ambicioso**	ambition	**ambición**
dangerous	**peligroso**	danger	**peligro**
famous	**famoso**	fame	**fama**
friendly	**amistoso**	friendship	**amistad**
funny	**chistoso**	joke	**chiste**
white-haired	**canoso**	white hair	**cana**
loud	**ruidoso**	noise	**ruido**
proud	**orgulloso**	pride	**orgullo**
valuable	**valioso**	value	**valor**
wonderful	**maravilloso**	wonder	**maravilla**

Hot Tips!

- If you are serious about describing someone, talk more about their looks. There are all kinds of people:

barefoot	**descalzo**	scar	**cicatriz**
glasses	**lentes**	tattoo	**tatuaje**
naked	**desnudo**	wig	**peluca**

- You've probably figured out that a lot of descriptive words in Spanish end in either the letters **ado** or **ido**. This participle verb form is a simple alteration of our base action word. Although we'll be talking more about this later, take a few minutes to read through these examples:

to confuse	**confundir**	confused	**confundido**
to surprise	**sorprender**	surprised	**sorprendido**
to tire	**cansar**	tired	**cansado**

- Seek out all the vocabulary that you can. Here are a few of my favorites:

I'm...	**Estoy...**
available	**disponible**
busy	**ocupado**
lost	**perdido**
ready	**listo**
wrong	**equivocado**

- Some descriptive words can go *before* the thing being described. This indicates a deeper quality or characteristic.

good food	**comida buena**	excellent food	**buena comida**

But watch out! A few letters are dropped when you describe in the masculine:

good car	**carro bueno**	big man	**hombre grande**
great car	**buen carro**	fine man	**gran hombre**

- At your new Spanish level, all the words below will be required. Look! It'll be easier if you learn them as opposites:

hard	**duro**	clear	**claro**
soft	**blando**	dark	**oscuro**
open	**abierto**	straight	**recto**
closed	**cerrado**	crooked	**torcido**
broad	**ancho**	wet	**mojado**
narrow	**estrecho**	dry	**seco**
deep	**profundo**	rough	**áspero**
shallow	**bajo**	smooth	**liso**
empty	**vacío**	heavy	**pesado**
full	**lleno**	light	**ligero**
thick	**grueso**	tight	**apretado**
thin	**delgado**	loose	**flojo**
better	**mejor**	dull	**romo**
worse	**peor**	sharp	**afilado**

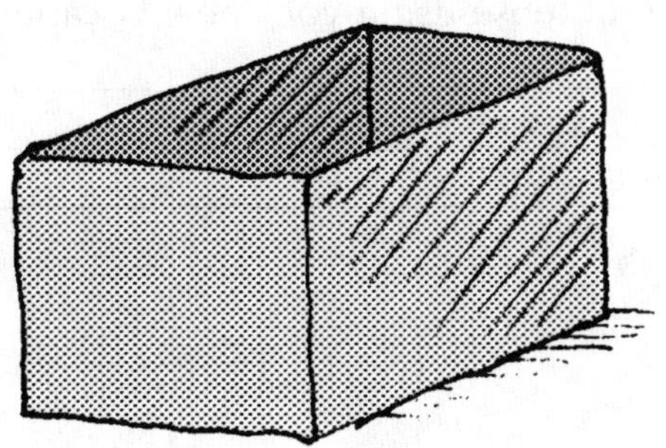

¡Yo recuerdo!

What's the opposite?

ancho	______
correcto	______
ruidoso	______
mojado	______
cobarde	______
vacío	______

Name the base verbs here:

abandoned	**abandonado**	______
calm	**calmado**	______
intoxicated	**intoxicado**	______
numb	**adormecido**	______
used	**usado**	______

Translate without any help. And say each word aloud:

necesario	______	**fantástico**	______
terrible	______	**profesional**	______
sentimental	______	**diligente**	______
magnífico	______	**romántico**	______
correcto	______	**cruel**	______
probable	______	**imaginativo**	______
posible	______	**intelectual**	______

What's happening here? That's right—the **in** means not:

correcto	______	**incorrecto**	______
quieto	______	**inquieto**	______
cómodo	______	**incómodo**	______

Now, write a few practice sentences in the present tense using your new vocabulary:

______

______

______

HOW'S IT GOING?
¡Qué tal!

In any language, describing what people look like is only part of the picture. It's also a good idea to discuss what's going on inside the person. Act out these emotions as you practice. For ladies, please change the final letter **o** to **a**:

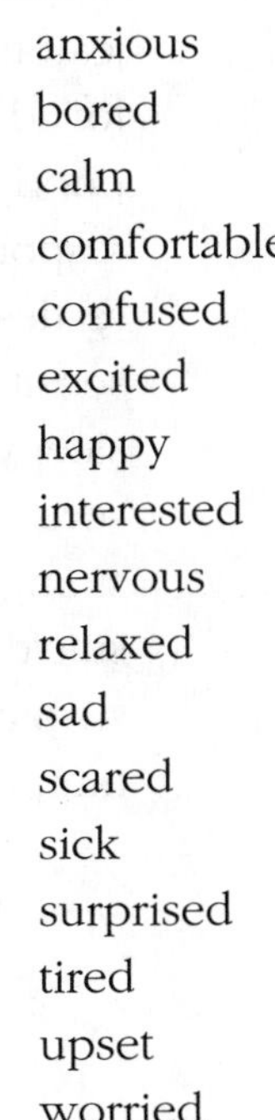

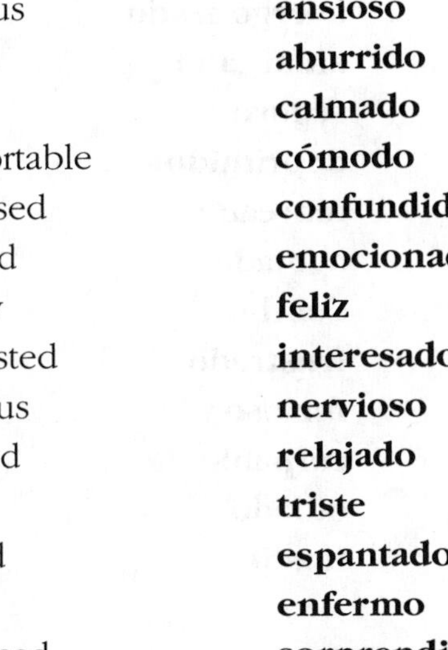

I am...	**Estoy...**
anxious	**ansioso**
bored	**aburrido**
calm	**calmado**
comfortable	**cómodo**
confused	**confundido**
excited	**emocionado**
happy	**feliz**
interested	**interesado**
nervous	**nervioso**
relaxed	**relajado**
sad	**triste**
scared	**espantado**
sick	**enfermo**
surprised	**sorprendido**
tired	**cansado**
upset	**enojado**
worried	**preocupado**

HOW DO YOU FEEL?
¿Cómo se siente?

Tell your therapist about your feelings!

I feel... **Me siento...**

abused	**abusado**	impatient	**impaciente**
apathetic	**apático**	insecure	**inseguro**
ashamed	**avergonzado**	jealous	**celoso**
bitter	**amargado**	loved	**amado**
confident	**seguro**	poorly	**mal**
depressed	**deprimido**	responsible	**responsable**
dizzy	**mareado**	restless	**inquieto**
exhausted	**agotado**	sensitive	**sensible**
faint	**débil**	sleepy	**soñoliento**
frustrated	**frustrado**	sore	**dolorido**
furious	**furioso**	strange	**raro**
guilty	**culpable**	suicidal	**suicida**
hated	**odiado**	suspicious	**sospechoso**
hostile	**hostil**	trapped	**atrapado**

Hot Tips!

Concentrate on those base verbs! It's a great way to learn descriptions:

Description	Base Verb	
agotado	**agotar**	(to exhaust)
amado	**amar**	(to love)
atrapado	**atrapar**	(to trap)
confundido	**confundir**	(to confuse)
deprimido	**deprimir**	(to depress)
odiado	**odiar**	(to hate)
sorprendido	**sorprender**	(to surprise)

THE HUMAN BODY
El cuerpo humano

Here's an overview of body parts in Spanish, in addition to useful command phrases, so that you can practice while you follow along!

Point to (the)...	**Señale...**
Look at (the)...	**Mire...**
Touch (the)...	**Toque...**

arm	**el brazo**
back	**la espalda**
chest	**el pecho**
ear	**la oreja**
elbow	**el codo**
eye	**el ojo**
finger	**el dedo**
foot	**el pie**
hand	**la mano**
head	**la cabeza**
knee	**la rodilla**
leg	**la pierna**
mouth	**la boca**
neck	**el cuello**
nose	**la nariz**
shoulder	**el hombro**
stomach	**el estómago**
toe	**el dedo del pie**
tooth	**el diente**

Stay on a roll, but this time try out these painful expressions:

My__________hurts.	**Me duele __________.**
My__________hurt.	**Me duelen __________.**

ankle	**el tobillo**	rib	**la costilla**
breasts	**los senos**	spine	**la columna**
buttocks	**las nalgas**	thigh	**el muslo**
calf	**la pantorrilla**	throat	**la garganta**
collarbone	**la clavícula**	tongue	**la lengua**
forearm	**el entebrazo**	wrist	**la muñeca**
hip	**la cadera**		

What a Face!
¡Qué cara!

Look at that mirror closely. What do you see?

cheek	**la mejilla**
chin	**la barbilla**
eyebrow	**la ceja**
eyelash	**la pestaña**
eyelid	**el párpado**
gums	**las encías**
jaw	**la mandíbula**
lip	**el labio**
nostril	**la fosa nasal**

And don't forget those internal organs. This time, think about making a medical commentary:

He/She has trouble with (the)... **Tiene problemas con...**

bladder	**la vejiga**
brain	**el cerebro**
gallbladder	**la vesícula**
heart	**el corazón**
kidney	**el riñón**
intestine	**el intestino**
liver	**el hígado**
lung	**el pulmón**
spleen	**el bazo**

Hot Tips!

- Here are some fun words that help describe folks in more detail:

He/She has (the)... **Tiene...**

beard	**la barba**
dimples	**los hoyuelos**
freckles	**las pecas**
mole	**el lunar**
pimples	**los granos**
ponytail	**la coleta**
sideburns	**las patillas**
warts	**las verrugas**
wrinkles	**las arrugas**

- More key words you can use:

It's (the)...	**Es...**
breath	**el aliento**
complexion	**el cutis**
feature	**la facción**
gesture	**el gesto**
speech	**el habla**
voice	**la voz**

- And be sure to mention the five senses or **los cinco sentidos**:

smell	hearing	sight	touch	taste
el olor	**la audición**	**la vista**	**el tacto**	**el sabor**

- You never know when these terms will come in handy:

I see (the)...	**Veo...**
blood	**la sangre**
bone	**el hueso**
flesh	**la carne**
hair	**el pelo**
muscle	**el músculo**
nerve	**el nervio**
skin	**la piel**
vein	**la vena**

- As long as we're talking about our health (**la salud**), don't hesitate to use those emergency one-liners you picked up in beginning Spanish. Here's a brief review:

I have (the)...	**Tengo...**
broken bone	**el hueso quebrado**
bruise	**la contusión**
burn	**la quemadura**
cold	**el resfriado**
cut	**la cortadura**
fever	**la fiebre**
flu	**la influenza**
headache	**el dolor de cabeza**
pain	**el dolor**
sore throat	**el dolor de garganta**
sprain	**la torcedura**
stomachache	**el dolor de estómago**
toothache	**el dolor de muela**

¡Yo recuerdo!

Translate:

Tiene arrugas en la cara. ____________________

Hay mucha sangre en las venas. ____________________

Me duelen las muñecas y los tobillos. ____________________

Señale la cortadura en la mano. ____________________

La quemadura está en la piel. ____________________

¡Ordénelo!

On Planet Present Tense, coming up with formal commands is easy, until you come across the irregular action words. Many fit into the pattern below. All you need is the **yo** form. Just change the last letter from an **o** to an **a**. You can add other verbs to this list if you feel like it:

to tell	**decir**	I tell	**Digo**	Tell!	**¡Diga!**
to come	**venir**	I come	**Vengo**	Come!	**¡Venga!**
to leave	**salir**	I leave	**Salgo**	Leave!	**¡Salga!**
to build	**construir**	I build	**Construyo**	Build!	**¡Construya!**
to bring	**traer**	I bring...	**Traigo**...	Bring...	**Traiga**...
to do	**hacer**	I do...	**Hago**...	Do...	**Haga**...
to put	**poner**	I put...	**Pongo**...	Put...	**Ponga**...
to think	**pensar**	I think...	**Pienso...**	Think...	**Piense...**
to return	**volver**	I return...	**Vuelvo...**	Return...	**Vuelva...**

Hot Tips!

- Don't forget to add an **n** for **ustedes**:

  Come, you guys! **¡Vengan ustedes!**

4

CHAPTER *CUATRO*
Practicaré mi español

FUTUREWORLD
El mundo del futuro

You have probably noticed that until now, all of our experiences in Spanish have taken place in the present tense. In other words, we are able to tell what we are doing (**¡Estamos estudiando ahora!**) and what we do (**¡Estudiamos todos los días!**). That's really great, but these two forms won't help us much when it's time to discuss what we will do! So we're off again, fellow **estudiantes**, to another land of Spanish action words—Futureworld, where everyone talks about what is yet to come!

WHAT WILL BE, WILL BE
Qué será, será

All set for the future? Limber up first with the stuff we learned on Planet Present Tense. Change each action word by following the examples. But watch out! Some of these verbs are rather irregular!

	Right now... **Ahora...**	Every day... **Todos los días...**
(Yo)	**estoy escribiendo en español.**	**escribo en español.**
(María)	**está durmiendo en la cama.**	**duerme en la cama.**
(Nosotros)	**estamos bailando mucho.**	________________
(Ellos)	**están cerrando las puertas.**	________________
(Yo)	**estoy bebiendo leche.**	________________

Now, on to *future* activities. Believe it or not, there are very few changes made to the base verb forms. Generally speaking, all you do is add a few letters at the end. The pattern is pretty much the same for the **-ar, -er,** and **-ir** endings. As you practice, exaggerate the accented syllable:

To Speak — Hablar

I'll speak **hablaré**
You'll, He'll, She'll speak **hablará**
You'll (pl.), They'll speak **hablarán**
We'll speak **hablaremos**

To Eat — Comer

I'll eat **comeré**
You'll, He'll, She'll eat **comerá**
You'll (pl.), They'll eat **comerán**
We'll eat **comeremos**

To Write — Escribir

I'll write **escribiré**
You'll, He'll, She'll write **escribirá**
You'll (pl.), They'll write **escribirán**
We'll write **escribiremos**

Now, using this same formula, give it a try with these:

Trabajar

____

____

____

Vender

____

____

____

Ir

____

____

____

HOT TIPS

Hot Tips!

- This form with "will" is called the future tense. However, to express "Will you...?" for willingness, a wish, or desire, use the word **¿Quiere...?**:

Will you go with me?	**¿Quiere ir conmigo?**

- "I'll hear" is **Oiré**. **Oír** (to hear) drops the accent over the **i**.

- Put these words somewhere within view and rehearse phrases in the future tense:

after	**después**	***Comeré después.***
tomorrow	**mañana**	__________
in a few days	**en pocos días**	__________
next year	**el próximo año**	__________
the day after tomorrow	**pasado mañana**	__________
some day	**algún día**	__________
in the future	**en el futuro**	__________
the following one	**el siguiente**	__________
later	**luego**	__________
later on	**más tarde**	__________
soon	**pronto**	__________

THE STRANGE ONES
Los raros

A few verbs in Futureworld display rather deviant behavior. The following "irregulars" are easy to recall since they follow a similar pattern. Go ahead and give them a try. You know what the four forms mean:

caber (to fit)	**cabré, cabrá, cabrán, cabremos**
decir (to say, tell)	**diré, dirá, dirán, diremos**
hacer (to do, make)	**haré, hará, harán, haremos**
poder (to be able to)	**podré, podrá, podrán, podremos**
poner (to put)	**pondré, pondrá, pondrán, pondremos**
querer (to want)	**querré, querrá, querrán, querremos**
saber (to know something)	**sabré, sabrá, sabrán, sabremos**
salir (to leave)	**saldré, saldrá, saldrán, saldremos**
tener (to have)	**tendré, tendrá, tendrán, tendremos**
valer (to be worth)	**valdré, valdrá, valdrán, valdremos**
venir (to come)	**vendré, vendrá, vendrán, vendremos**

Oh, sure, there are more irregular verbs in Spanish—but these irregulars from Futureworld need to be handled first!

Hot Tips!

- Card-makers! Try to recall these endings: **é, á, án, emos**
- **Haber** (to have) is a verb you'll need very soon. Hold onto its future forms for later use: **habré, habrá, habrán, habremos**
- The future tense in Spanish may also be used to express activities that must, can, or probably take place. Notice how these sentences can be translated:

Estará en Cuba.	He'll be in Cuba. He must be in Cuba. He's probably in Cuba.
¿Quién será?	Who will it be? Who can it be? I wonder who it is.
No vendrán.	They won't come. They probably won't come. They must not come.

¡Yo recuerdo!

Take the simple sentence and send it to the future. Study these examples:

Estudio en mi cuarto.	***Estudiaré en mi cuarto.***
Viene a las cinco.	***Vendrá a las cinco.***
Vendemos carros aquí.	______________________
No oigo nada.	______________________
Tienen muchas fiestas.	______________________
Ella come su cena.	______________________

I'M GOING TO DO IT!
Voy a hacerlo!

Do you recollect the irregular verb **ir** (to go) from Planet Present Tense? Well, guess what? It's also the form used to talk about actions that are going to happen in the future. Read on:

Ir (To Go) voy, va, van, vamos

Voy a mi casa. (I'm going to my house.)
Voy a *comer*. (I'm going *to eat*.)

You see—all you add is a verb infinitive! Let's try a few more:

We're going to read.	**Vamos a leer.**
They're going to cook.	**Van a cocinar.**
She's going to come.	**Ella va a venir.**

Go ahead—you try it. Follow the sample given, and discover *two* ways to discuss future events!

Manejaré mañana.	***Voy a manejar mañana.***
Limpiarán el baño.	***Van a limpiar el baño.***
José saldrá a las ocho.	______________
Haremos una fiesta.	______________

Hot Tips!

- Another way to increase your Spanish skills is to lengthen your sentences by adding little phrases. It's real easy to do once you learn the linking words. This one is my favorite:

  que (who, whom, which, that)

  It's the man who lives in the big house.
  Es el hombre que vive en la casa grande.

  I'll eat the food that's on the table.
  Comeré la comida que está en la mesa.

CITY SPANISH
El español urbano

In the world of future-talk, everybody's on the go. Refresh your memory with these translations:

building	**el edificio**	sidewalk	**la acera**
city block	**la cuadra**	street	**la calle**
corner	**la esquina**	traffic light	**el semáforo**
highway	**la carretera**		

Practice these frequently visited establishments. Which place do you like the best?

I will visit... **Visitaré...**
I'm going to visit (the)... **Voy a visitar...**

airport	**el aeropuerto**	park	**el parque**
bank	**el banco**	office	**la oficina**
beauty salon	**el salón de belleza**	museum	**el museo**
		movie theater	**el cine**
bookstore	**la librería**	market	**el mercado**
bus station	**la estación de autobús**	library	**la biblioteca**
		hospital	**el hospital**
church	**la iglesia**	pharmacy	**la farmacia**
college	**el colegio**	police station	**la estación de policía**
factory	**la fábrica**	post office	**el correo**
fire department	**el departamento de bomberos**	school	**la escuela**
		store	**la tienda**
gas station	**la gasolinera**	university	**la universidad**

WHAT PLACE?
¿Qué lugar?

Call out everything as you pass by!

Where's (the)...? **¿Dónde está...?**

billboard	**el letrero**
bridge	**el puente**
bus stop	**la parada de autobús**
car lot	**el lote de carros**
fountain	**la fuente**
railroad track	**la vía del ferrocarril**
skyscraper	**el rascacielos**
stop sign	**el señal de parada**
telephone pole	**el poste de teléfono**
toll booth	**la caseta de peaje**
tower	**la torre**
tunnel	**el túnel**

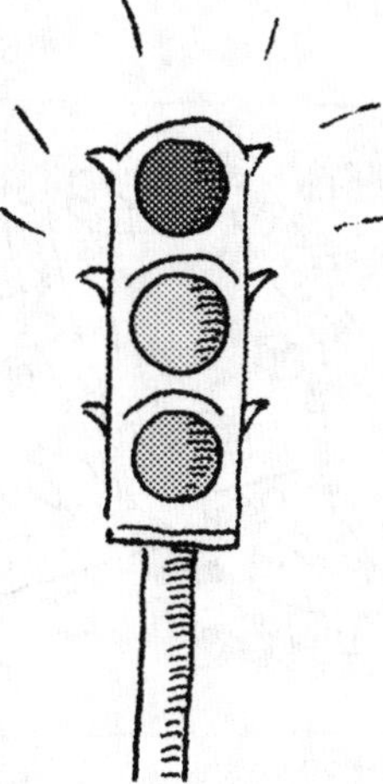

What's going on indoors? Keep chattering away:

We're at (the)... **Estamos en...**

We'll be at (the)... **Estaremos en...**

rotating door	**la puerta giratoria**
elevator	**el ascensor**
entrance	**la entrada**
escalator	**la escalera mecánica**
exit	**la salida**
floor	**el piso**
lobby	**el salón**
mailbox	**el buzón**
restroom	**el baño**
stairs	**las escaleras**

Here's some more street Spanish:

I'm going to park at (the)... **Voy a estacionar en...**

alley	**el callejón**
avenue	**la avenida**
boulevard	**el bulevar**
path	**el sendero**
parking lot	**el estacionamiento**
road	**el camino**
route	**la ruta**

Describe the place where you live. Use more than one word:

I live in (the)... **Vivo en...**

I'll drive to (the)... **Manejaré a...**

area	**el área**
border	**la frontera**
city	**la ciudad**
community	**la comunidad**
county	**el condado**
district	**el distrito**
downtown	**el centro**
neighborhood	**el vecindario**
outskirts	**las afueras**
site	**el sitio**
state	**el estado**
town	**el pueblo**
village	**la villa**
zone	**la zona**

Hot Tips!

- Have you ever seen this pattern before? The **-ería** ending informs us that it's a shop or factory:

bakery	**la panadería**	jewelry store	**la joyería**
barber shop	**la peluquería**	laundromat	**la lavandería**
florist	**la floristería**	meat market	**la carnicería**
furniture store	**la mueblería**	shoe store	**la zapatería**

- Has anyone ever shown you these special places—in Spanish?

bar	**el bar**
campgrounds	**el campamento**
cemetery	**el cementerio**
city hall	**el municipio**
jail	**la cárcel**
pier	**el muelle**
warehouse	**el almacén**
zoo	**el zoológico**

- And can you relate to any of these places of worship?

We go to (the)...	**Vamos a...**
We'll go to (the)...	**Iremos a...**

cathedral	**la catedral**
chapel	**la capilla**
church	**la iglesia**
mosque	**la mezquita**
synagogue	**la sinagoga**
temple	**el templo**

Finished? Are you kidding? There's so much more to learn!

It's a _______ zone.	**Es una zona _______.**
business	**de negocios**
commercial	**comercial**
construction	**de construcción**
residential	**residencial**
tourism	**turística**
traffic	**de tráfico**

¡Yo recuerdo!

Take a few city-related vocabulary items, and plug them into the sentence patterns below. Don't be shy. Clear your throat and read each one aloud!

I'm working at (the)...	**Estoy trabajando en...**
She works at (the)...	**Ella trabaja en...**
We're going to work at (the)...	**Vamos a trabajar en...**

Now link each item with its related location:

la mueblería	**el criminal**
el mercado	**el dinero**
el banco	**el carro**
la biblioteca	**el tren**
la gasolinera	**el cartero**
la vía del ferrocarril	**la comida**
el buzón	**el libro**
la cárcel	**la mesa**

And guess at these translations:

la clínica ____________________

la prisión ____________________

el estudio ____________________

el supermercado ____________________

la agencia ____________________

el canal ____________________

el motel ____________________

el hotel ____________________

la cafetería ____________________

el mall ____________________

¡Ordénelo!

To tell a friend or family member to do something, you'll have to give commands in the **tú** or informal form. Notice the difference between the formal and informal commands as you practice. Keep your eye on the final letter:

Verb	Formal Command	Informal Command
(to walk) **habl<u>ar</u>**	**¡Hable!**	**¡Habla!**
(to eat) **com<u>er</u>**	**¡Coma!**	**¡Come!**
(to write) **escrib<u>ir</u>**	**¡Escriba!**	**¡Escribe!**

With regular verbs the **ar**s end in **a**, while the **er**s and **ir**s end in **e**. Here are some more formal and informal command words:

(to walk) **caminar**	**¡Camine!**	**¡Camina!**
(to read) **leer**	**¡Lea!**	**¡Lee!**
(to insist) **insistir**	**¡Insista!**	**¡Insiste!**

TRANSPORTATION
El transporte

No one moves around town much unless they have transportation. How do you get around in Futureworld?

I'll go by...	**Iré por...**
I'm going to travel by...	**Voy a viajar por...**

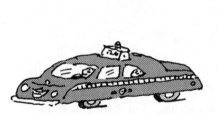

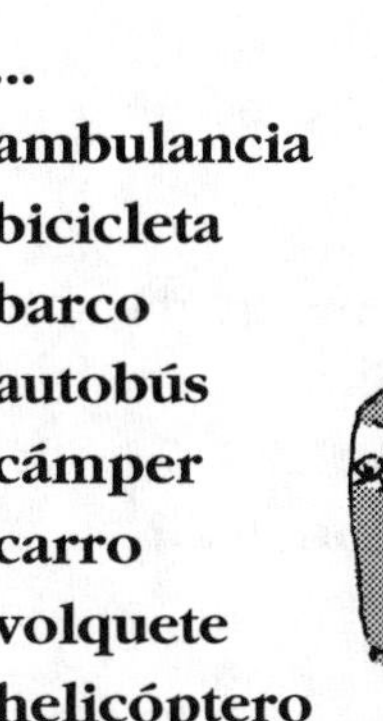

ambulance	**ambulancia**
bicycle	**bicicleta**
boat	**barco**
bus	**autobús**
camper	**cámper**
car	**carro**
dump truck	**volquete**
helicopter	**helicóptero**
house trailer	**coche habitación**
moped	**bicicleta motorizada**
motorcycle	**motocicleta**
streetcar	**tranvía**
subway	**metro**
taxi	**taxi**
tow truck	**grúa**
tractor	**tractor**
train	**tren**
truck	**camión**

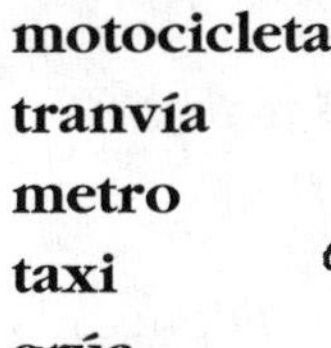

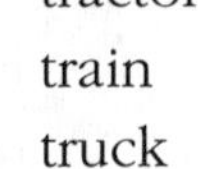

Hot Tips!

- Car can be **carro, coche,** or **automóvil,** depending on where a person is from.

- There's always something going on at the airport. Learn how to talk about air travel:

airstrip	**la pista de aterrizaje**	terminal	**el terminal**
flight	**el vuelo**		

- Travelers may need these phrases as well:

by foot	**a pie**	by horse	**a caballo**

- Look at all the family vehicles:

I'm selling (the)...	**Estoy vendiendo...**
I have (the)...	**Tengo...**
I'll buy (the)...	**Compraré...**
convertible	**el descaportable**
jeep	**el jip**
pickup	**la camioneta**
sedan	**el sedán**
sportscar	**el carro deportivo**
van	**la vagoneta, la furgoneta**

- Speaking of traveling, try these helpful one-liners used by tourists:

¿A qué distancia?	How far?
¿Hay agua potable?	Is there drinking water?
¿Puedo pagar con esto?	Can I pay with this?
¿Está incluída?	Is it included?
¿Está lista?	Is it ready?
¿Está ocupada?	Is it taken?
¿Puede ayudarme?	Can you help me?
¿Puede recomendar uno?	Can you recommend one?
¿Puede repararlo?	Can you fix it?

- To move (to change residence) is **mudarse**:

Are they going to move?	**¿Se van a mudar?**
No, they're going to stay.	**No, se van a quedar.**

See how the **se** words sound in the future tense? Here's a quick overview of all the tenses we've learned. Put the **se**, **me**, and **nos** in front:

We're moving *now.*	**Nos estamos mudando ahora.**
They move *every year.*	**Se mudan cada año.**
I'll move *next month.*	**Me mudaré el próximo mes.**

- **Ir** (to go) is usually followed by **a** (to). But beware of the **a** + **el** = **al** formula. Watch:

I'm going to the bank.	**Voy al banco.**

Consejos verbales

In the present or future, this verb belongs with your infinitives:

He knows how to speak French...	**El sabe hablar francés...**
and he will know how to speak Spanish.	**y sabrá hablar español.**

AUTO PARTS
Las piezas del auto

Not many parts of the car can be labeled, so rely on your command words so you won't forget:

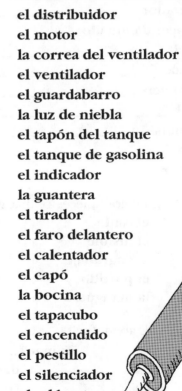

Touch (the)... **Toque...**
Look at (the)... **Mire...**
Point to (the)... **Señale...**

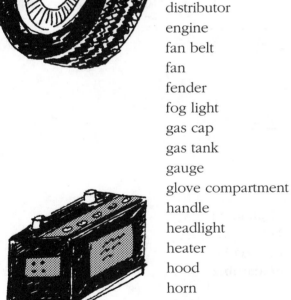

axle	**el eje**
battery	**la batería**
brake	**el freno**
brake light	**la luz de frenada**
bumper	**el parachoques**
carburetor	**el carburador**
catalytic converter	**el convertidor catalítico**
clutch	**el embrague**
dashboard	**el tablero de instrumentos**
distributor	**el distribuidor**
engine	**el motor**
fan belt	**la correa del ventilador**
fan	**el ventilador**
fender	**el guardabarro**
fog light	**la luz de niebla**
gas cap	**el tapón del tanque**
gas tank	**el tanque de gasolina**
gauge	**el indicador**
glove compartment	**la guantera**
handle	**el tirador**
headlight	**el faro delantero**
heater	**el calentador**
hood	**el capó**
horn	**la bocina**
hubcap	**el tapacubo**
ignition	**el encendido**
lock	**el pestillo**
muffler	**el silenciador**
odometer	**el odómetro**

rearview mirror	**el espejo retrovisor**	stick shift	**el cambio manual**
safety belt	**el cinturón de seguridad**	tail light	**el faro trasero**
		tape deck	**la casetera**
seat	**el asiento**	tire	**el neumático**
shock absorber	**el amortiguador**	trunk	**la maletera**
spare tire	**el neumático de repuesto**	turn signal	**la señal de dirección**
spark plug	**la bujía**	upholstery	**la tapicería**
speedometer	**el indicador de velocidad**	visor	**la visera**
		wheel	**la rueda**
starter	**el arrancador**	windshield	**el parabrisas**
steering wheel	**el volante**	windshield wiper	**el limpia-parabrisas**

Hot Tips!

- Lots of auto parts are similar in both languages. Pull over and translate these:

  antena ______________________________

  acelerador ______________________________

  aire acondicionado ______________________________

  exterior ______________________________

  radiador ______________________________

  instrumento ______________________________

  pedal ______________________________

  transmisión ______________________________

  radio ______________________________

  interior ______________________________

- Here are some more pieces of that vehicle:

cable	**el cable**	lever	**el palanca**
fuse	**el fusible**	pump	**la bomba**
gear	**el engranaje**	valve	**la válvula**
hatch	**el portillo**	wire	**el alambre**
hose	**la manguera**		

- This time, talk about fuel:

It'll take...	**Tomará...**
diesel	**diésel**
regular	**regular**
unleaded	**sin plomo**

READ THE SIGN!
¡Lea el letrero!

On the streets of Spanish cities the rules are posted everywhere:

Curve	**Curva**
Detour	**Desviación**
Do Not Enter	**Prohibido Entrar**
Do Not Litter	**No Tirar Basura**
Do Not Pass	**Prohibido Pasar**
Don't Walk	**No Caminar**
Entrance	**Entrada**
Exit	**Salida**
Narrow Road	**Camino Estrecho**
No Left Turn	**No Doblar a la Izquierda**
No Parking	**Estacionamiento Prohibido**
No U Turn	**Prohibida la Vuelta en "U"**
One Way	**Dirección Unica**
Passing Lane	**Pista para Pasar**
Railroad Crossing	**Cruce de Ferrocarril**
Road Closed	**Camino Cerrado**
Road Crossing	**Cruce de Caminos**
School Zone	**Zona Escolar**
Slow	**Despacio**
Speed Limit	**Velocidad Máxima**
Stop	**Parada** (or **Alto**)
Stop Ahead	**Parada Próxima**
Traffic Circle	**Glorieta**
Wait	**Espere**
Walk	**Camine**
Wrong Way	**Vía Equivocada**
Yield	**Ceda el Paso**

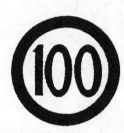

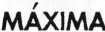

- Learn the translations of all the signs you can:

Closed	**Cerrado**	Open	**Abierto**
Emergency	**Emergencia**	Out of Order	**Descompuesto**
For Rent	**Se Alquila**	Pull	**Jale**
Handicapped	**Minusválidos**	Push	**Empuje**
No Smoking	**No Fumar**	Restrooms	**Servicios Sanitarios**

WORK WORDS
Palabras del trabajo

A job is an essential part of our lives! Read the vocabulary below and follow the examples provided to create your own questions (and then *answer* them!).

appointment	**la cita**	***¿Tiene ella una cita?***
benefits	**los beneficios**	
career	**la carrera**	***¿Le gusta la carrera?***
conference	**la conferencia**	
interview	**la entrevista**	
investment	**la inversión**	
invoice	**la factura**	
loss	**la pérdida**	
meeting	**la reunión**	
opportunity	**la oportunidad**	
paycheck	**el cheque de pago**	
position	**el puesto**	
product	**el producto**	
profit	**la ganancia**	
program	**el programa**	
purchase	**la compra**	
raise	**el aumento**	
receipt	**el recibo**	
salary	**el salario**	
sale	**la venta**	
schedule	**el horario**	
strike	**la huelga**	
success	**el éxito**	***¿Va a tener éxito?***
time card	**la tarjeta de registro horario**	
training	**el entrenamiento**	
vacations	**las vacaciones**	***¿Está tomando las vacaciones?***

IT'S YOUR BUSINESS!
¡Es su negocio!

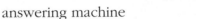

Stick removable labels on everything around the office until you learn the names of the objects by heart:

I'll look for the...	**Buscaré...**
I'm looking for the...	**Voy a buscar...**

answering machine	**el contestador automático**
computer	**la computadora**
copier	**la copiadora**
fax	**el fax**
file	**el archivo**
folder	**la carpeta**
form	**el formulario**
mail	**el correo**
printer	**la impresora**
scissors	**las tijeras**
stapler	**la engrapadora**
typewriter	**la máquina de escribir**

Hot Tips!

- You may hear these one-liners, too.

part time	**trabajo parcial**
full time	**trabajo completo**
day off	**día de descanso**

- **Trabajo** comes in a variety of forms. Try these three:

job	**el trabajo**	chore	**la tarea**	errand	**el mandado**

¡Yo recuerdo!

Name three auto parts in Spanish:

____________________ ____________________ ____________________

Translate these words:

purchase	______________	sale	______________
gain	______________	loss	______________
invoice	______________	receipt	______________
computer	______________	stapler	______________

More opposites! Make the connection:

abierto	**jale**
empuje	**entrada**
salida	**cerrado**

TOOLS OF THE TRADE
Las herramientas de la profesión

Build up your skills with new vocabulary. Pound away at these items using a few command words:

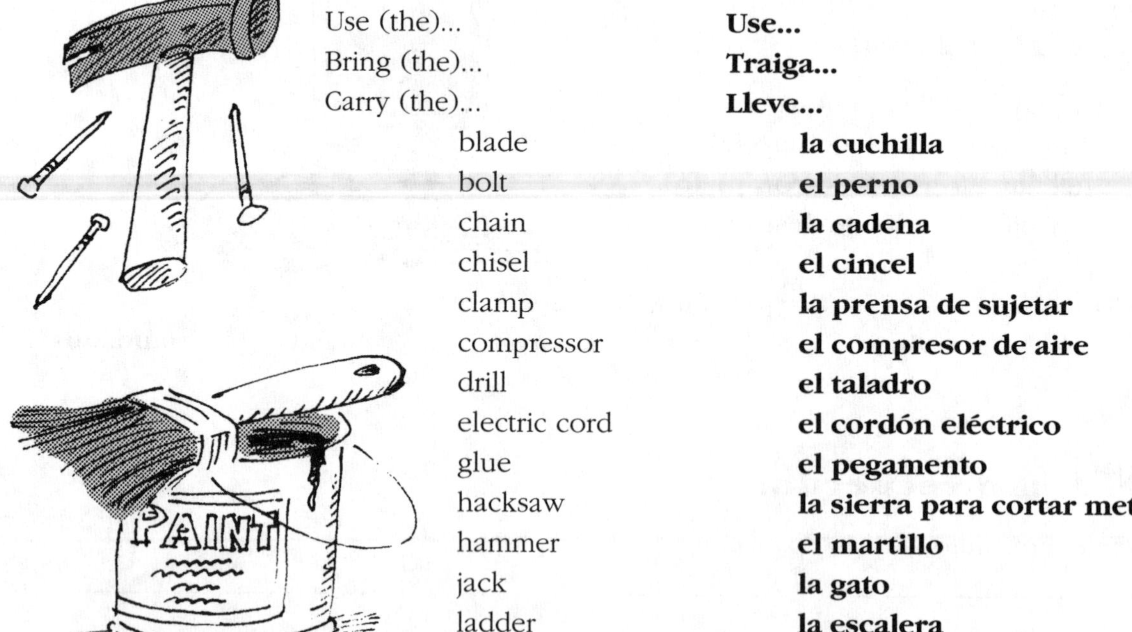

Use (the)...	**Use...**
Bring (the)...	**Traiga...**
Carry (the)...	**Lleve...**
blade	**la cuchilla**
bolt	**el perno**
chain	**la cadena**
chisel	**el cincel**
clamp	**la prensa de sujetar**
compressor	**el compresor de aire**
drill	**el taladro**
electric cord	**el cordón eléctrico**
glue	**el pegamento**
hacksaw	**la sierra para cortar metal**
hammer	**el martillo**
jack	**la gato**
ladder	**la escalera**
level	**el nivel**

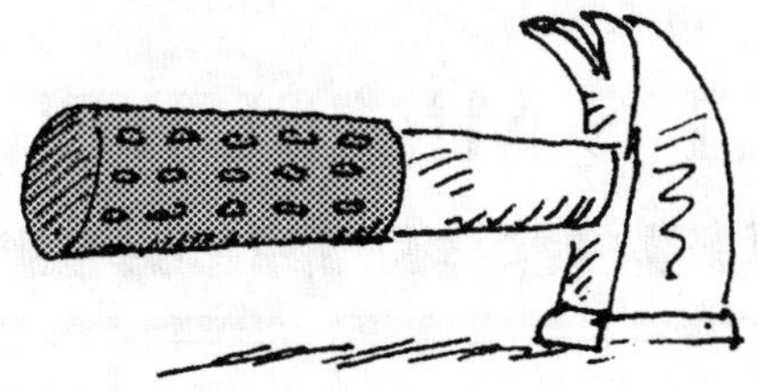

measuring tape	**la cinta para medir**
nail	**el clavo**
nut	**la tuerca**
paint	**la pintura**
paint brush	**la brocha de pintar**
pliers	**las pinzas**
ramp	**la rampa**
safety glasses	**los lentes de protección**
sandpaper	**el papel de lija**
saw	**el serrucho**
scaffold	**el andamio**
scraper	**el raspador**
screw	**el tornillo**
screwdriver	**el desarmador**
shovel	**la pala**
staple	**la grapa**
tape	**la cinta**
toolbox	**la caja de herramientas**
trowel	**la llana**
wrench	**la llave inglesa**

Ready to do a little yardwork?

Will you need (the)...? **¿Necesitará usted...?**

ax	**el hacha**
bag	**la bolsa**
blower	**el soplador**
box	**la caja**
chainsaw	**la motosierra**
clippers	**las tijeras podadoras**
fertilizer	**el abono**
gloves	**los guantes**
hoe	**el azadón**
hose	**la manguera**
insecticide	**el insecticida**
lawnmower	**la cortadora de césped**
manure	**el estiércol**
pick	**el pico**
pitchfork	**la horquilla**
poison	**el veneno**
rake	**el rastrillo**
rope	**la soga**
shovel	**la pala**
sprayer	**el rociador**
trimmer	**el podador**
wheelbarrow	**la carretilla**

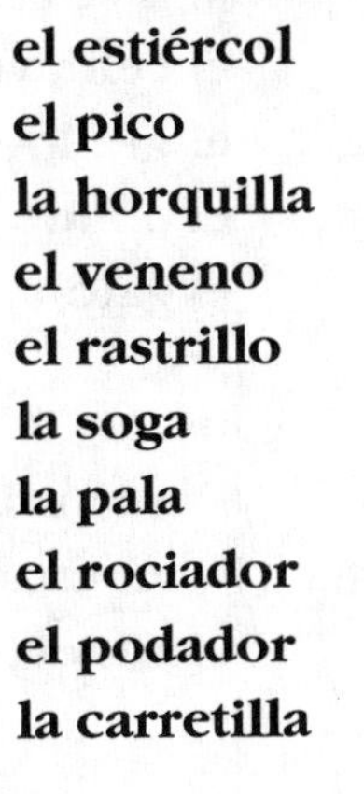

LET'S MEASURE!
¡Vamos a medir!

Since we've got tools in our hands, take a second to confirm those proper measurements. You'll probably need a little help in Spanish, so add these terms to your total:

Where's (the)...	**¿Dónde está...?**
bag	**la bolsa**
bottle	**la botella**
box	**la caja**
can	**la lata**
dozen	**la docena**
handful	**el puñado**
package	**el paquete**
pair	**el par**
piece	**el pedazo**
ton	**la tonelada**

What's (the)...	**¿Cuál es...**
height	**la altura**
length	**el largo**
percentage	**el porcentaje**
size	**el tamaño**
weight	**el peso**
width	**el ancho**

And have you memorized these conversions?

5/8 mi. = **el kilómetro**
2.2 lbs. = **el kilógramo**
32° F = **0° C**

Workers require this selection also:

cent	**el centavo**	inch	**la pulgada**
degree	**el grado**	mile	**la milla**
dollar	**el dólar**	ounce	**la onza**
gallon	**el galón**		

- And which part?

a half **una mitad**
a quarter **un cuarto**
a third **un tercero**

HOUSECLEANING
La limpieza de la casa

While doing your chores, shift everything from the present tense to the future, just like the examples below. Use one of the three action words provided:

usar
tener
necesitar

box	**la caja**
Usamos la caja.	***Usaremos la caja.***
We use the box.	We'll use the box.
broom	**la escoba**
Tenemos la escoba.	***Tendremos la escoba.***
We have the broom.	We'll have the broom.
brush	**el cepillo**
Necesitamos el cepillo.	***Necesitaremos el cepillo.***
We need the brush.	We'll need the brush.

bucket	**el balde**
dustpan	**el cogedor de basura**
hose	**la manguera**
mask	**la máscara**
mop	**el trapeador**
rag	**el trapo**
scouring pad	**el estropajo**
scrub brush	**el cepillo de fregar**
sponge	**la esponja**
towel	**la toalla**
trashbag	**la bolsa para basura**
trashcan	**el cubo de basura**
vacuum cleaner	**la aspiradora**

¡Yo recuerdo!

In this activity, you've got to join each verb with its appropriate object:

subir	**la pala**
pegar	**la brocha**
pintar	**las tijeras**
cortar	**la escalera**
excavar	**el pegamento**
limpiar	**la esponja**

¡Ordénelo!

The **tu** command form can also be negative. Don't forget—this only applies in informal situations:

Work!	**¡Trabaja!**	Don't work!	**¡No trabajes!**
Drink!	**¡Bebe!**	Don't drink!	**¡No bebas!**
Write!	**¡Escribe!**	Don't write!	**¡No escribas!**

For regular verbs, **-ar** becomes **-es**, and the **-er** or **-ir** becomes **-as**. Now notice the pattern for those irregular commands:

Hang-up!	**¡Cuelga!**	Don't hang up!	**¡No cuelgues!**
Start!	**¡Comienza!**	Don't start!	**¡No comiences!**
Go!	**¡Ve!**	Don't go!	**¡No vayas!**
Leave!	**¡Sal!**	Don't leave!	**¡No salgas!**
Put!	**¡Pon!**	Don't put!	**¡No pongas!**
Hear!	**¡Oye!**	Don't hear!	**¡No oigas!**
Tell!	**¡Di!**	Don't tell!	**¡No digas!**
Give!	**¡Da!**	Don't give!	**¡No des!**
Follow!	**¡Sigue!**	Don't follow!	**¡No sigas!**
Bring!	**¡Trae!**	Don't bring!	**¡No traigas!**
Do!	**¡Haz!**	Don't do!	**¡No hagas!**
Be!	**¡Sé!**	Don't be!	**¡No seas!**
Come!	**¡Ven!**	Don't come!	**¡No vengas!**
Have!	**¡Ten!**	Don't have!	**¡No tengas!**

FOOD!
¡La comida!

Practice this selection of food words as you continue to change verbs from the present to the future tense.

bread	**el pan**	**Necesito el pan.**	**Necesitaré el pan.**
meat	**la carne**	**Come la carne.**	**Comerá la carne.**
cheese	**el queso**	**Tienen el queso.**	**Tendrán el queso.**
fish	**el pescado**	**Vendemos el pescado.**	**Venderemos el pescado.**
chicken	**el pollo**	**Compro el pollo.**	________________
steak	**el bistec**	**Corta la carne.**	________________
soup	**la sopa**	**Toman la sopa.**	________________
salad	**la ensalada**	**Mezclo la ensalada.**	________________
ham	**el jamón**	**Servimos el jamón.**	________________
butter	**la mantequilla**	**Pone la mantequilla.**	________________
egg	**el huevo**	**Cocinan el huevo.**	________________
turkey	**el pavo**	**Sacamos el pavo.**	________________
rice	**el arroz**	**Preparo el arroz.**	________________
pork	**el cerdo**	**Quiere el cerdo.**	________________
roast beef	**el rosbif**	**Piden el rosbif.**	________________
seafood	**el marisco**	**Limpia el marisco.**	________________
noodle	**el fideo**	**Compramos el fideo.**	________________
roll	**el panecillo**	**Pasan el panecillo.**	________________

VEGETABLES
Los vegetales

Let's toss in these additional lists dealing with food. Combine the three verbs below with the new vocabulary to create sentences as complex as you can make them.

Eat (the)...	**Come...**
Bring (the)...	**Trae...**
Put (the)...	**Pon...**

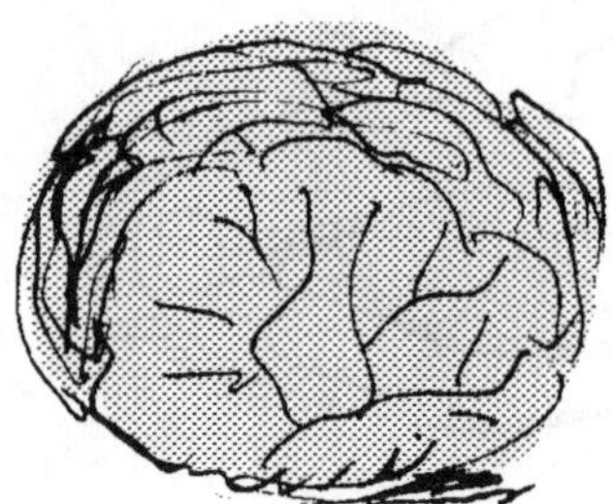

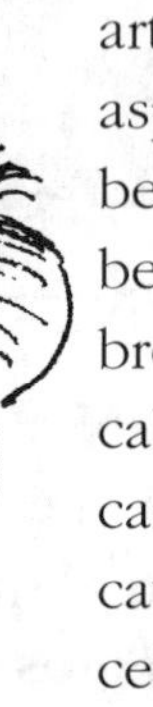

artichoke	**la alcachofa**
asparagus	**el espárrago**
beans	**los frijoles**
beet	**la remolacha**
broccoli	**el brécol**
cabbage	**el repollo**
carrot	**la zanahoria**
cauliflower	**el coliflor**
celery	**el apio**
corn	**el maíz**
cucumber	**el pepino**
eggplant	**la berenjena**
green bean	**la judía verde**
green onion	**la cebollana**
lettuce	**la lechuga**
mushroom	**el champiñón**
onion	**la cebolla**
peas	**las arvejitas**
potato	**la papa**
pumpkin	**la calabaza**
radish	**el rábano**
spinach	**la espinaca**
sweet potato	**el camote**
tomato	**el tomate**
turnip	**el nabo**
watercress	**el berro**
zucchini	**la calabacita verde**

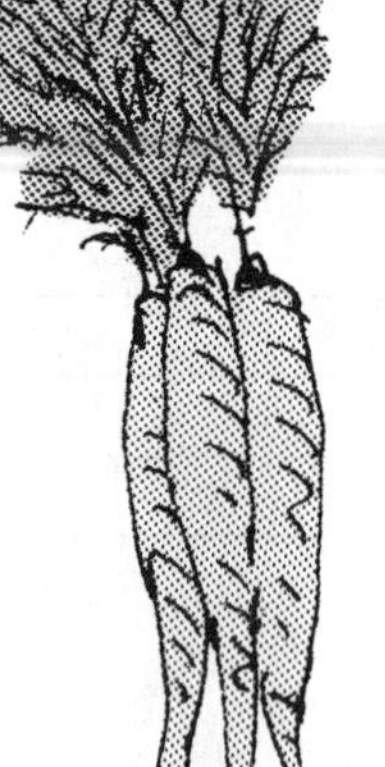

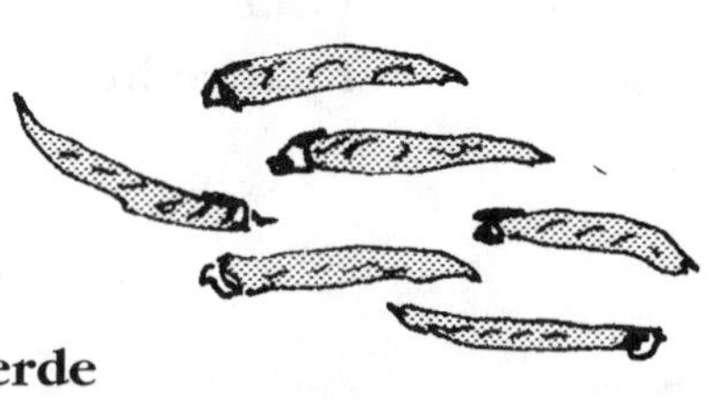

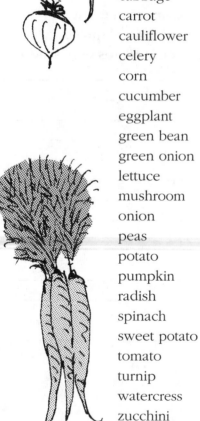

FRUIT
La fruta

Cut (the)...	**Corta...**
Pick up (the)...	**Recoge...**
Look for (the)...	**Busca...**
apple	**la manzana**
apricot	**el albaricoque**
banana	**el plátano**
blackberry	**la mora**
blueberry	**el arándano**
cantaloupe	**el melón**
cherry	**la cereza**
coconut	**el coco**
fig	**el higo**
grape	**la uva**
grapefruit	**la toronja**
lemon	**el limón**
orange	**la naranja**
peach	**el melocotón**
pear	**la pera**
pineapple	**la piña**
plum	**la ciruela**
prune	**la ciruela pasa**
raisin	**la pasa**
strawberry	**la fresa**

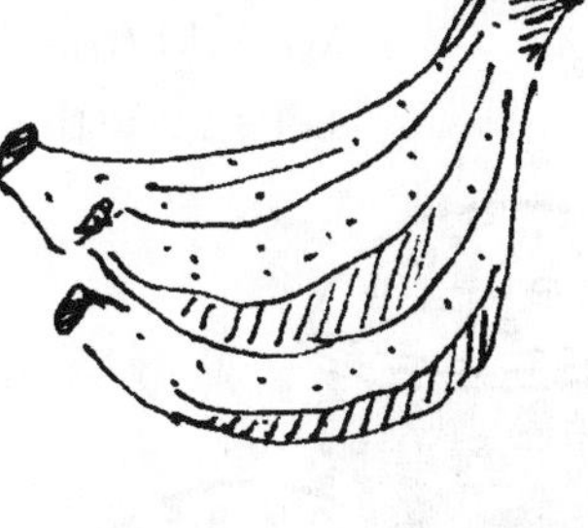

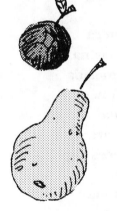

Desserts
Los postres

We'll get (the)...	**Conseguiremos...**
cake	**la torta**
candy	**el dulce**
chewing gum	**el chicle**
cookie	**la galleta**
cracker	**la galleta salada**
ice cream	**el helado**
gelatin	**la gelatina**
pie	**el pastel**

Ingredients, Spices, and Condiments
Los ingredientes, las especias y los condimentos

Making sure that you know all the basic foods is important, but if you really enjoy hanging around the kitchen, flavor your Spanish with the following words. Continue playing with verbs using the present and future tenses and forming full sentences.

We add (the)...	**Añadimos...**
Let's add (the)...	**Vamos a añadir...**

baking powder	**el polvo de hornear**
broth	**el caldo**
chocolate	**el chocolate**
cinnamon	**la canela**
cornstarch	**el almidón de maíz**
flour	**la harina**
garlic	**el ajo**
honey	**la miel**
hot pepper	**el ají**
lard	**la manteca**
margarine	**la margarina**
marmalade	**la mermelada**
mayonnaise	**la mayonesa**
mint	**la menta**
mustard	**la mostaza**
nuts	**las nueces**
oil	**el aceite**
olive	**la aceituna**
parsley	**el perejil**
peanut butter	**la crema de maní**
pepper	**la pimienta**
pickle	**el encurtido**
salad dressing	**el aliño de ensalada**
salt	**la sal**
sauce	**la salsa**
sugar	**el azúcar**
tomato sauce	**la salsa de tomate**
vanilla	**la vainilla**
vinegar	**el vinagre**

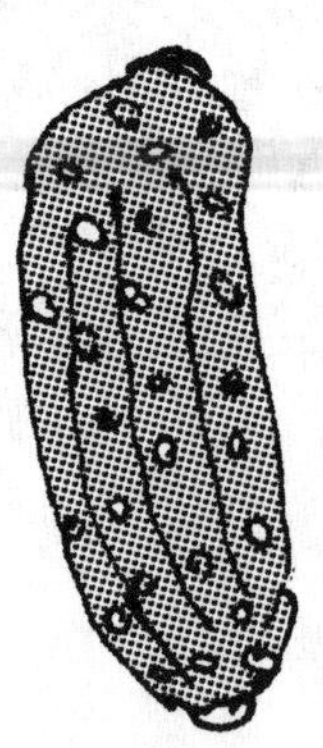

Hot Tips!

- Don't skip your meals. You learned about them in *Level One*:

breakfast	**el desayuno**
lunch	**el almuerzo**
dinner	**la cena**
snack	**la merienda**

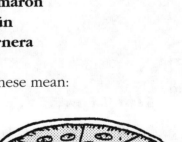

- Now, speak to the butcher and the fish seller:

I'll need (the)...	**Necesitaré...**
bacon	**el tocino**
clams	**las almejas**
crab	**el cangrejo**
ground beef	**la carne molida**
hamburger	**la hamburguesa**
hot dog	**el perro caliente**
lamb	**el cordero**
lobster	**la langosta**
meatball	**la albóndiga**
sausage	**la salchicha**
shrimp	**el camarón**
tuna	**el atún**
veal	**la ternera**

- You're in big trouble if you can't figure out what these mean:

el yogurt
el cereal
la pizza
el ketchup

- Sauce it up!

teriyaki sauce	**la salsa japonesa**
Worcestershire sauce	**la salsa inglesa**
soy sauce	**la salsa de soya**
barbecue sauce	**la salsa de barbacoa**

- People from Latin America and Spain don't all agree on what these food items are called, so be prepared to learn other names for everything!

HAVE A DRINK
Tome una bebida

Thirsty? Wash down your meals with the appropriate beverage. While giving instructions, use either "to take" (**tomar**) or "to drink" (**beber**). Develop comments using all the verb tenses:

Is she drinking tea?	**¿Está bebiendo té?**
No, she takes coffee.	**No, toma café.**
Do you want to drink wine?	**¿Quieren tomar vino?**
Yes, we'll take white wine.	**Sí, tomaremos el vino blanco.**

beer	**la cerveza**	lemonade	**la limonada**
coffee	**el café**	milk	**la leche**
decaffeinated coffee	**el café descafeinado**	shake	**el batido**
diet soda	**la soda dietética**	skim milk	**la leche descremada**
hot chocolate	**el chocolate caliente**	soft drink	**el refresco**
iced tea	**el té helado**	tea	**el té**
juice	**el jugo**	water	**el agua**
		wine	**el vino**

Hot Tips!

- If you're still at the market, why not shop for some of these important items:

batteries	**las pilas**
cigarettes	**los cigarrillos**
envelopes	**los sobres**
light bulbs	**los focos**
magazines	**las revistas**
matches	**los fósforos**
medicines	**las medicinas**
newspapers	**los periódicos**
post cards	**las tarjetas postales**
rolls of film	**los rollos de foto**
stamps	**las estampillas**
sunglasses	**los lentes del sol**

- The idea of "un-" is usually translated as **des-** in Spanish verbs. Watch:

to hook	**enganchar**	to unhook	**desenganchar**
to do	**hacer**	to undo	**deshacer**
to plug in	**enchufar**	to unplug	**desenchufar**

¡Yo recuerdo!

Fill out this chart. Take as much time as you need:

las carnes	**los vegetales**	**las frutas**	**las bebidas**
________	________	________	________
________	________	________	________
________	________	________	________

Use logic to finish these phrases:

bread and...	**pan y...**
soup and...	**sopa y...**
pie and...	**pastel y...**
salt and...	**sal y...**
oil and...	**aceite y...**

Consejos verbales

Ponder these new tips on how to use those verb infinitives. Just stick one of these expressions in front. Study each translation:

Además de cocinar,	Besides cooking,
Al pagar,	Upon paying,
Antes de ordenar,	Before ordering,
Después de tomar,	After drinking,
Para aprender,	In order to learn,
Sin comer,	Without eating,

CLOTHING
La ropa

Now take a shot at the articles of clothing. Most of them should look familiar. Keep experimenting with the future tense.

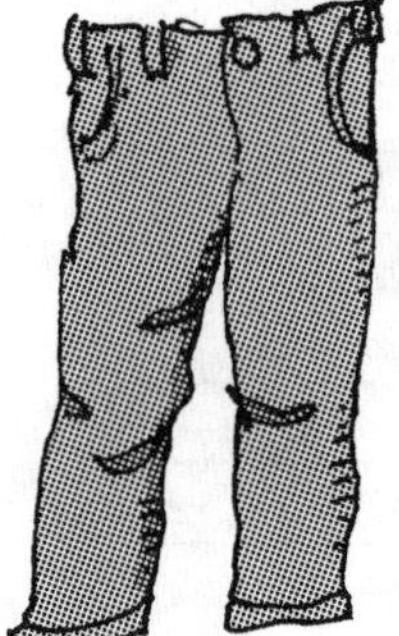

I'm going to wear (the)...	**Voy a usar...**
We'll buy (the)...	**Compraremos...**
Put on (the)...	**Póngase...**
bathing suit	**el traje de baño**
bathrobe	**la bata de baño**
belt	**el cinturón**
blouse	**la blusa**
boots	**las botas**
brassiere	**el sostén**
cap	**la gorra**
dress	**el vestido**
girdle	**la faja**
gloves	**los guantes**
jacket	**la chaqueta**
mittens	**los mitones**
overcoat	**el abrigo**
pajamas	**el pijama**
panties	**las bragas**
pants	**los pantalones**
raincoat	**el impermeable**
sandals	**las sandalias**
scarf	**la bufanda**
shirt	**la camisa**
shoes	**los zapatos**
shorts	**los calzoncillos**
skirt	**la falda**
slip	**la combinación**
slippers	**las zapatillas**
socks	**los calcetines**
sportcoat	**el saco**
stockings	**las medias**
suit	**el traje**
sweater	**el suéter**

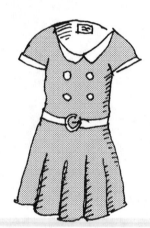

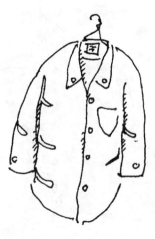

sweatsuit	**la sudadera**
T-shirt	**la camiseta**
tennis shoes	**los tenis**
tie	**la corbata**
underwear	**la ropa interior**
vest	**el chaleco**

Hot Tips!

- Details, details! Interject other phrases that refer to clothes and continue using the verbs you have learned. Use both tenses:

She's putting on (the)...	**Se viste con...**
She's taking off (the)...	**Se saca...**
She's wearing...	**Lleva...**

buckle	**la hebilla**
button	**el botón**
collar	**el cuello**
cuff	**el puño**
embroidery	**el bordado**
hem	**el ruedo**
pocket	**el bolsillo**
shoulder pad	**la hombrera**
sleeve	**la manga**
strap	**la correa**
zipper	**el cierre**

5

CHAPTER *CINCO*
Practiqué mucho

PAST TENSE TERRITORY
El territorio del tiempo pasado

Buckle up, **mis amigos**! In previous chapters, we hopped all over the present and future tenses. Now, we're moving into rougher country—Past Tense Territory, where life is a bit more challenging.

It's time to talk about past activities. Though most Spanish students complain about this tense, there are plenty of shortcuts in this chapter that can make your experience here as painless as possible!

WHAT HAPPENED? IT'S THE PRETERIT!
¿Qué pasó? ¡Es el pretérito!

Spanish has two basic past tenses—the preterit and the imperfect. Sorry, but you'll have to remember their names.

The preterit is a little more common, because it refers to actions that were completed in past time. We'll get to the imperfect tense a little later on.

Let's take a look at a simple formula that shows how to create preterit forms with most action words.

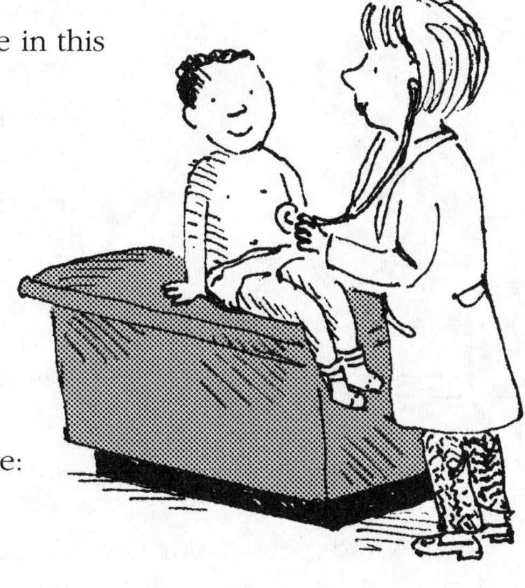

For regular **-ar** verbs, change the endings just like in this example:

To Work	**Trabajar**
I worked	**trabajé**
You, He, She worked	**trabajó**
You (pl.), They worked	**trabajaron**
We worked	**trabajamos**

In other words, drop the **-ar** and add one of these:

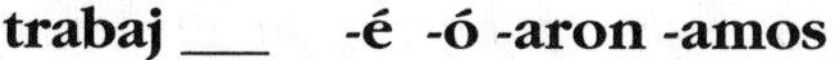

trabaj ___ -é -ó -aron -amos

I worked yesterday.	**Trabajé ayer.**
Did they work?	**¿Trabajaron?**
We didn't work.	**No trabajamos.**

For regular **-er** and **-ir** actions, change the forms to look like these:

To Eat	**Comer**
I ate	**comí**
You, He, She ate	**comió**
You (pl.), They ate	**comieron**
We ate	**comimos**

Again, keep things simple. These are the letters you'll need to know:

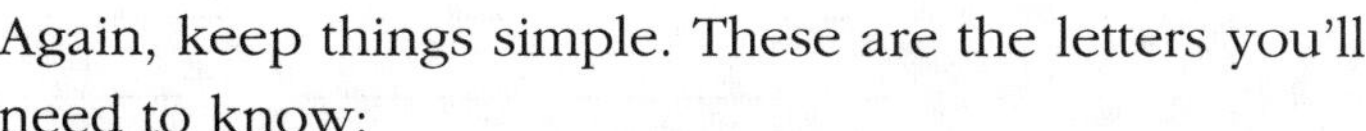

com ___ -í -ió -ieron -imos

They ate last night.	**Comieron anoche.**
Did you eat?	**¿Comió usted?**
I didn't eat.	**No comí.**

To Write **Escribir**

Most **-ir** verbs are handled the same as the **-er** verbs. Notice the resemblance:

escrib_____ -í -ió -ieron -imos

I wrote two weeks ago.	**Escribí hace dos semanas.**
He did not write.	**No escribió.**
Did you guys write?	**¿Escribieron ustedes?**

Review the preterit forms again, then practice these past tense patterns using the verbs below. Translate each phrase into Spanish:

(**correr**)	I ran.	**Corrí**
(**cantar**)	She sang.	**Cantó**
(**manejar**)	We didn't drive.	**No manejamos**
(**subir**)	They climbed.	**Subieron**
(**terminar**)	Did you guys finish?	**¿Terminaron ustedes?**
(**besar**)	They kissed.	______________
(**caminar**)	He walked.	______________
(**ganar**)	They won.	______________
(**pescar**)	She fished.	______________
(**escribir**)	I didn't write.	______________
(**nadar**)	Did you swim?	______________
(**pelear**)	We fought.	______________
(**navegar**)	They sailed.	______________
(**hablar**)	He spoke.	______________
(**estacionar**)	I didn't park.	______________

Hot Tips!

- See how the "we" form looks exactly like the one on Planet Present Tense!

- You knew I'd mention the **tú** form:

You (informal) worked.	**Trabajaste.**
You (informal) ate.	**Comiste.**
You (informal) wrote.	**Escribiste.**

THE CRAZY ONES
Las palabras locas

It figures! Like everywhere else in our travels, not all the preterits like to follow the rules. Take on this next group carefully, and notice any consistencies in their changes. Here, the **e** becomes an **i** in two of the forms:

(to ask for) ***pedir*: pedí, pidió, pidieron, pedimos**
(to feel) ***sentir*: sentí, sintió, sintieron, sentimos**
(to serve) ***servir*: serví, sirvió, sirvieron, servimos**

Collect more members of this unique band of **-ir** verbs. Just follow the pattern above:

(to choose) ***elegir:*** ____________ ____________ ____________ ____________
(to compete) ***competir:*** ____________ ____________ ____________ ____________
(to measure) ***medir:*** ____________ ____________ ____________ ____________
(to repeat) ***repetir:*** ____________ ____________ ____________ ____________

And here's another cluster of irregulars in the preterit. They all end in the letters **-uir**. As you practice reading each word aloud, pay special attention to the spelling:

(to build) ***construir:* construí, construyó, construyeron, construimos**
(to destroy) ***destruir:* destruí, destruyó, destruyeron, destruimos**
(to include) ***incluir:* incluí, incluyó, incluyeron, incluimos**

Here's more of the same. It's your turn to complete the forms:

(to contribute) ***contribuir:* contribuí, contribuyó** ____________ ____________
(to conclude) ***concluir:*** ____________ ____________ ____________ ____________
(to obstruct) ***obstruir:*** ____________ ____________ ____________ ____________

HOT TIPS

Hot Tips!

- Members of the **cir** series are a lot alike, too! All these words end in the exact same letters, and have no accent marks:

  (to produce) ***producir:* produje, produjo, produjeron, produjimos**
  (to introduce) ***introducir:* introduje, introdujo,** ____________ ____________
  (to reduce) ***reducir:*** ____________ ____________ ____________ ____________
  (to translate) ***traducir:*** ____________ ____________ ____________ ____________

MORE EXAMPLES OF IRREGULARITIES
Más ejemplos de irregularidades

You should know by now that the key to remembering irregular verbs is to focus on key patterns instead of each individual word. For example, in the preterit, anything with **poner** inside gets treated the same:

(to put) ***poner:* puse, puso, pusieron, pusimos**
(to suppose) ***suponer:* supuse, supuso, supusieron, supusimos**
(to oppose) ***oponer:* opuse, opuso, opusieron, opusimos**
(to fix) ***componer:* compuse, compuso, compusieron, compusimos**
(to propose) ***proponer:* propuse, porpuso, propusieron, propusimos**

Stay on a roll. Note the awkward shift in these verbs that include the word **traer**. Finish the forms below:
(to bring) ***traer:* traje, trajo, trajeron, trajimos**
(to attract) ***atraer:* atraje, atrajo, atrajeron, atrajimos**
(to distract) ***distraer:*** ____________ ____________ ____________ ____________
(to subtract) ***substraer:*** ____________ ____________ ____________ ____________

And look at **tener**. All its friends are just as strange!
(to have) ***tener:* tuve, tuvo, tuvieron, tuvimos**

Keep going:
(to contain) ***contener:*** ____________ ____________ ____________ ____________
(to detain) ***detener:*** ____________ ____________ ____________ ____________
(to entertain) ***entretener:*** ____________ ____________ ____________ ____________
(to maintain) ***mantener:*** ____________ ____________ ____________ ____________
(to obtain) ***obtener:*** ____________ ____________ ____________ ____________

Also, any verb with **venir** looks like this on preterit property:

(to come) ***venir:* vine, vino, vinieron, vinimos**

Go on—it's your turn:
(to agree) ***convenir:*** ____________ ____________ ____________ ____________
(to intervene) ***intervenir:*** ____________ ____________ ____________ ____________
(to foresee) ***prevenir:*** ____________ ____________ ____________ ____________

¡Yo recuerdo!

Now that you've read about preterits, can you translate?

Tuvimos una fiesta. ____________________
Sandra no vino. ____________________
Pidieron comida. ____________________
Destruyeron todo. ____________________
Compuse la música. ____________________
¿Trajo el papel? ____________________
Mantuvimos el carro. ____________________
Traduje el libro. ____________________

Hot Tips!

- When you deal with irregulars, you're bound to meet up with a few **-se** verbs, or reflexives. This is what happens to them:

(to surrender)	**rendirse**	**Nos rendimos ayer.**
(to get dressed)	**vestirse**	**Me vestí muy temprano.**
(to become)	**ponerse**	**La fruta se puso verde.**

PRETERIT PESTS
Pestes pretéritas

A handful of verbs in the preterit tense are really zany, but that doesn't mean you can't figure them out. Keep track of each one as you practice these next forms aloud. Stay alert for patterns:

(to believe)	***creer:*** **creí, creyó, creyeron, creímos**
(to fall)	***caer:*** **caí, cayó, cayeron, caímos**
(to hear)	***oír:*** **oí, oyó, oyeron, oímos**
(to laugh)	***reír:*** **reí, rió, rieron, reímos**
(to read)	***leer:*** **leí, leyó, leyeron, leímos**

(to die) ***morir:* morí, murió, murieron, morimos**
(to follow) ***seguir:* seguí, siguió, siguieron, seguimos**
(to give) ***dar:* di, dio, dieron, dimos**
(to sleep) ***dormir:* dormí, durmió, durmieron, dormimos**

(to walk) ***andar:* anduve, anduvo, anduvieron, anduvimos**
(to be) ***estar:* estuve, estuvo, estuvieron, estuvimos**

(to be able to) ***poder:* pude, pudo, pudieron, pudimos**
(to fit) ***caber:* cupe, cupo, cupieron, cupimos**
(to know) ***saber:* supe, supo, supieron, supimos**

(to do, to make) ***hacer:* hice, hizo, hicieron, hicimos**
(to say) ***decir:* dije, dijo, dijeron, dijimos**
(to want) ***querer:* quise, quiso, quisieron, quisimos**

Hot Tips!

- A couple of verbs change meaning when you speak in the preterit:

I know.	**Yo sé.**	I found out.	**Yo supe.**
I know him.	**Le conozco.**	I met him.	**Le conocí.**
I don't want to.	**No quiero.**	I refused to.	**No quise.**

¿Cómo se escribe?

Some preterits must be spelled differently, although they're pronounced as normal as can be:

(to touch) ***tocar:* toqué, tocó, tocaron, tocamos**
(to pay) ***pagar:* pagué, pagó, pagaron, pagamos**
(to pray) ***rezar:* recé, rezó, rezaron, rezamos**
(to find out) ***averiguar:* averigüé, averiguó, averiguaron, averiguamos**
(to polish) ***bruñir:* bruñí, bruñó, bruñeron, bruñimos**

TO GO OR TO BE?
¿Ir o Ser?

Don't ask me why, but the following two well-known verbs have exactly the same forms in the preterit. It's really no big deal, since the context of your sentence will determine which of the two you're referring to. Try them out—they're terribly important:

I went/I was	**fui**
You, He, She, It went/You were; He, She, It was	**fue**
You (pl.), They went/You (pl.), They were	**fueron**
We went/We were	**fuimos**

These examples will help you out:

I went to my house	**Fui a mi casa.**
I was the person.	**Fui la persona.**
Where did you go?	**¿Adónde fue?**
Who was it?	**¿Quién fue?**
They went to work.	**Fueron al trabajo.**
They were responsible.	**Fueron responsables.**
We didn't go late.	**No fuimos tarde.**
We weren't students.	**No fuimos estudiantes.**

Hot Tips!

- "Went," "was," and "were" can be expressed in several ways in Spanish. You'll learn all of these words very soon:

She went to college.	**Iba al colegio.**	They were friends.	**Eran amigos.**
I was at my house.	**Estaba en mi casa.**		

Consejos verbales

Infinitives fit in with your preterit forms:

I saw your sister dance.	**Yo vi bailar a su hermana.**
A knock at the door was heard.	**Se oyó tocar la puerta.**
They let us enter.	**Nos dejaron entrar.**

¡Yo recuerdo!

Change these present tense phrases to the preterit, just like the example. Look out—they're irregular!

Voy a mi trabajo. ***Fui a mi trabajo.*** ____________
Duermo en mi cama. ____________________.
Hago la ensalada. ____________________.
Pago el dinero. ____________________.
Rezo a Dios. ____________________.
Leo mucho. ____________________.

THE WORLD OF SPORTS
El mundo del deporte

Before we tackle any new turf during our excursion to Past Tense Territory, let's play with another set of Spanish vocabulary words. In this chapter, all our terms refer to fun and leisure. Start off with a universal theme—sports! Note the similarities to English:

I played...	**Jugué...**
I watched...	**Miré...**

baseball	**el béisbol**
basketball	**el básquetbol**
bowling	**el boliche**
boxing	**el boxeo**
football	**el fútbol americano**
golf	**el golf**
hockey	**el hockey**
lacrosse	**el lacrosse**
racquetball	**el ráquetbol**
soccer	**el fútbol**
tennis	**el tenis**
volleyball	**el vóleibol**

These **actividades** are pretty fun, too! Continue to use the preterit:

I like...	**Me gusta...**
I liked...	**Me gustó...**
boating	**el paseo en bote**
dancing	**el baile**
fishing	**la pesca**
hiking	**la caminata**
horseback riding	**la equitación**
jogging	**el trote**
running	**la carrera**
sailing	**la navegación a vela**
skating	**el patinaje**
skiing	**el esquí**
Did you learn how...?	**¿Aprendió cómo...?**
to lift weights	**levantar pesas**
to do exercise	**hacer ejercicio**
to ride bikes	**andar en bicicleta**

Hot Tips!

- If you're into sports, learn those words that relate to what you do:

I went to (the)...	**Fui a...**
arena	**el anfiteatro**
court	**la cancha**
field	**el campo**
game	**el juego**
gym	**el gimnasio**
match	**el partido**
playground	**el campo de recreo**
pool	**la piscina**
practice	**la práctica**
stadium	**el estadio**
bowling alley	**la bolera**
bull ring	**la plaza de toros**
golf course	**el campo de golf**
skating rink	**el patinadero**

- Many Spanish-speakers use English when it comes to **deportes**:

  el ping pong
  el rollerblading
  los aerobics

Sports Equipment
Equipo deportivo

Don't give up on those commands!

Use...	**Use...**
Take...	**Tome...**
Bring...	**Traiga...**
ball	**la pelota**
basket	**la canasta**
bat	**el bate**
bow and arrow	**el arco y la flecha**
darts	**los dardos**
mitt	**el guante**
net	**la red**
pool table	**la mesa de billar**
racket	**la raqueta**
treadmill	**el molino**
weights	**las pesas**

Care to add anything to the list above?

________________ ________________ ________________

________________ ________________ ________________

________________ ________________ ________________

And now some exercises:

I watched the match. ________________________________

I liked the gym. ________________________________

Do you like the ball? ________________________________

Did you learn to use the bat? ________________________________

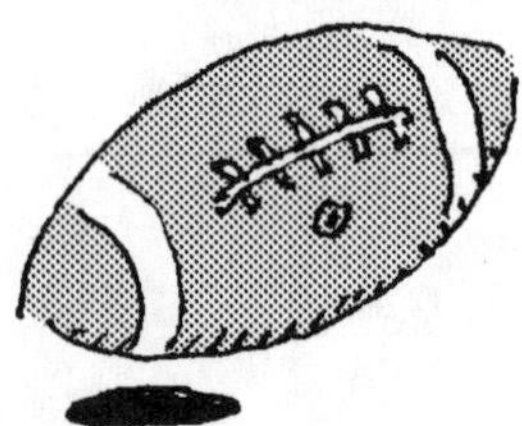

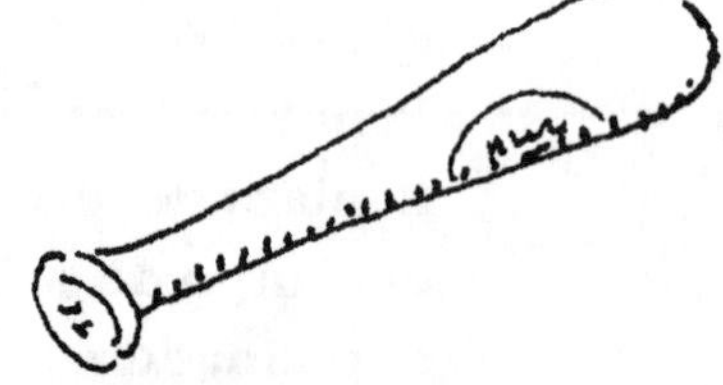

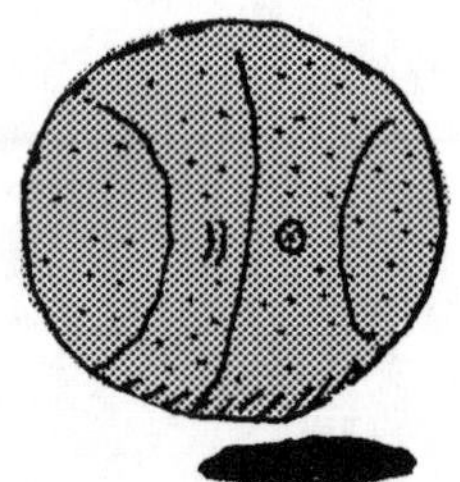

WHAT USED TO HAPPEN? HERE IS THE IMPERFECT!
¿Qué pasaba? ¡Aquí está el imperfecto!

We're not out of the woods yet. Get ready for the other major verb form here in the Land of Past Tenses. It's called the imperfect.

Unlike the preterit, which expresses a completed action, the imperfect expresses a continued, customary, or repeated action in the past. In other words, it's used to express what was happening or what used to happen before.

Let's take a look at a simple formula that shows how to create imperfect forms with most action words. Fortunately, it's a whole lot easier than the preterit.

For regular **-ar** actions, change the endings just like this example:

To Work	**Trabajar**
I was working	**trabajaba**
You were working; He, She was working	**trabajaba**
You (pl.), They were working	**trabajaban**
We were working	**trabajábamos**

Check out these translations. Unlike the preterit, these actions were never really started and completed:

I used to work in Mexico.	**Trabajaba en México.**
Were they working?	**¿Trabajaban?**
We wouldn't work there.	**No trabajábamos allí.**

For regular **-er** and **-ir** actions, the endings are formed differently:

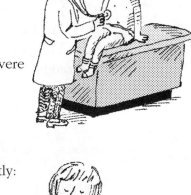

To Eat	**Comer**
I was eating	**comía**
You were eating; He, She was eating	**comía**
You (pl.), They were eating	**comían**
We were eating	**comíamos**

Fill in the English. You don't need any help:

To Write	**Escribir**
______________________________	**escribía**
______________________________	**escribía**
______________________________	**escribían**
______________________________	**escribíamos**

Again, notice how these differ from the preterit:

We used to write letters.	**Escribíamos cartas.**
She was writing a novel.	**Ella escribía una novela.**
I wouldn't eat breakfast.	**Yo comía el desayuno.**
Were they eating meat?	**¿Comían la carne?**

Hot Tips!

- You need to study. These examples will get you started. Notice how different the translations are from the preterit:

I was running.	**Corría.**
She used to sing.	**Cantaba.**
We wouldn't drive.	**No manejábamos.**
They were climbing.	**Subían.**
Did you guys used to finish?	**¿Terminaban ustedes?**

- As always, drop the subject pronoun if it's understood who you're talking about:

I used to play. **(Yo) jugaba**

- Here are the shortcut formulas for regular verbs in the imperfect tense. Take notes, you card-makers!

hablar	**comer**	**escribir**
hablaba (n)	**comía (n)**	**escribía (n)**
hablábamos	**comíamos**	**escribíamos**

- Have you noticed how often we use these past tense expressions? Look over all the words that were just presented. They'll prepare you for real-life conversations!

- Talking about past experiences, don't forget those reflexive verbs with **se**. Bear in mind that these "little words" usually go at the beginning. Look at both the preterit and the imperfect:

To Stand Up — **Levantarse**

He stood up in the class. — **Se levantó en la clase.**
He was standing up in the class. — **Se levantaba en la clase.**

To Fall Asleep — **Dormirse**

She fell asleep at 2:00. — **Se durmió a las dos.**
She used to fall asleep at 2:00. — **Se dormía a las dos.**

- And, how about the personal **tú** form? Try it out in the imperfect. The "you" is informal.

You used to buy.	**Tú comprabas.**
You were playing.	**Tú jugabas.**
You would read.	**Tú leías.**

¡Ordénelo!

Things get real strange in commands when all the "little words" come together. Object pronouns can get confusing, so try to follow along. Just remember that general principle—people go before things!

Look how they all go at the end!

Tell me.	**Dígame.**	Tell it to me.	**Dígamelo.**
Bring us.	**Tráiganos.**	Bring it to us.	**Tráiganosla.**

Watch out! The **le** can't be with the **lo**. It changes to **se**:

Give him.	**Dele.**	Give it to him.	**Déselo.**
Buy her.	**Cómprele.**	Buy them for her.	**Cómpreselas.**

What about the negative? Watch the word order:

Don't tell it to me. **No me lo diga.**
Don't bring it to us. **No nos la traiga.**
Don't give it to him. **No se lo dé.**
Don't buy it for her. **No se la compre.**

Hot Tips!

- A few phrases with **se** don't obey regulations.

I forgot the book. **Se me olvidó el libro.**
Our car stopped. **Se nos paró el carro.**
My dog escaped. **Se me escapó el perro.**

¡Yo recuerdo!

Follow the examples and fill in the blanks:

Preterit:		Imperfect:	
Ella corrió.	She ran.	**Ella corría.**	She used to run.
Ellos ganaron.	They won.	**Ellos ganaban.**	They__________.
__________.	We fished.	**Pescábamos.**	__________.
Nadé mucho.	__________.	__________.	I used to swim.
¿__________?	Did you fight?	¿__________?	__________?
__________.	__________.	**No peleaban.**	__________.

- Connect the sport with its related object:

el tenis	**el caballo**
el básquetbol	**el patinadero**
el béisbol	**la canasta**
el hockey	**el guante**
la equitación	**la raqueta**
la pesca	**el barco**

HIGHLY IRREGULAR!
¡Muy irregular!

That's right, the imperfect has irregularities, just like all the other tenses. But, surprisingly, there are only three verbs you'll have to worry about. And the good news is that these are words you'll be using all the time.

See how they contrast with the preterit tense:

(to go) **ir:**
Imperfect: iba, iba(n), íbamos

He used to go there.
Iba ahí. (imperfect)

He went there.
Fue ahí. (preterit)

(to be) **ser:**
Imperfect: era, era(n), éramos

He used to be a teacher.
Era maestro. (imperfect)

He was a teacher.
Fue maestro. (preterit)

(to see) **ver:**
Imperfect: veía, veía(n), veíamos

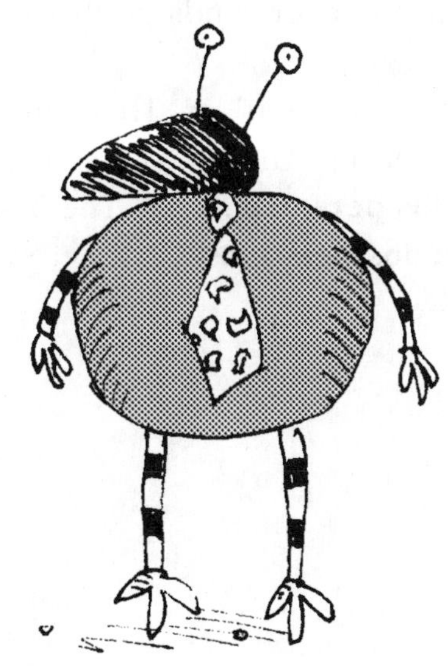

He used to see the countryside.
Veía el campo. (imperfect)

He saw the countryside.
Vio el campo. (preterit)

Hot Tips!

- Here are the **tú** forms. You figure out the translations:

  ibas ______________________

  eras ______________________

- Try not to confuse **ser** with **estar**. Remember they're used very differently.

- Here's an easy guide to differentiating between the preterit and the imperfect. You may want to cut this part out and post it somewhere:

Use the preterit to tell what happened in the past.

It implies...
...that an action began.
...that an action ended.
...that an action was completed within a definite period of time.

Use the imperfect to tell what was happening or what used to happen in the past.

It describes...
...persons or things when the action is past.
...customary, repeated, or habitual activities in the past.
...an action, scene, or condition that was continuing for an indefinite period of time.

- **Hay** means "There is" or "There are."
  Había means "There was" or "There were."

  Hay dos personas. There are two people.
  Había dos personas. There were two people.

- Jot down these key words somewhere. They are the popular time words that go with your past tense verb forms:

before	**antes**
yesterday	**ayer**
the day before yesterday	**anteayer**
last night	**anoche**
last week	**la semana pasada**
a year ago	**hace un año**
in the past	**en el pasado**
the night before last	**anteanoche**

¡Yo recuerdo!

Translate to Spanish:

She used to go there. ______________________________

He used to be a doctor. ______________________________

They used to see the mountains. ______________________________

¡Ordénelo!

Both the formal and informal command forms put the **se** words in the same place. It becomes a **te** in the **tú** form:

	Formal	Informal
Stand up	**Levántese**	**Levántate**
Sit down	**Siéntese**	**Siéntate**
Lie down	**Acuéstese**	**Acuéstate**
Get dressed	**Vístase**	**Vístete**
Leave	**Váyase**	**Vete**

Here's the pattern for negations:

Don't stand up	**No se levante**	**No te levantes**
Don't sit down	**No se siente**	**No te sientes**
Don't lie down	**No se acueste**	**No te acuestes**
Don't get dressed	**No se vista**	**No te vistas**
Don't leave	**No se vaya**	**No te vayas**

MORE FUN!
¡Más diversión!

Let's get back to those much-needed Spanish vocabulary words. Sure, you know the names for some of these things, but how long before you learn them all? Notice the past tense patterns:

We were playing with (the)... **Jugábamos con...**
We played with (the)... **Jugamos con...**

balloon	**el globo**
blocks	**los bloques de madera**
cards	**la baraja**
cartoons	**los dibujos animados**
checkers	**el juego de damas**
chess	**el ajedrez**
costume	**el disfraz**
crayons	**los gises**
doll	**la muñeca**
fireworks	**los fuegos artificiales**
game	**el juego**
jump rope	**la cuerda para brincar**
kite	**la cometa**
marbles	**las canicas**
puzzle	**el rompecabezas**
skateboard	**la patineta**
skates	**los patines**
sled	**el trineo**
stuffed animal	**el animal de peluche**
toy	**el juguete**

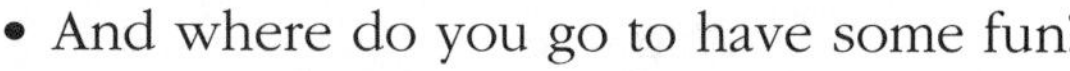

- And where do you go to have some fun?

  We went to... **Fuimos a...**
  We used to go to... **Ibamos a...**

amusement park	**el parque de atracciones**
circus	**el circo**
festival	**el festival**
movie theater	**el cine**
parade	**el desfile**
party	**la fiesta**
theater	**el teatro**

WHAT WERE YOU DOING? LOOK AT THE PAST PROGRESSIVE!
¿Qué estaba haciendo? ¡Mire al pretérito progresivo!

Here's one more way to talk about previous experiences. Instead of saying what they did or what they used to do, Spanish-speakers sometimes share what they were actually doing. This verb has two parts, so pay attention.

First, give your **ar** actions the **ando** endings and the **er** or **ir** verbs the **iendo** endings. You've done this before:

hablar	**hablando**
comer	**comiendo**
escribir	**escribiendo**

Second, change the verb **estar** to the imperfect forms:

estar **estaba, estaba(n), estábamos**

Now, put them together. This past progressive is like the present progressive because it gets easier the more you practice.

Concentrate as you read each verb form:

I was working.	**Estaba trabajando.**
You were eating; He, She was eating.	**Estaba comiendo.**
You (pl.), They were writing.	**Estaban escribiendo.**
We were speaking.	**Estábamos hablando.**

Hot Tips!

- The negative and question forms are simple:

We weren't eating.	**No estábamos comiendo.**
Were you guys leaving?	**¿Estaban saliendo?**

- Sometimes the past progressive is used just like the imperfect:

I was dancing all night.	**Bailaba toda la noche.**
	Estaba bailando toda la noche.

HOBBIES!
¡Los pasatiempos!

Everyone around Past Tense Territory is sharing what they were doing recently in their spare time. How about you?

I was...	**Yo estaba...**
collecting coins	**coleccionando monedas**
drawing	**dibujando**
listening to CDs	**escuchando los discos compactos**
painting	**pintando**
playing music	**tocando música**
reading	**leyendo**
seeing movies	**viendo películas**
singing	**cantando**
taking pictures	**tomando fotos**
using the computer	**usando la computadora**
watching videos	**mirando videos**

Hot Tips!

- Are you having fun yet?

I used to enjoy...	**Me gustaba...**
art	**el arte**
ballet	**el ballet**
concert	**el concierto**
opera	**la ópera**
play	**la obra de teatro**

I would read the book of...	**Leía el libro de...**
coloring	**pintar**
jokes	**chistes**
magic tricks	**trucos de magia**
riddles	**adivinanzas**
songs	**canciones**
stories	**cuentos**

- How about a little music? Recognize the English?

I used to play (the)...	**Tocaba...**
I was playing (the)...	**Estaba tocando...**

clarinet	**el clarinete**
drum	**el tambor**
guitar	**la guitarra**
organ	**el órgano**
piano	**el piano**
saxophone	**el saxófono**
trombone	**el trombón**
trumpet	**el trompeta**
violin	**el violin**

- And, these opposites are always good to know!

(frown) **el ceño**	(smile) **la sonrisa**
(tears) **las lágrimas**	(laughter) **la risa**
(tragedy) **la tragedia**	(comedy) **la comedia**

¡Yo recuerdo!

Join the English word with its translation:

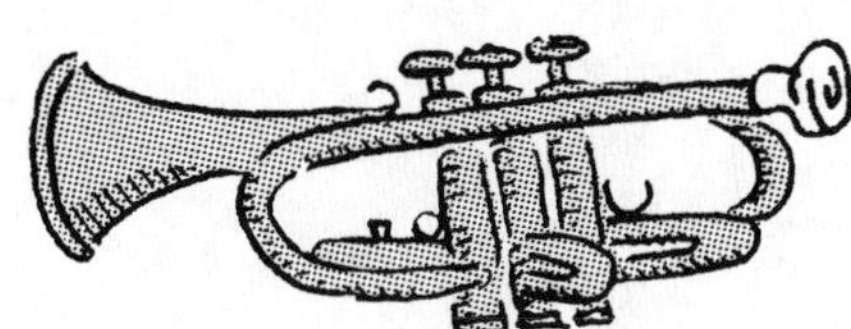

chess	**el tambor**
drum	**el juguete**
parade	**el ajedrez**
puzzle	**la sonrisa**
smile	**el columpio**
song	**el rompecabezas**
swing	**la canción**
toy	**el desfile**

Now change these words from the preterit to the past progressive:

comí	*estaba comiendo*
bailó	*estaba bailando*
trabajé	______________
compraron	______________
escribimos	______________
habló	______________
bebí	______________

6

CHAPTER *SEIS*
¡Sí, he practicado!

PERFECT WORDS
Las palabras perfectas

During our trek through the worlds of intermediate and advanced Spanish skills, we often come across verb forms that seem to appear again and again. The past participle form is a perfect example. The past participles of most **-ar**, **-er**, and **-ir** verbs are easy to form and even easier to use. And as you'll discover soon, they're perfect for everyday use!

To form the past participle, follow this simple pattern. The **-ar** verbs change to **-ado**, while the **-er**s and **-ir**s change to **-ido**:

Infinitive:	to speak (**habl<u>ar</u>**)	to sell (**vend<u>er</u>**)	to serve (**serv<u>ir</u>**)
Past Participle:	spoken (**habl<u>ado</u>**)	sold (**vend<u>ido</u>**)	served (**serv<u>ido</u>**)

Now, here are some ways these words can be used:

Go for it. Create a few past participles without assistance:

comer	*comido*	**mover**	________
comprar	*comprado*	**llegar**	________
cerrar	________	**cocer**	________
dormir	________	**ir**	________
jugar	________	**estar**	________

And what's so special about the past participle? A lot! Just look at this awesome new tense:

The Present Perfect
El presente perfecto

Here's another verb tense with a fancy name, and plenty of practical uses. The present perfect tense is actually made up of two words. The past participle, which we just learned, is used with the verb **haber** (to have), in order to discuss actions that have already been completed. In short, it's another way to talk about the past.

Compare these sentences:

Bailé.	(preterit)	I danced.
Bailaba.	(imperfect)	I used to dance.
Estaba bailando.	(past progressive)	I was dancing.
He bailado.	(present perfect)	I have danced.

Let's take a look at a formula that shows how to create present perfect forms with most action words. First, form the past participle by changing the endings of your verbs to **ado** or **ido**:

manejar (to drive)	**manejado** (driven)
comer (to eat)	**comido** (eaten)

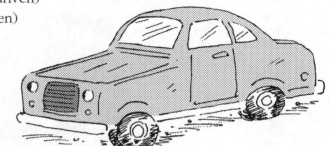

Now, add these unique forms of **haber**:

I have	**he**
You have; He, She has	**ha**
You (pl.), They have	**han**
We have	**hemos**

And then, put the two parts together:

Yo he manejado.	I have driven.
No hemos manejado.	We haven't driven.
Pablo ha comido.	Paul has eaten.
¿Han comido?	Have they eaten?

These phrases are for you to translate:

Hemos estudiado. ________________________________

No he terminado. ________________________________

¿Han salido? ________________________________

Hot Tips!

- **Haber** will be worked on throughout this chapter, so take a second look at the forms above. Also, note how **haber** isn't of much use without the participle.

- Whatever you do, try not to confuse the **-ado** and **-ido** endings with the **-ando** and **-iendo** endings found in the present participle. They're not the same thing!

THE REBELS
Los rebeldes

Don't ask! Just memorize this next set of irregular past participles, and then practice them as soon as you can! As you can tell, they break all the rules. Read each sample aloud as you fill in the English:

escribir (to write)		
escrito (written)	**He escrito el libro.**	*I've written the book.*
ver (to see)		
visto (seen)	**He visto el doctor.**	*I've seen the doctor.*
poner (to put)		
puesto (put)	**He puesto todo en la mesa.**	______
hacer (to do, to make)		
hecho (done, made)	**He hecho el trabajo.**	______
abrir (to open)		
abrieto (opened)	**He abierto las ventanas.**	______
decir (to say)		
dicho (said)	**He dicho muchas cosas.**	______
volver (to return)		
vuelto (returned)	**He vuelto temprano.**	______
romper (to break)		
roto (broken)	**He roto la silla.**	______
cubrir (to cover)		
cubierto (covered)	**He cubierto el carro.**	______

Hot Tips!

- To avoid mixing up your tenses, think before you translate. Always ask yourself, "What am I trying to say? Has it happened, or did it happen?" In no time, your messages will surface automatically!

Focus on the difference:

He has opened the door.	**Ha abierto la puerta.**	(present perfect)
He opened the door.	**Abrió la puerta.**	(preterit)
He used to open the door.	**Abría la puerta.**	(imperfect)

- The informal **tú** form in this tense is obvious:

Have you eaten? **¿*Has* comido?**

- Don't lose track of these little words, which are more common irregular participles:

ser (to be)	**sido** (been)	She's been a doctor.
ir (to go)	**ido** (gone)	She's gone to Spain.
dar (to give)	**dado** (given)	She's given her money.

¿Cómo se escribe?

Some past participle forms ending in **-ido** take a written accent. Pronounce these examples:

traer (to bring)	**traído**	**Han traído el dinero.**
oír (to hear)	**oído**	**Hemos oído la música.**
reir (to laugh)	**reído**	**He reído mucho.**
caer (to fall)	**caído**	**Ha caído en el agua.**
leer (to read)	**leído**	**Hemos leído dos libros.**

¡Yo recuerdo!

Change these verbs to past participles:

manejar	____________	**ir**	____________
correr	____________	**escribir**	____________
escuchar	____________	**volver**	____________

Now, add the forms of **haber** to complete the present perfect tense:

I have driven. ______________________________

She has run. ______________________________

They have listened. ______________________________

Has he gone? ______________________________

We haven't written. ______________________________

They've returned. ______________________________

Consejos verbales

Look at all the forms you know!

Voy a...	**bailar.**
Fuimos a...	**bailar.**
Han ido a...	**bailar.**

I'm going dancing.
We went dancing.
They've gone dancing.

¡Ordénelo!

We saw earlier how formal commands are put together when all the pronouns get involved. This time, let's check out those same action words in an informal scenario. Use this stuff with family and friends:

Tell me.	**Dime.**	Tell it to me.	**Dímelo.**
Bring us.	**Tráenos.**	Bring it to us.	**Tráenosla.**
Give him.	**Dale.**	Give it to him.	**Dáselo.**
Buy her.	**Cómprale.**	Buy them for her.	**Cómpraselas.**

Don't tell it to me!	**¡No me lo digas!**
Don't bring it to us!	**¡No nos la traigas!**
Don't give it to him!	**¡No se lo des!**
Don't buy it for her!	**¡No se las compres!**

THE PAST PERFECT
El pasado perfecto

Adjust one part of the present perfect tense, and you're prepared to deal with previous experiences that *had* happened before. This is called the past perfect tense. Practice each form while looking over the translation below.

I, you, she, he, it had	**había**	**(hablado)**
You (pl.), They had	**habían**	**(comido)**
We had	**habíamos**	**(escrito)**

Notice how the forms of **haber** resemble the imperfect tense. Keep practicing, and don't be afraid to add your own:

I had driven	**Había manejado.**
She had laughed.	**Había reído.**
They had gone.	**Habían ido.**
We had danced.	**Habíamos bailado.**

____

____

____

Hot Tips!

- In some texts, the past perfect tense is called the pluperfect.
- That's right—**habías** is the **tú** form.
- As with every verb form, learn how to express negative comments as well as questions. Notice how the two-part verbs aren't separated:

Have you eaten?	**¿Ha comido usted?**
No, I haven't eaten.	**No, no he comido.**
Had they eaten?	**¿Habían comido?**
No, they hadn't eaten.	**No, no habían comido.**

- In the land of perfect tenses, those verbs with **se** don't get treated any differently. The **-me**, **-se**, and **-nos** go at the beginning:

Has he taken a bath?	**¿Se ha bañado?**
We hadn't gotten dressed.	**No nos habíamos vestido.**
I had stood up.	**Me había levantado.**

- A few other forms of **haber** may surface in conversation or literature, so set aside this next band of words for such an emergency. Chances are, you won't have to use them much. They, too, go in front of the past participles:

Preterit Perfect	I'd	**Hube**	**mostrado**
	You'd, He'd, She'd	**Hubo**	**andado**
	You'd (pl.), They'd	**Hubieron**	**trabajado**
	We'd	**Hubimos**	**ganado**
Future Perfect	I'll have	**Habré**	**parado**
	You'll, She'll, He'll have	**Habrá**	**colgado**
	You (pl.), They'll have	**Habrán**	**dado**
	We'll have	**Habremos**	**comprado**
Conditional Perfect	I would have	**Habría**	**comido**
	You, She, He would have	**Habría**	**levantado**
	You (pl.), They would have	**Habrían**	**jugado**
	We would have	**Habríamos**	**manejado**

- Don't be afraid to interject **le** or **lo**:

Le he dicho.	I have told him.
Lo había dicho.	I had told it.
Se lo he dicho.	I have told it to him.

Consejos verbales

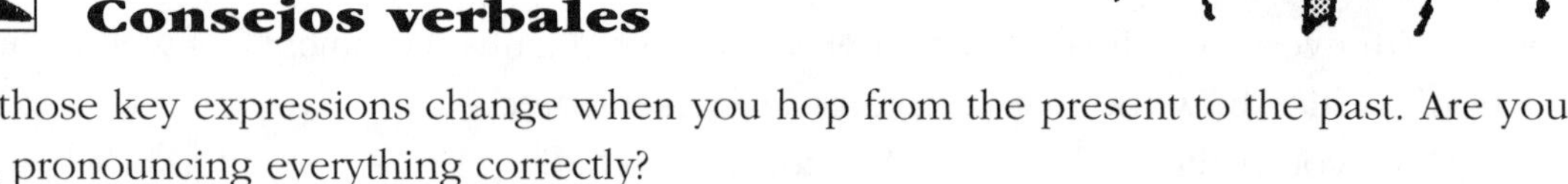

All those key expressions change when you hop from the present to the past. Are you still pronouncing everything correctly?

Tengo que salir. I have to leave.
Tenía que salir. I had to leave.

Hay que estudiar. It is necessary to study.
Había que estudiar. It was necessary to study.

Hace mucho frío. It's very cold.
Hacía mucho frío. It was very cold.

La policía acaba de llegar. The police just arrived.
La policía acababa de llegar. The police had just arrived.

Quiere salir con ella. He wants to go out with her.
Ha querido salir con ella. He has wanted to go out with her.

Now try out your perfect forms with these key phrases:

It had been easy to... ...do.
Había sido fácil de... ...hacer.

They had been tired of... ...work.
Habían estado cansados de... ...trabajar.

¡Yo recuerdo!

Translate into English:

Ellos habían ido. ____________________
Ella había hablado. ____________________
Me había levantado. ____________________
Le había hablado. ____________________
Había que estudiar. ____________________

DYNAMIC DESCRIPTIONS
Descripciones dinámicas

By now, you should have realized that the **ado** and **ido** endings in Spanish are similar to our "ed" endings in English. This is clearly seen when you compare descriptive words. Not all action words fit this next pattern, but look carefully at the creative way participles can be used:

to paint **pintar** painted **pintado**
Las casas están pintadas.
to close **cerrar** closed **cerrado**
La puerta está cerrada.
to arrange **arreglar** arranged **arreglado**
Los papeles están arreglados.

Notice how the "description word" changes according to the object being described. Using the examples above, fill in the missing description!

to bore	**aburrir**	bored	*aburrido*
to dress	**vestir**	dressed	________
to love	**amar**	loved	________
to prepare	**preparar**	prepared	________
to separate	**separar**	separated	________
to tire	**cansar**	tired	________
to worry	**preocupar**	worried	________

These aren't "ed" words, but they describe anyway. Continue to translate:

to anger	**enojar**	angry	*enojado*
to cut	**cortar**	cut	________
to freeze	**congelar**	frozen	________
to sell	**vender**	sold	________
to stick	**pegar**	stuck	________

Hot Tips!

- Irregular past participles can describe, also. Remember these?

It's done!	**¡Está hecho!**
It's open!	**¡Está abierto!**
It's written!	**¡Está escrito!**

- Some verbs can be substituted for **estar** when you try to describe. These all imply, "It is open":

encontrarse	**Se encuentra abierto.**
hallarse	**Se halla abierto.**
verse	**Se ve abierto.**

- Are you able to alter **hay** without any help?

Hay	There is or There are
Había	There was or There were
Ha habido	There has been or There have been
Había habido	There had been

PASSIVE PASSAGES
Voces pasivas

I told you the past participle performed wonders! Another important use is found in passive voice expressions, which generally tell what is, what was, what will be, what has been, or what had been done. To form the passive voice, simply combine a form of the verb **ser** with any past participle. Here are some examples. Again, note how the endings can change:

The book was written by Sam.	**El libro fue escrito por Samuel.**
The meat has been cut by Anne.	**La carne ha sido cortada por Ana.**
The children are loved by her.	**Los niños son amados por ella.**
We will be married by him.	**Seremos casados por él.**
It had been built by them.	**Había sido contruida por ellos.**

The key to the passive voice is to know the forms of **ser**. Why not review and practice them today!

(present)	**soy, es, son, somos**
(future)	**seré, será, serán, seremos**
(preterit)	**fui, fue, fueron, fuimos**
(imperfect)	**era, era, eran, éramos**
(progressive)	**siendo**
(past participle)	**sido**

IT'S NATURAL!
¡Es natural!

Pause to refuel your vocabulary tank with new lists of Spanish terms. The theme below is "nature," and we'll be grappling with topics such as geography, plants, and animals.

I have lived near (the)...	**He vivido cerca de...**
We had traveled to (the)...	**Habíamos viajado a...**

beach	**la playa**
cave	**la cueva**
coast	**la costa**
desert	**el desierto**
field	**el campo**
forest	**el bosque**
gulch	**la barranca**
hill	**el cerro**
jungle	**la selva**
lagoon	**la laguna**
lake	**el lago**
mountain	**la montaña**
ocean	**el océano**
pond	**la charca**
river	**el río**
sea	**el mar**
stream	**el arroyo**
swamp	**el pantano**
valley	**el valle**

Hot Tips!

- Now may be as good a time as any to add a few more location words in Spanish. Make sure no one gets lost.

north	**el norte**
south	**el sur**
east	**el este**
west	**el oeste**
along	**a lo largo**
around	**alrededor**
back	**atrás**
between	**entre**
forward	**adelante**
in the middle	**en medio**
over	**sobre**
towards	**hacia**

Now point to everything you see in the wild. And keep using the perfect tense:

We had already seen (the)...	**Ya habíamos visto...**
Have you touched (the)...	**¿Ha tocado...?**

bush	**el arbusto**
dirt	**la tierra**
dust	**el polvo**
flower	**la flor**
foliage	**el follaje**
grass	**el pasto**
gravel	**la grava**
land	**el terreno**
mud	**el lodo**
plant	**la planta**
rock	**la piedra**
sand	**la arena**
tree	**el árbol**
weed	**la hierba**

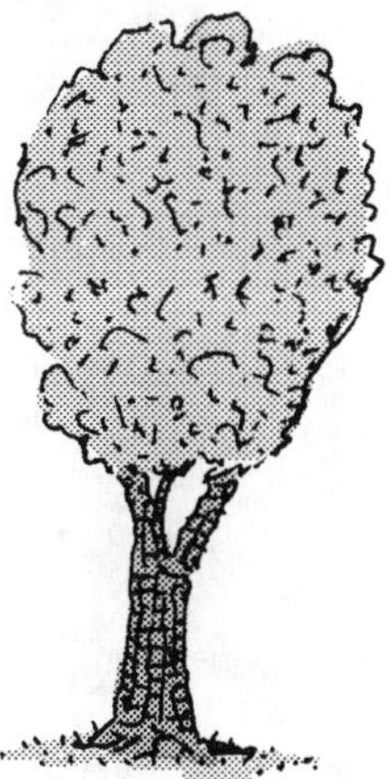

THE PLANTS!
¡Las plantas!

What do you know about plant life in Spanish? Put this vocabulary alongside some action words and practice the verb forms we've learned in this chapter:

I've bought (the)...	**He comprado...**
I had planted (the)...	**Había plantado...**

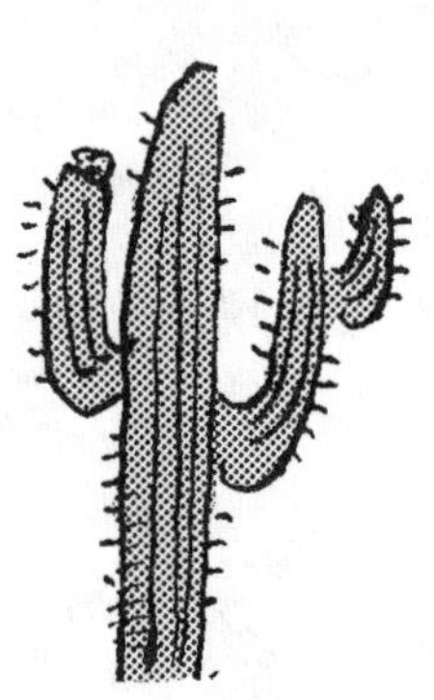

birch	**el abedul**
cactus	**el cacto**
carnation	**el clavel**
cedar	**el cedro**
elm	**el olmo**
fern	**el helecho**
geranium	**el geranio**
ivy	**la hiedra**
maple	**el arce**
oak	**el roble**
palm	**la palmera**
pine	**el pino**
rose	**la rosa**
sunflower	**el girasol**
tulip	**el tulipán**
violet	**la violeta**
walnut	**el nogal**
willow	**el sauce**

Hot Tips!

- Advanced Spanish speakers can identify all of its parts!

bark	**la corteza**
branch	**la rama**
bud	**el botón**
bulb	**el bulbo**
leaf	**la hoja**
root	**la raíz**
seed	**la semilla**
stem	**el tallo**
trunk	**el tronco**
twig	**la ramita**

- Now name these places where plants are found:

crop	**la cosecha**
garden	**el jardín**
grove	**la arboleda**
lawn	**el césped**
orchard	**la huerta**

¡Yo recuerdo!

Be very careful as you translate:

Está hecho. ____________________

Están congelados. ____________________

Estamos cerrados. ____________________

Son casados. ____________________

Fue vendido. ____________________

Había sido perdido. ____________________

Now test your memory:

Name three flowers: __________ __________ __________

Name three trees: __________ __________ __________

Name three parts of a plant: __________ __________ __________

THE ANIMALS
Los animales

Every good Spanish student knows the names for most pets and untamed beasts, so don't be left out! But how do we learn them? Putting labels on animals won't help, so you may have to point. Start off at the pet store or farm:

I've had (the)... **He tenido...**
We'd lost (the)... **Habíamos perdido...**

canary	**el canario**
cat	**el gato**
chicken	**la gallina**
cow	**la vaca**
dog	**el perro**
duck	**el pato**
fish	**el pez**
goat	**el chivo**
hamster	**el hámster**
horse	**el caballo**
parakeet	**el perico**
pig	**el cerdo**
rabbit	**el conejo**
sheep	**la oveja**
turtle	**la tortuga**

Keep pointing. And use all your Spanish skills!

Put it in the... **Póngalo en...**

aquarium	**el acuario**
box	**la caja**
doghouse	**la perrera**
pen	**el corral**
stable	**el establo**
yard	**el patio**

It likes to...	Le gusta...		
bark	**ladrar**	play	**jugar**
bite	**morder**	run	**correr**
climb	**subir**	scratch	**rascar**
do tricks	**hacer trucos**	sit	**sentarse**
eat this	**comer esto**	sleep	**dormir**
hunt	**cazar**	swim	**nadar**
make noise	**hacer ruido**		

Hot Tips!

- Keep talking about your special animal friend:

It's eating...	**Está comiendo...**
It eats...	**Come...**
It ate...	**Comió...**
anything	**cualquier cosa**
everything	**todo**
grain	**trigo**
hay	**heno**
meat	**carne**
plants	**plantas**
seeds	**semillas**

Its name is ____________________. **Su nombre es ____________________.**

It's ____________________ years old. **Tiene ____________________ años.**

It's a female.	**Es hembra.**
It's a male.	**Es macho.**
It's friendly.	**Es amistoso.**
It's trained.	**Está entrenado.**

It needs...	**Necesita...**
It will need...	**Necesitará...**
a bath	**un baño**
a collar	**un collar**
a haircut	**un corte de pelo**
a leash	**una traílla**

THE WILD ONES
Los salvajes

This time, head for the hills, the circus, or the zoo!

We've never seen (the)...!	**¡Nunca hemos visto...!**
bear	**el oso**
beaver	**el castor**
camel	**el camello**
coyote	**el coyote**
deer	**el venado**
elephant	**el elefante**
fox	**el zorro**
frog	**el rana**
giraffe	**la jirafa**
hippopotamus	**el hipopótamo**
lion	**el león**
lizard	**el lagarto**
mole	**el topo**
monkey	**el mono**
moose	**el alce**
mouse	**el ratón**
opossum	**el zarigüeya**
porcupine	**el puercoespín**
raccoon	**el mapache**
rat	**la rata**
rhinoceros	**el rinocerante**
skunk	**el zorrillo**
snake	**la culebra**
squirrel	**la ardilla**
tiger	**el tigre**
wolf	**el lobo**
zebra	**la cebra**

Hot Tips!

And for the birdwatcher...

Look at the...	**Mire...**
bird	**el pájaro**
crow	**el cuervo**
goose	**el ganso**
hawk	**el halcón**
owl	**el buho**
robin	**el petirrojo**
sparrow	**el gorrión**
swan	**el cisne**
woodpecker	**el picaposte**
wren	**el reyezuelo**

- These creepy crawlers aren't always pleasant, but go for them anyway:

She's found (the)...	**Ha encontrado...**
He'd killed (the)...	**Había matado...**
ant	**la hormiga**
bee	**la abeja**
beetle	**el escarabajo**
cricket	**el grillo**
dragonfly	**la libébula**
flea	**la pulga**
fly	**la mosca**
grasshopper	**el saltamontes**
hornet	**el avispón**
ladybug	**la mariquita**
mosquito	**el zancudo**
moth	**la polilla**
scorpion	**el escorpión**
slug	**la babosa**
snail	**el caracol**
spider	**la araña**
wasp	**la avispa**
worm	**el gusano**

¡Yo recuerdo!

Connect the animal with its related action word:

el perro	**nadar**
el pez	**volar**
el pájaro	**ladrar**

Which animal is bigger?

el sapo o el alce ____________________

el oso o el cerdo ____________________

el venado o la ardilla ____________________

Can you name three birds and three insects in Spanish?

____________________ ____________________

____________________ ____________________

____________________ ____________________

More practice! Time to use the compound tenses and the new vocabulary.
Translate the following:

The hawks have hunted the rabbit. ____________________

The crow had eaten all the grain. ____________________

The tiger has found the meat. ____________________

The mouse had found the cheese. ____________________

The boy has bought two turtles. ____________________

The frogs had already seen the flies. ____________________

The ants have gone to the house. ____________________

The rat had gone to the kitchen. ____________________

LOOK, UP IN THE SKY!
¡Mire, arriba en el cielo!

Speaking of natural beauty, have you ever stared into the heavens and just wondered? Now, do the same thing in Spanish! Use compound tenses!

I have studied (the)... **He estudiado...**
He had explained (the)... **Había explicado...**

comet	**la cometa**
constellation	**la constelación**
distance	**la distancia**
galaxy	**la galaxia**
gravity	**la gravedad**
light years	**los años luz**
moon	**la luna**
orbit	**la órbita**
planet	**el planeta**
rocket	**el cohete**
satellite	**el satélite**
solar system	**el sistema solar**
space	**el espacio**
star	**la estrella**
sun	**el sol**
universe	**el universo**
world	**el mundo**

Consejos verbales

This is easy...

Off to study! **¡A estudiar!**
Off to work! **¡A trabajar!**
Off to eat! **¡A comer!**

7

CHAPTER *SIETE*
Espero que practique usted

TOUGH TERRAIN
Terreno difícil

From Planet Present Tense, to Futureworld, to Past Tense Territory… what could possibly lie ahead? It seems we've entered a cloudy haze, with no real verb tense to stand on. Can we learn anything from this uncharted mass of mysteries?

Stay tuned, **super-estudiantes**, as we close out the final leg of our journey through advanced Spanish skills. Welcome to Subjunctive Space, where creatures of all sizes speak a language of their own. Soon, you will hold the keys to their secrets, and will have conquered the toughest part of learning Spanish—the subjunctive mood!

THE CONDITIONAL
El tiempo condicional

Before you slip into Subjunctive Space, you'll have to know how to form the conditional tense in Spanish. It's used to talk about what would happen next.

The conditional tense is a lot like the future tense, because letters are added at the end of the base verbs. As you practice reading the following words, pay attention to the accent marks:

	I, You, He, She would speak	**hablaría**
-ar verbs	You (pl.), They would speak	**hablarían**
	We would speak	**hablaríamos**
	I, You, He, She would eat	**comería**
-er, **ir** verbs	You (pl.), They would eat	**comerían**
	We would eat	**comeríamos**

Ready for some more? Let's begin!

She said that she would buy the car.	**Ella dijo que compraría el carro.**
We knew that we would learn Spanish.	**Sabíamos que aprenderíamos el español.**
I thought that I would go to Chicago.	**Yo creía que iría a Chicago.**
He would like to study with you guys.	**Le gustaría estudiar con ustedes.**
They promised they would arrive early.	**Prometieron que llegarían temprano.**

Hot Tips!

- Write this down: Conditional (would) = **ía(n)**, **íamos**

THE NIGHTMARES
Las pesadillas

You can't hide from those irregular verbs, so you might as well learn them while you can! See how the following words resemble the irregular forms we studied in the preterit. Study the pattern, and then fill in the remaining blanks:

(to be able to)	**poder:**	**podría,**	***podrían,***	***podríamos***
(to know)	**saber:**	**sabría,**	***sabrían,***	***sabríamos***
(to fit in)	**caber:**	**cabría,**	________,	________
(to leave)	**salir:**	**saldría,**	________,	________
(to have)	**tener:**	**tendría,**	________,	________
(to be worth)	**valer:**	**valdría,**	________,	________
(to come)	**venir:**	**vendría,**	________,	________
(to say)	**decir:**	**diría,**	________,	________
(to do, to make)	**hacer:**	**haría,**	________,	________
(to want)	**querer:**	**querría,**	________,	________
(to put)	**poner:**	**pondría,**	________,	________

Now read these examples aloud:

We would say a lot of good things. **Diríamos muchas cosas buenas.**
They would always leave at night. **Siempre saldrían en la noche.**
She would put the flowers on the table. **Ella pondría las flores en la mesa.**

- Once you feel comfortable around the conditional, try out a few sentences with "if" (**si**), when you want it to mean "whether." Note how they're always in the negative:

  We didn't know if (whether) we would come. **No sabíamos si vendríamos.**
  She didn't say if (whether) she would drive. **No decía si manejaría.**
  They didn't decide if (whether) they would go. **No decidían si irían.**

- The sentences above can also be expressed in the future tense. Check out the changes:

  We don't know if we will come. **No sabemos si vendremos.**
  She doesn't say if she will drive. **No dice si manejará.**
  They don't decide if they will go. **No deciden si irán.**

- "Would" is also used to represent a repeated past action in English, in which case it's translated by the imperfect tense in Spanish:

  When I was younger, I would work late. **Cuando era menor, trabajaba tarde.**

- The conditional form of **haber** is **habría**, and it's used quite a bit:

  I thought that there would be more money. **Pensaba que habría más dinero.**
  I would have danced. **Yo habría bailado.**

- Both the conditional and future tenses can also be used for probability or conjecture:

  I wonder what time it is. **¿Qué hora será?**
  It was probably three o'clock. **Serían las tres.**

- Did you see how the conditional tense often follows **que** phrases? Keep that in mind.

- Anytime you use "would" in Spanish to communicate doubt or preference, you'll have to include the subjunctive mood. We'll cover this just ahead:

  I would go if I had the money! **Iría se *tuviera* el dinero.**

¡Yo recuerdo!

Look at all the tenses you've learned! Now you should be able to express action in a variety of ways. This next exercise will get you to shift your thoughts from tense to tense, so focus on when each verb takes place. Concentrate on these examples:

To Leave **Salir (yo)**

(every day) ***todos los días***	***Yo salgo todos los días.***
(right now) ***ahora***	***Yo estoy saliendo ahora.***
(tomorrow) ***mañana***	__________
(yesterday) ***ayer***	__________
(before) ***antes***	__________

To Come **Venir (ellos)**

todos los días	__________
ahora	__________
mañana	__________
ayer	__________
antes	***Ellos han venido antes.***

To Arrive **Llegar (Martín)**

todos los días	__________
ahora	__________
mañana	***Martín llegará mañana.***
ayer	***Martín llegó ayer.***
antes	__________

THE SUBJUNCTIVE MOOD
El subjuntivo

Have you ever experienced feelings of doubt, desire, hope, preference or other emotions? Or have you ever felt like making a suggestion or giving a command?

If you have, and would like to share such feelings in Spanish, you'll have to learn how to use the subjunctive mood. It's called a mood rather than a tense because it's used to express important changes in the speaker's attitude.

There are numerous ways to use the subjunctive, so refer back to this section until you're familiar with all of its forms and meanings. Here are three of its primary uses:

- First, the subjunctive is used when a situation involves something indefinite, uncertain, or contrary to fact:

  It's possible that he might not come!

- Second, the subjunctive is used to express hope, desires, and emotions.

  I wish I were home!

- Third, it's used when one person expresses his or her will that someone else do something:

  He suggested that we come at once!

You'll get the hang of this once we get started. Practice each of the following examples one at a time, and say everything aloud with plenty of feeling.

I hope I can see her today.	**Ojalá que *pueda* verle hoy.**
They want me to write the letter.	**Quieren que yo *escriba* la carta.**
I don't allow him to smoke.	**No permito que él *fume*.**

Notice the spelling changes in the second verb. See if you can find a pattern:

It's probable that I may finish.	**Es probable que yo *termine*.**
No one likes to do it.	**No hay nadie que le *guste* hacerlo.**
We'll leave whenever you want.	**Saldremos cuando usted *quiera*.**
I'm giving you the book so you can read it.	**Le doy el libro para que lo *lea* usted.**
We allow him to work in the garage.	**Permitimos que él *trabaje* en el garaje.**

As you can tell, these sentences are a little different from the kind we've learned before. There's some kind of feeling tied into each one. That's the way it is in Subjunctive Space.

Did you also notice the new pattern in the verb forms? For the present subjunctive, it's a lot like the command form we learned earlier. Watch:

I hope he works.	**Espero que él *trabaje*.**	Work!	**¡Trabaje!**
We want you to eat.	**Queremos que usted *coma*.**	Eat!	**¡Coma!**
She prefers that I go.	**Prefiere que yo *vaya*.**	Go!	**¡Vaya!**

In most cases, the **-ar** verbs change to **-e**, and the **-er** or **-ir** verbs change to **-a**. Here are the forms:

Hablar	Comer	Escribir
hable	coma	escriba
hable	coma	escriba
hablen	coman	escriban
hablemos	comamos	escribamos

¡Yo recuerdo!

You try it. Use the verb **manejar** (to drive):

Espero que él ____________________.

Espero que ellos ____________________.

Espero que nosotros ____________________.

Hot Tips!

- Card-makers, beware! Don't get these mixed up with any of your other tenses. The subjunctive is actually a mood, and should be filed separately.

- As always, the informal **tú** form is simple:

  hables **comas** **escribas**

- Do you recall the stem-changers from Planet Present Tense? They also get their endings reversed. We won't worry about the translations here:

Pensar	Mover	Pedir
piense	mueva	pida
piensen	muevan	pidan
pensemos	movamos	pidamos

Using the same system, fill in these forms on your own:

Perder	Dormir	Servir
__________	__________	__________
__________	__________	__________
__________	__________	__________

THE ABNORMAL ONES
Los verbos anormales

You guessed it! These are some exceptions to this easy-to-follow pattern, and a handful of verbs are a little out of the ordinary. Recognize any command words? Look up their meanings if you have to:

Ser	**Ver**	**Saber**	**Caber**	**Ir**	**Haber**
sea	**vea**	**sepa**	**quepa**	**vaya**	**haya**
sean	**vean**	**sepan**	**quepan**	**vayan**	**hayan**
seamos	**veamos**	**sepamos**	**quepamos**	**vayamos**	**hayamos**

Notice this next pattern. Just add the **-n** for plural, and the **-mos** for we. It's just like that for all these verbs—the base word stays the same. Again, you do the translations:

Valer	**Tener**	**Venir**	**Decir**	**Hacer**
valga	**tenga**	**venga**	**diga**	**haga**
valgan	**tengan**	**vengan**	**digan**	**hagan**
valgamos	**tengamos**	**vengamos**	**digamos**	**hagamos**

Traer	**Caer**	**Oír**	**Poner**
traiga	**caiga**	**oiga**	**ponga**
traigan	**caigan**	**oigan**	**pongan**
traigamos	**caigamos**	**oigamos**	**pongamos**

Practice time:

He is pleased that I've arrived.	**Se alegra de que yo *haya llegado.***
I believe he'll do it, even though it's late.	**Creo que lo hará, aunque *sea* tarde.**
I forbid you to leave the room.	**Te prohibo que *salgas* del cuarto.**
We doubt that she'll go.	**Dudamos que ella *vaya.***
They're looking for someone who knows how to cook.	**Buscan a alguien que *sepa* cocinar.**

THE *QUE* PHRASES
Las frases con que

Since the subjunctive usually follows a phrase that includes **que**, why not learn the top **que** expressions that Spanish speakers use all the time? Their function is to communicate desires, requests, and doubts. So get in the "mood" to practice these. And remember, only use the subjunctive when you *feel* like it:

I hope that...	**Espero que...**	**...salga.**
I pray that...	**Ojalá que...**	
I'm afraid that...	**Temo que...**	
I insist that...	**Insisto en que...**	
I'm happy that...	**Me alegro que...**	
I'm sorry that...	**Siento que...**	
I want that...	**Quiero que...**	
I wish that...	**Deseo que...**	
I prefer that...	**Prefiero que...**	
I suggest that...	**Recomiendo que...**	
I'm surprised that...	**Me sorprende que...**	
I like that...	**Me gusta que...**	
I doubt that...	**Dudo que...**	
I prohibit that...	**Prohibo que...**	
I demand that...	**Exijo que...**	
I lament that...	**Lamento que...**	
I deny that...	**Niego que...**	

Hot Tips!

- Do not try to learn all of this at once! Study only those phrases that you know you'll put to practice.

- See how the **yo**, **usted**, **él**, and **ella** forms are all the same? This makes remembering easier!

- **Se** verbs get the same treatment:

  Espero que ella se levante y se bañe temprano.

  I hope that she gets up and bathes early.

- There are plenty of ways to make a request. Begin with one of these:

I'm begging you to...	**Le ruego que...**	**...salga.**
I'm telling you to...	**Le digo que...**	
I'm asking you to...	**Le pido que...**	
I'm advising you to...	**Le aconsejo que...**	
I'm ordering you to...	**Le ordeno que...**	

- The most common use of the subjunctive is after verbs of desire or command, when the two verbs have different subjects:

I want *him* to fall to sleep.	**Quiero que él se duerma.**
Thomas tells *us* to eat here.	**Tomás nos dice que comamos aquí.**

- By the way, if there is only *one* subject, then you use the infinitive:

Mary wants to eat here.	**María quiere comer aquí.**

- Always bear in mind that the subjunctive mood is only used in special cases, often based upon one's personal opinions:

(request)	It's necessary that...	**Es necesario que...**	**...salga.**
(feeling)	It's a pity that...	**Es una lástima que...**	
(doubt)	It's possible that...	**Es posible que...**	

¿Cómo se escribe?

These two verbs are strange because of the accent marks:

dar (to give)	**dé**	**den**	**demos**
estar (to be)	**esté**	**estén**	**estemos**

¡Yo recuerdo!

Finish these common phrases using the subjunctive mood:

Ojalá que ________________________________.

Prefiero que ________________________________.

Temo que ________________________________.

Me alegro que ________________________________.

Le pido que ________________________________.

Es una lástima que ________________________________.

WITHOUT A DOUBT!
¡Sin duda!

Occasionally, we all make statements that aren't exactly based on documented facts. That is to say, we guess! Here are a few phrases that you can use along with the subjunctive whenever you just hope that something happens. Notice how nothing is certain:

We'll ask him when he comes. (If he ever comes!)
Le preguntaremos cuando venga.
Tell her before she leaves. (If she ever leaves!)
Dígale antes de que se vaya.
I'll wait until she calls me. (If she ever calls!)
Voy a esperar hasta que me llame.
As soon as they arrive, we'll eat. (If they ever arrive!)
Tan pronto como lleguen, comeremos.
I'm giving you this book so that you can read it.
(If you ever read it!)
Le doy este libro para que lo lea.

Hot Tips!

- Have you seen how easy it is to insert those little words, like **se**, **le**, **me**, and **lo**? Check back on the previous sentences to see how they're used!

- Play around with these other phrases when it's time to use the subjunctive:

in case that	**en caso de que**
in order that	**a fin de que**
so that	**de manera que**
in spite of the fact that	**a pesar de que**
without	**sin que**
although	**aunque**
unless	**a menos que**
provided that	**con tal que**
while	**mientras**

Practice:

I work so that you can eat.
Trabajo de manera que puedas comer.

Peter works even though his wife has money.
Pedro trabaja aunque su esposa tenga dinero.

They talk to us in spite of the fact they don't know much Spanish.
Hablan con nosotros a pesar de que no sepan mucho español.

- Any comment that suggests unknown information gets the subjunctive mood. Look:

We're looking for someone who might speak Spanish.
Buscamos a alguien que hable español.

I can't find a Spanish book that might be good.
No puedo encontrar un libro de español que sea bueno.

There's no one here who might dance well.
No hay nadie aquí que baile bien.

- Never forget that this present subjunctive mood only works with the present or future tenses.

It's important that you guys bring it. (present)
***Es* importante que lo traigan.**

It will be important that you guys bring it. (future)
***Será* importante que lo traigan.**

¡Yo recuerdo!

Observe the differences between the following sentences. Translate those that belong in the subjunctive:

He always asks him for money. **Siempre le pide dinero.**
He always asks him to leave. ______________________________.

I want to eat. **Quiero comer.**
I want you to eat. ______________________________.

It's true that they're sick. **Es cierto que están enfermos.**
It's possible that they're sick. ______________________________.

¡Ordénelo!

Specify when it comes to command words! Tailor your actions to fit your lifestyle. They're effective for work or play. Could some of these be put to use?

Agarre	Grab	**Haga**	Do
Apague	Turn off	**Instale**	Install
Ayude	Help	**Jale**	Pull
Baje	Go down	**Lea**	Read
Cambie	Change	**Llame**	Call
Compre	Buy	**Prenda**	Turn on
Consiga	Get	**Quite**	Take off
Dé	Give	**Repare**	Repair
Diga	Tell	**Salga**	Leave
Empiece	Begin	**Saque**	Take out
Empuje	Push	**Suba**	Go up
Entre	Enter	**Termine**	Finish
Escriba	Write	**Tome**	Take
Firme	Sign	**Venda**	Sell

THE PAST SUBJUNCTIVE
El imperfecto de subjuntivo

Out in Subjunctive Space, it's also possible to discuss one's desires, requests, and doubts in the past tense. So, when you share your thoughts or opinions in the preterit or imperfect, then the other verb must change a bit. Keep your eye on these **-ar**, **-er**, and **-ir** words in the past subjunctive. Again, each verb has three forms:

Hablar

hablara, hablaran, habláramos

She wanted	him to speak	them to speak	us to speak
Quería que	**hablara**	**hablaran**	**habláramos**

Comer

comiera, comieran, comiéramos

He insisted that	you eat	they eat	we eat
Insistía que	**comiera**	**comieran**	**comiéramos**

Escribir

escribiera, escribieran, escribiéramos

He doubted that	I wrote	they wrote	we wrote
Dudaron que	**escribiera**	**escribieran**	**escribiéramos**

And when it comes to those irregular verbs, the past subjunctive has the same base word as the preterit in the **usted**, **él** and **ella** form. Look closely:

He said it.	**Lo dijo.**
She denied that he said it.	**Negaba que lo dijera.**
He slept.	**Durmió.**
I insisted that he sleep.	**Insistía que durmiera.**
He read.	**Leyó.**
We would prefer that he reads.	**Preferiríamos que él leyera.**

Hot Tips!

- The past subjunctive also works with the conditional tense:
  We would prefer that you study Spanish.
  Preferiríamos que usted estudiara español.

- There is also a present perfect subjunctive, so you may want to learn these forms of **haber**:
  haya hayan hayamos

  It's possible that you've lost your book!
  ¡Es posible que haya perdido su libro!

- You may come across **-ese** or **-iese** forms instead of the **-ara** or **-iera** forms. They mean the same thing and are totally interchangeable:

comera	**comieran**	**comiéramos**
or	or	or
comiese	**comiesen**	**comiésemos**

- Don't forget that **ser** and **ir** have the same forms in the past subjunctive:
  fuera, fueran, fuéramos

¡Yo recuerdo!

Go back and review a little. Then, fill in the blanks below with the past subjunctive form of your choice:

Juan quería que ella ____.
Yo insistía que usted no ____.
Ellas negaron que nosotras ____.
Nosotros preferimos que ustedes ____.
Sandra dudaba que él ____.

IF...
Si...

All this chatter about the unknown in Subjunctive Space eventually leads to statements that include the word "if." We used it earlier when we practiced the conditional tense:

If Mary comes, she'll bring the food.
***Si* María viene, traerá la comida.**

But, what if you're not so sure? Obviously, when a comment is a little unreal or contrary-to-fact, you'll need the subjunctive. The following "if" statements need both the conditional and the past subjunctive. As you read aloud, get in the "mood":

If I had a car, I'd go to the beach.
Si tuviera un carro, iría a la playa.

If he knew how to cook, he'd work in a restaurant.
Si supiera cocinar, trabajaría en un restaurante.

If we studied, we'd speak Spanish.
Si estudiáramos, hablaríamos español.

See? Nothing's certain. Use these forms for your wishes, hopes, aspirations, and dreams!

Hot Tips!

- Since the following words also express uncertainty, add the subjunctive to them, too!

  Whoever met him, admired him a lot.
  ***Quienquiera* que le encontrara, le admiraba mucho.**

  Wherever she went, she was able to speak Spanish.
  ***Dondequiera* que fuera ella, podía hablar español.**

  Whatever we did, we enjoyed ourselves.
  ***Todo* lo que hiciéramos, nos divertíamos.**

- The unique expression **ojalá** is often used to express hopes and wishes:

  I wish I had more money.

  Ojalá tuviera más dinero.

- **Quisiera** is another key word that refers to "want, wish, or desire." Check out all of its uses:

What would you like?	**¿Qué quisiera?**
They wish that she'd stay.	**Quisieran que se quedara.**
We don't want to dance.	**No quisiéramos bailar.**

- Interject this one-liner when you get the chance:

as if	You talk as if you were the president!
como si	**¡Habla como si fuera el presidente!**

THE TWO-PART SUBJUNCTIVE
El subjuntivo de dos partes

As we learned in the previous chapter, Spanish verb forms include compound tenses, the same as in English, but with intriguing differences. Now we will see one of the most common tenses, one that uses the verb **haber**:

I have eaten...	**He comido...**
I had eaten...	**Había comido...**
Having eaten...	**Habiendo comido...**

In Subjunctive Space, one of the most popular two-part verb forms is the past perfect subjunctive. It's a lot like the other compound forms, which are made up of forms of **haber** and a past participle. Since you already know your **-ado** and **-ido** words, the only parts missing are the past subjunctive forms of **haber**. These two-part subjunctives are generally used with if. Here's the first half:

(If) I, you, he, she had	spoken,	(If) we had	written,
(Si) ***hubiera***	**hablado,**	**(Si)** ***hubiéramos***	**escrito,**
(If) you (pl.), they had	eaten,		
(Si) ***hubieran***	**comido,**		

Now, let's finish these sentences. We've seen the conditional form of **haber** before. Again, this half of your sentence has two parts, also:

I, you, he, she would have...	spoken.
habría	**hablado.**
You (pl.), they would have...	eaten.
habrían	**comido.**
we would have...	written.
habríamos	**escrito.**

And here's what they look like together. Think of ways to use this creative structure in everyday situations around the house:

If I had bought lettuce, I would have prepared a salad.
Si hubiera comprado lechuga, habría preparado una ensalada.

If they had read the book, they would have learned the language.
Si hubieran leído el libro, habrían aprendido el lenguaje.

If she had earned more money, she would have traveled to Spain.
Si hubiera ganado más dinero, habría viajado a España.

Note how the conversations in the subjunctive are often based on opinion, instead of fact. If you like to tell others what you want, think, or feel, then Subjunctive Space is the right place for you!

Hot Tips!

- The two-part subjunctive is worthless without past participles. Have you memorized all the important irregular ones? Go ahead—prove it:

written	***escrito*** ______	said	______
opened	______	hacer	***hecho*** ______
gone	***ido*** ______	poner	______
ver	______	volver	______

- Use the negative and question forms, too:

  If she hadn't planted the flowers, we wouldn't have had the garden.

  Si no hubiera plantado las flores, no habríamos tenido el jardín.

  If you had danced last night, would you have slept all day?

  Si hubiera bailado anoche, ¿habría dormido todo el día?

- Keep on using those reflexive verbs!:

  If I had bathed, I would have shaved.

  Si me hubiera bañado, me habría afeitado.

- Great news! You can reverse both parts of your sentences if you feel like it. It won't affect the message:

  Si me hubiera bañado, me habría afeitado.

  Me habría afeitado si me hubiera bañado.

¡Yo recuerdo!

Take as long as you want to translate these:

If you had married a Cuban, you would have learned Spanish.

____.

If I had left at seven, I would have arrived early.

____.

If they had studied, they would have finished the class.

____.

¡Ordénelo!

We saw a group of simple commands a while ago. Now we'll play with the big boys. Memorize each of these as if they were single words. If you want, use what you know to shape your own!

Follow me	**Sígame**	Take it away	**Quítelo**
Turn around	**Voltéese**	Do it	**Hágalo**
Take it out	**Sáquelo**	Tell it to me	**Dígamelo**
Give it to me	**Démelo**	Write it	**Escríbalo**
Show it to me	**Muéstremelo**	Throw it to me	**Tíremelo**
Lift them up	**Levántelos**	Help me	**Ayúdeme**
Lower them	**Bájelos**	Bring it to me	**Tráigamelo**
Look at me	**Míreme**	Turn it off	**Apáguelo**
Close it	**Ciérrelo**	Turn it on	**Préndalo**

OTHER THINGS TO TALK ABOUT
Otras cosas para conversar

There's always room for more discussion! These next few topics are a bit more thought-provoking than those covered earlier, and will raise your proficiency in Spanish to a whole new level. As you develop phrases and sentences with these words, consider using those verb forms from Subjunctive Space.

Start off by sharing your thoughts on current events:

I'd like to discuss (the)...	**Quisiera discutir...**
abuse	**el abuso**
AIDS	**el SIDA**
budget	**el presupuesto**
crime	**el crimen**
drugs	**las drogas**
gangs	**las pandillas**
government	**el gobierno**
law	**la ley**
political parties	**los partidos políticos**
pollution	**la contaminación**
population	**la población**
poverty	**la pobreza**
rights	**los derechos**
war	**la guerra**
weapons	**las armas**

Some concepts are a little tough to explain:

freedom	**la libertad**	peace	**la paz**
hate	**el odio**	respect	**el respeto**
hope	**la esperanza**	sacrifice	**el sacrificio**
kindness	**la bondad**	security	**la seguridad**
love	**el amor**	stress	**el estrés**
patience	**la pacienca**	trust	**la confianza**

Guess at the meanings of these topics. Look for the English:

la elección	________________	**el terrorismo**	________________
la crisis	________________	**la violencia**	________________
el voto	________________	**la inmigración**	________________
la justicia	________________	**el racismo**	________________
el aborto	________________	**el sexo**	________________

If they didn't have the laws, they would have more crime!
¡Si no tuvieran leyes, tendrían más crimen!

THE LEGAL SYSTEM
El sistema legal

Have you ever noticed how serious conversations often lead to legal issues and concerns? Be prepared. When law and order are the theme, use these terms:

Describe (the)...	**Describa...**
bail	**la fianza**
charge	**la acusación**
court	**el tribunal**
defendant	**el acusado**
defense	**la defensa**
evidence	**la evidencia**
guilty one	**el culpable**
innocence	**la inocencia**
jail	**la cárcel**
judge	**el juez**
jury	**el jurado**
lawsuit	**el pleito**
lawyer	**la abogado**
lies	**las mentiras**
prison	**la prisión**
punishment	**el castigo**
trial	**el juicio**
truth	**la verdad**
verdict	**el veredicto**
witness	**el testigo**

The judge told him to talk to his lawyer.
El juez le dijo que hablara con su abogado.

DO YOU BELIEVE?
¿Cree usted?

Everyone believes in something. It may be personal, but say a few words in Spanish anyway.

angel	**el ángel**	Lord	**el Señor**
astrology	**la astrología**	meditation	**la meditación**
atheist	**el ateo**	Mormon	**el mormón**
belief	**la creencia**	Moslem	**el musulmán**
Bible	**la Biblia**	nature	**la naturaleza**
Catholic	**el católico**	power	**el poder**
Christian	**el cristiano**	prayer	**el rezo**
confession	**la confesión**	Protestant	**el protestante**
creation	**la creación**	psychology	**la psicología**
cross	**la cruz**	reason	**la razón**
cult	**el culto**	religion	**la religión**
disciple	**el discípulo**	sacred	**sagrado**
evolution	**la evolución**	Savior	**el Salvador**
heaven	**el cielo**	science	**la ciencia**
hell	**el infierno**	suffering	**el sufrimiento**
hero	**el héroe**	thought	**el pensamiento**
Jesus Christ	**Jesucristo**	value	**el valor**
Jew	**el judío**	worship	**la adoración**

If he were a Christian, he would believe in angels.
Si fuera cristiano, creería en los ángeles.

Hot Tips!

Link the opposite words:

la paz	**la inocencia**
el odio	**el infierno**
la verdad	**la guerra**
el cielo	**el amor**
el culpable	**la mentira**

LOVE
El amor

Embrace this next set of Spanish words and phrases with lots of care. You never know when you'll need them! By the way, this is a perfect place for the **tú** form:

I had a nice time.	**Me divertí mucho.**
Did you enjoy it?	**¿Te gustó?**
You make me so happy!	**¡Qué feliz me haces!**

Would you...?	**¿Podrías...?**
kiss me	**besarme**
hug me	**abrazarme**
marry me	**casarte conmigo**
see me later	**verme más tarde**
call me soon	**llamarme pronto**
caress me	**acariciarme**

I would like...	**Quisiera...**
to dance	**bailar**
to go out with you	**salir contigo**
to visit you	**visitarte**
to take a walk	**dar un paseo**
to chat	**platicar**
to discuss it	**conversarlo**

It's (the)...	**Es...**
anniversary	**el aniversario**
compliment	**el cumplido**
date	**la cita**
honeymoon	**la luna de miel**
hug	**el abrazo**
kiss	**el beso**
love letter	**la carta amorosa**
promise	**la promesa**
secret	**el secreto**
wedding	**la boda**
gossip	**el chisme**
jealousy	**el celos**
marriage	**el matrimonio**

Are you close enough to look them in the eyes?

You are (the)...	**Eres...**
adorable	**el adorable**
angel	**el ángel**
beloved	**el amado**
darling	**el querido**
king	**el rey**
life	**la vida**
love	**el amor**
lover	**el amante**
precious	**el precioso**
prince	**el príncipe**
princess	**la princesa**
queen	**la reina**
sweet	**el dulce**
sweetheart	**el corazoncito**
treasure	**el tesoro**

We are...	**Somos...**
engaged	**novios**
married	**casados**
a couple	**una pareja**
promised	**prometidos**
together	**juntos**

He's or She's...	**Es...**		
affectionate	**cariñoso/a**	intimate	**íntimo/a**
amorous	**amoroso/a**	nice	**simpático/a**
charming	**encantador/a**	passionate	**apasionado/a**
considerate	**considerado/a**	pleasant	**agradable**
cute	**mono/a**	respectful	**respetuoso/a**
faithful	**fiel**	responsible	**responsable**
flirtatious	**coqueto/a**	romantic	**romántico/a**
friendly	**amistoso/a**	shy	**tímido/a**
funny	**chistoso/a**	sincere	**sincero/a**
handsome	**guapo/a**	well-mannered	**educado/a**
honest	**honesto/a**	wonderful	**maravilloso/a**

Hot Tips!

- Be poetic! Use your imagination if you have to:

I love you with all my heart.	**Te amo con todo mi corazón.**
I'm in love truly.	**Estoy enamorado de verdad.**

- And use all your grammar skills:

  If you only knew how much I love you.
  Si supieras cuánto lo que te amo.

- Some descriptive vocabulary refers to women only!

She would be...	**Ella sería...**
beautiful	**bella**
graceful	**graciosa**
lovely	**hermosa**
pretty	**bonita**
seductive	**seductiva**
very pretty	**linda**

- All this talk about love sounds great in Subjunctive Space. What are these folks saying here?

  Si fueras mi novia, te besaría todo el día.
  Si tuviera un amante, sería simpático, honesto, y guapo.
  Espero que encuentre un amor sincero.

  Now, it's your turn:

  ____

  ____

  ____

8

CHAPTER *OCHO*
¡Más y más práctica!

WE'RE BACK HOME!
¡Regresamos a casa!

Our trip through Spanish has been long and hard, as we've bounced from tense to tense gathering up verbs and vocabulary. Now we're "back on Earth," and here's where the real work must be done. You'll only get better if you practice, so don't delay. Remember what they say about learning a foreign language:
"If you don't use it, you'll lose it!"

Practice Makes Perfect
La práctica lleva a la perfección

At the intermediate and advanced levels of language learning, the best ways to practice include the assistance of a fluent Spanish speaker. If that's not feasible, then seriously commit to some, if not all, of the following activities.

Listen and Speak!
¡Escuche y repita!

You know how effective listening can be when it comes to language learning. Audio tapes, videos, CDs, radio, TV, and even CD ROM products are great teaching tools. But often, consistent real-life exposure to the spoken language is still the best technique.

No matter how you practice, nothing will be retained unless you try to have some fun. These next few techniques are ideal for the more advanced Spanish student, and guarantee a good time for learners at every level!

Sing a Song!
¡Cante una canción!

Get somebody who knows something about music to play or sing traditional Spanish serenades for you. Memorize them, and you'll fit right in at any Hispanic social event! Start off with the well-known example below. As you practice, notice all the verb tenses:

Estas son las mañanitas	These are the little songs
que cantaba el rey David	that King David would sing
a las muchachas bonitas,	to the pretty girls,
se las cantaban así:	he'd sing to them like this:
Despierta, mi bien, despierta.	Wake up, my love, wake up.
Mira, que ya amaneció.	Look, the dawn has come.
Ya los pajaritos cantan.	The birds are already singing.
La luna ya se metió.	The moon is already down.

Dance to the Rhythm!
¡Baile al ritmo!

Dancing is yet another excellent approach to practicing conversational Spanish skills. It's true! Learn Latin dance from a friend or attend a class and you'll be chattering away in no time. The **cha-cha**, **cumbia**, **salsa**, **samba**, **mambo**, and **merengue** are the most popular steps, and Latin tunes are available everywhere on CDs or audio cassettes. By listening to the chorus time and again, the words will stick, and your Spanish will improve. More importantly, you'll be having fun, and be able to join in at Latino parties or clubs. Who knows? Maybe your fancy steps will lead you to exciting new relationships!

Hot Tips!

- Song and dance can be tremendous language experiences, but don't stop there. Here's a list of other extracurricular activities that are filled with Hispanic cultural enrichment. Consult your local news media about upcoming events involving folks from Spain or Latin America, including:

holiday celebrations	shows
sports competitions	museum displays
operas	business meetings
ballets	family parties
plays	festivals
movies	arts and crafts workshops
cooking classes	diversity seminars
concerts	

Add more ideas if you're in the mood!

____

____

Tongue Twisters
Trabalenguas

Speaking of language fun, why not try this other effective practice technique. They're called **trabalenguas!** This exercise will not only help your pronunciation skills, but you can acquire new Spanish words as well. How fast can you say these one-liners without hurting yourself?

Tres tristes tigres trillaron trigo en un trigal.
Three sad tigers threshed wheat in a wheat field.

Compre poca capa parda, porque el que poco capa parda compra poco por capa parda paga.
Buy only a little brown cape, for he who buys only a little brown cape pays only for a little brown cape.

Hot Tips!

- Dialog practice is fine, but it can get boring unless you get help from a native speaker. As you read through this conversation sample about wedding problems, try to picture all the non-verbal movements and changes in tone:

  Octavio: **¡Hola, Andrea!**
  Andrea: **¡Octavio! ¡Buenos días! ¿Cómo estás?**
  Octavio: **Bien, gracias. Y tú, ¿qué pasa?**
  Andrea: **Algo increíble—me voy a casar.**
  Octavio: **¡No puede ser! ¿Con quién?**
  Andrea: **Con Rogelio Morales. ¿Le conoces?**
  Octavio: **Claro, es dentista, ¿no? Su hermano es policía.**
  Andrea: **¿Hermano? No me dijo que tiene un hermano.**
  Octavio: **Sí, yo trabajaba con ellos cuando vivía en San Antonio.**
  Andrea: **¿San Antonio? Nunca me dijo él que vivió en San Antonio.**
  Octavio: **¿No? ¡Qué raro! ¿Y no te dijo que ha estado casado antes?**
  Andrea: **¡Casado! ¡Casado antes! ¡Con permiso, Octavio, pero tengo que hacer una llamada!**
  Octavio: **¿Vas a llamar a Rogelio?**
  Andrea: **¡No! A la iglesia, a la aerolínea y al hotel. ¡Este matrimonio está concelado!**

- How are your phone skills in Spanish? Practice these expressions:

Hello!	**¡Aló!** or **¡Diga!** or **¡Bueno!**
This is _______.	**Este es _______.**
Please don't hang up.	**No cuelgue, por favor.**
Please wait a moment.	**Espere un momento, por favor.**
Could I speak with _______?	**¿Puedo hablar con _______?**
He/she is not home.	**No está en casa.**
When will he/she return?	**¿Cuándo regresa?**
May I leave a message?	**¿Puedo dejar un mensaje?**
Could I take a message?	**¿Puedo tomar un mensaje?**
I'll call back later.	**Llamaré más tarde.**
Please call me at _______.	**Por favor, llámeme al _______.**

Is there someone there who speaks English?
¿Hay alguien allí que hable inglés?

PROVERBS
Los proverbios

Spanish sayings are exchanged in conversations everyday. Proverbs are meaningful words to the wise. Check out the following jewels, and memorize those that suit you best. As always, notice how each verb is used:

El que madruga, Dios lo ayuda.
He who gets up early, God helps.

Dime con quién andas, y te diré quién eres.
Tell me who you hang around with, and I'll tell you who you are.

En boca cerrada no entran moscas.
Flies do not enter a closed mouth.

No todo lo que brilla es oro.
All that glitters is not gold.

Más vale pájaro en mano que cien volando.
A bird in hand is worth more than one hundred flying.

No dejes para mañana lo que puedes hacer hoy.
Don't leave for tomorrow what you can do today.

Camarón que se duerme, se lo lleva la corriente.
The shrimp that sleeps, the current takes away.

Donde una puerta se cierra, otra se abre.
Whenever a door closes, another opens.

Donde no hay amor, no hay dolor.
Where there is no love, there is no pain.

Consejos verbales

One-line expressions are full of infinitives:

There's nothing to eat.	**No hay nada que comer.**
I don't know what to say.	**No sé que decir.**
It's better to play than to work.	**Es mejor jugar que trabajar.**

Hot Tips!

This set of suggestions has been mentioned before:

- Label and command: For new vocabulary items, especially around work or at home, stick removable labels on objects, with their names in Spanish clearly in sight. Then, have a friend or family member order you to touch, lift, look at, or move whatever it is you're learning.

- Interview other Spanish students: List a variety of non-threatening questions in Spanish, using different verb tenses. Then meet regularly with fellow students of Spanish, and pencil in their responses to your home-made questionnaire.

- Make flashcards: It may take self-discipline and commitment, but one of the best methods to remember the meanings and conjugations of Spanish verbs is to use color-coded 3x5 cards. Start off with white cards for regular verbs. Then try brightly colored cards for those pesky irregular ones. They even make ultra-bright cards, which work great for those awkward subjunctives and commands.

- And here's the standard guide to Spanish sound-making. Use it as a quick-check reference to basic pronunciation:

✔ Spanish words are pronounced exactly the way they are written.

✔ Knowing the five vowels is the key to speaking and understanding Spanish.

✔ Poor pronunciation in Spanish does not seriously affect communication.

✔ Turn up the volume for the accented (´) parts of words. Spanish words without accents get more volume at the end, unless they end in A, E, I, O, U, N, or S. These get more volume on the next to the last part.

✔ Spanish words are "run-together" in short, choppy pieces, usually pronounced in the front part of the mouth, with little or no air being used to make the sounds.

READ AND WRITE
Lea y escriba

At the higher levels of language learning, more emphasis is placed on reading and writing skills. Although we've mentioned several tips on how to improve in this area, there's still a need to outline some simple practice suggestions:

Read!
¡Lea!

The more Spanish you read, the faster you'll pick up grammar skills. It's that simple. Gather all the Spanish reading materials you can. Leaflets, receipts, and brochures are readily available, and most libraries include a foreign language section.

To prepare for any reading activity, make sure you understand the differences between your verb tenses. See if you can figure out what's happening in each of these paragraphs, and which tenses are being used:

Raúl López trabaja mucho en su casa. Siempre limpia la casa, lava la ropa y cocina la comida. Vive con su hermano Marcos. Marcos no trabaja. Come todo el día, bebe cerveza, y mira televisión. Los dos hermanos son muy diferentes.

Cada lunes, Carla se despierta a las seis. Se baña, se peina y se viste rápido. Ella es enfermera en un hospital grande. Tiene que llegar temprano para ayudarle al doctor. Carla no duerme mucho porque estudia medicina en la universidad.

Mañana voy a Miami. Visitaré a mis primos en el centro. Vamos a salir en la noche a comer y a bailar a los restaurantes latinos. Estaré con ellos dos semanas. ¡Será fantástico!

La semana pasada fui a las montañas con mi familia. Nos divertimos mucho. Dormí bajo las estrellas y vi muchos animales. Mi hermano pescó y mis hermanitas jugaron con nuestro perro. Comimos muy bien. Me gustó mi viaje a las montañas y quiero volver el próximo año.

Cuando tenía veinte años, Rosa trabajaba en una tienda. Vendía juguetes a los niños. Era una tienda pequeña y siempre venían muchos jóvenes para ver los nuevos juegos, las muñecas y las pelotas. Rosa abría la puerta a las nueve y la cerraba a las seis. Cada sábado había una fiesta en la tienda, con globos, música y un desfile de juguetes. Rosa era una vendedora excelente porque amaba a los niños.

He tenido una buena vida. Mi esposa y yo hemos vivido los últimos cincuenta años en la misma casa y ahora tenemos una familia grande aquí en Colorado. Nuestros hijos y nietos nos han ayudado mucho. Nos han lavado la ropa, nos han traído comida y nos han visitado todos los domingos. Creo que he tenido una vida hermosa porque hemos recibido mucho amor de la familia.

Espero que mi amiga venga mañana. Me alegra que estemos de vacaciones, pero temo que no vaya a llegar temprano. Si ella tuviera un auto nuevo, yo no estaría preocupada. Yo insistía en que tomara el autobús, pero ella quería usar su propio auto. Es muy probable que no tenga ningún problema y que todo salga bien.

CATEGORIES
Las categorías

Group your words into separate categories, and they'll be easier to learn. Not just vocabulary words, but action verbs as well. Use the "opposite technique" if you can. That way, you'll learn two key words at the same time:

to love	**amar**	to hate	**odiar**
to arrive	**llegar**	to leave	**salir**
to go	**ir**	to come	**venir**
to turn on	**prender**	to turn off	**apagar**
to ask	**preguntar**	to answer	**contestar**

¡Yo recuerdo!

All fired up for more review? Find the opposites to these verbs and vocabulary. Only use the glossary if you have to!

detrás	________	**gordo**	________	**bonito**	________
infierno	________	**subir**	________	**no**	________
triste	________	**correr**	________	**limpio**	________
joven	________	**entrada**	________	**mismo**	________
temprano	________	**corto**	________	**claro**	________
caro	________	**tío**	________	**primero**	________
tonto	________	**sin**	________	**techo**	________
blanco	________	**ancho**	________	**adiós**	________
sol	________	**fuerte**	________	**menos**	________
odiar	________	**encontrar**	________	**trabajar**	________
bajo	________	**pequeño**	________	**comprar**	________
abajo	________	**día**	________	**ganar**	________
frío	________	**mucho**	________	**izquierda**	________
menor	________	**fácil**	________	**mujer**	________
pobre	________	**empujar**	________	**malo**	________
mejor	________	**despacio**	________	**vacío**	________

WHAT DOES THAT MEAN?
¿Que significa eso?

Another good language exercise is to research the meanings of the names of cities and countries around the globe—in Spanish, of course. I'll get you started:

Los Angeles	angels	**Nevada**	snow-covered
San Antonio	St. Anthony	**Ecuador**	equator
Colorado	red	**Florida**	flowered
Costa Rica	rich coast		

Use a Spanish-English dictionary to continue:

San José ________________

Puerto Rico ________________

Sacramento ________________

Game Time
La hora de los juegos

No matter what your age is, games are incredible teaching tools. So shop around and check into mail order possibilities or the internet for any board games in Spanish. Concentration, Bingo, Crosswords, or Word Search are the best kinds to begin with. Once you master the children's games, move on to those activities that are geared for adults.

bien f
s r
p í
trabajo
ñ
o
inglés
e
d

Lots of Words
Muchas palabras

Here's a neat activity. Pull a "time word" from column **4,** and develop a sentence that's grammatically correct. Choose one word from each list for every sentence you create. The key is to conjugate the verb correctly. The word order doesn't matter that much. Watch:

Siempre Juan trabaja en el mercado.______________________

Nosotros hablábamos español ayer.______________________

____

____

1.	**2.**	**3.**	**4.**
Yo	**SER**	**profesor**	**ahora**
Juan	**ESTUDIAR**	**en el hospital**	**siempre**
Ustedes	**HABLAR**	**bien**	**mañana**
Ana y Luisa	**NECESITAR**	**frío**	**ayer**
Nosotros	**TRABAJAR**	**en el mercado**	**antes**
La señorita	**APRENDER**	**doctor**	
Tú	**VIVIR**	**inglés**	
	ESCRIBIR	**sed**	
	TENER	**trabajo**	
	LEER	**veinte años**	
	BEBER	**de México**	
	COMER	**cerveza**	
		el periódico	
		dinero	
		en la casa	

MORE ADVICE!
¡Más consejos!

- Always search for shortcuts to remembering your verb forms. Spanish is full of general trends, so take note of all you can:
  - ✔ The imperfect has three irregulars: **ser**, **ver**, and **ir**.
  - ✔ Most verbs ending in **cer** or **cir** have **zc** in their forms.
  - ✔ Irregular preterit forms end the same, except for **dar**, **ser**, **ir**.
  - ✔ The **-n** ending on a verb form indicates "they" or "you," plural.
  - ✔ The **-mos** ending at the end of a verb form means "we."
  - ✔ The **-o** ending usually means "I" in the present tense.
  - ✔ The **ó** ending usually means "You, He, She," or "It" in the preterit.
  - ✔ **Tú** forms in the present end in **s**, and **ste** in the preterit.

And what have you observed?

✔ ______________________________

✔ ______________________________

✔ ______________________________

- Use a timeline to remember your verb forms. The preterit, for example, is like a point in the past (—•—), because it's over and done with. The imperfect, however, is more like a wavy line (〰〰), without a specific beginning or end. The future is an arrow forward (⟶), and the perfect tenses are broken lines (- - - - -), since they have happened at various times before. For many learners, this timeline approach helps them see what their verb forms look like.

¿Cómo se escribe?

Prepare a special list of verbs that require spelling changes in their forms. Indicate the change at the top, and add to the list as you learn more Spanish. These are only samples:

(c)	(j)	(z)	(que)	(gue)
gozar	**coger**	**vencer**	**sacar**	**pagar**
abrazar	**corregir**	**cocer**	**tocar**	**colgar**
alcanzar	**dirigir**	**convencer**	**acercar**	**jugar**
amenazar	**elegir**	**torcer**	**atacar**	**juzgar**
avanzar	**escoger**		**buscar**	**llegar**
cazar	**recoger**		**publicar**	**negar**
cruzar	(ü)		**explicar**	**obligar**
comenzar	**averiguar**		**indicar**	**pegar**
			secar	**cargar**
			suplicar	**agregar**
			rascar	**apagar**
			marcar	**tragar**

QUESTIONS!
¡Preguntas!

This isn't a bad way to review. Just answer as many questions as you can! All the ones below are directed at you, so it isn't really necessary to write down the responses:

1. **¿Dónde trabajan los doctores y las enfermeras?**
2. **¿Quién es su mejor amigo?**
3. **¿Tiene usted una camisa azul?**
4. **¿Están hablando español las personas en su familia?**
5. **¿De qué color son sus zapatos?**
6. **¿Es usted una persona muy inteligente?**
7. **¿Tiene usted muchos primos?**
8. **¿Cuál comida le gusta más?**
9. **¿Qué va a hacer usted pasado mañana?**
10. **¿Comprende usted bien el francés?**
11. **¿Cuáles son tres animales grandes?**
12. **¿Tiene usted miedo de Drácula?**
13. **¿Dónde llueve y nieva mucho?**
14. **¿Es nuevo, bonito y blanco su carro?**
15. **¿Adónde va usted después del trabajo?**

16. ¿Cuáles son tres deportes importantes?
17. ¿Le gusta comprar ropa a usted?
18. ¿Tiene que ir al dentista mucho?
19. ¿Prefiere bailar o estudiar?
20. ¿Cuáles son tres profesiones importantes?
21. ¿Cierra las ventanas cuando hace mucho calor?
22. ¿Usted va al cine mucho?
23. ¿Qué estaba haciendo anoche a la medianoche?
24. ¿Quién le dijo "hi" ahora?
25. ¿De dónde es usted?
26. ¿Cuándo tendrá las vacaciones?
27. ¿Dice usted muchas mentiras?
28. ¿Adónde fue usted ayer por la mañana?
29. ¿Son las ocho y cuarto todavía?
30. ¿Qué quiere comer usted para el desayuno?
31. ¿Puede usted levantar dos sillas con una mano?
32. ¿Sabe usted manejar un tren?
33. ¿Nos dice cosas importantes el presidente?
34. ¿Necesita llegar temprano al trabajo?
35. ¿Quisiera usted ir a la luna?
36. ¿Miraba televisión anoche?
37. ¿Conoce usted a Santa Claus?
38. ¿Estudió español la semana pasada?
39. ¿Ha comido mucho chocolate este año?
40. ¿Había hablado mucho español antes de leer este libro?
41. ¿Qué haría si tuviera cinco millones de dólares?
42. ¿Hubiera estudiado español si hubiera nacido en Francia?

Hot Tips!

- Here's a great tip for advanced players. Keep searching for synonyms! Pick up words from different dialects, idioms, and even slang if necessary. Believe me—they'll all be useful! Put the translation next to each one of these synonym sets:

estudiante, alumno	________________	**foco, bombilla**	________________
pájaro, ave	________________	**maíz, elote**	________________
cara, rostro	________________	**acera, banqueta**	________________

¡Yo recuerdo!

Use your knowledge about cognates to translate these next words to Spanish. You may need to consult a dictionary:

physical ***físico*** ____________
plastic ____________
public ____________
Catholic ____________
analytical ____________

studious ***estudioso*** ____________
ambitious ____________
religious ____________
delicious ____________
famous ____________

university ***universidad*** ____________
liberty ____________
necessity ____________
possibility ____________
infirmity ____________

independent ***independiente*** ____________
important ____________
sufficient ____________
absent ____________
deodorant ____________

education ***educación*** ____________
invitation ____________
operation ____________
action ____________
application ____________

dictionary ***diccionario*** ____________
laboratory ____________
necessary ____________
anniversary ____________
secretary ____________

distance ***distancia*** ____________
ambulance ____________
difference ____________
experience ____________
reference ____________

impossible ***imposible*** ____________
terrible ____________
probable ____________
responsible ____________
amiable ____________

STILL MORE ADVICE
Todavía más consejos

- Shortcuts, memory tricks, and simplifications are always helpful. But the time always comes when you need a table that will tell you—at a glance—when and how a verb must end.

Regular-Verb Ending: -AR

Example: habl**ar**

Present Tense		**Future Tense**		**Preterit Tense**		**Imperfect Tense**	
Yo	hablo	Yo	hablaré	Yo	hablé	Yo	hablaba
El / Ella / Usted	habla	El / Ella / Usted	hablará	El / Ella / Usted	habló	El / Ella / Usted	hablaba
Ustedes	hablan	Ustedes	hablarán	Ustedes	hablaron	Ustedes	hablaban
Nosotros	hablamos	Nosotros	hablaremos	Nosotros	hablamos	Nosotros	hablábamos

Regular-Verb Ending: -ER

Example: com**er**

Present Tense		**Future Tense**		**Preterit Tense**		**Imperfect Tense**	
Yo	como	Yo	comeré	Yo	comí	Yo	comía
El / Ella / Usted	come	El / Ella / Usted	comerá	El / Ella / Usted	comió	El / Ella / Usted	comía
Ustedes	comen	Ustedes	comerán	Ustedes	comieron	Ustedes	comían
Nosotros	comemos	Nosotros	comeremos	Nosotros	comimos	Nosotros	comíamos

Regular-Verb Ending: -IR

Example: sal**ir**

Present Tense		**Future Tense**		**Preterit Tense**		**Imperfect Tense**	
Yo	salgo	Yo	saldré	Yo	salí	Yo	salía
El / Ella / Usted	sale	El / Ella / Usted	saldrá	El / Ella / Usted	salió	El / Ella / Usted	salía
Ustedes	salen	Ustedes	saldrán	Ustedes	salieron	Ustedes	salían
Nosotros	salimos	Nosotros	saldremos	Nosotros	salimos	Nosotros	salíamos

Neither all tenses nor the irregular verbs are covered in this table, but enough information is provided to help you with most situations.

- Things get easier once your brain has a system for putting all the words together. Many Spanish students have found the following steps to work for them:

   1. Let most of the key vocabulary and verbs surface first. If the majority of the words are there, and you know more or less what it is you're going to say, move on to Step 2. Otherwise, keep listening and wait awhile.

   2. Focus on what time or tense your comments are referring to. For instance, is it happening right now (present progressive), all the time (present indicative), or yesterday (preterit, imperfect)? Change your verbs to fit the correct time, and get ready to speak.

   3. As you begin to say something, concentrate on the person or thing involved in the action. The verb form must match. For example, are you talking about yourself (**yo** form) or another person (**él** or **ella** form)? Simply conjugate the verb tense in the appropriate form.

What happens next is the fun part. Let everything emerge naturally and follow where your language leads you! There will be pauses and mistakes, along with some pronunciation errors. But at least if the main verbs and vocabulary are mentioned in Spanish, the message is generally understood. So what are you waiting for?

Hot Tips!

- Create your own personal set of power-lines that can be used with any infinitive. This list will get you going. Go ahead and stick your favorite **-ar**, **-er**, or **-ir** verbs next to these:

   Tiene que... (You have to...) ____________________

   Hay que... (One must...) ____________________

   Debe... (You should...) ____________________

   Favor de... (Please...) ____________________

   No... (Don't...) ____________________

   Voy a... (I'm going to...) ____________________

   Acabo de... (I just finished...) ____________________

   ¿Quiere...? (Do you want...?) ____________________

¿Puede...? (Can you...?)__________
¿Le gusta...? (Do you like...?) __________
¿Prefiere...? (Do you prefer...?) __________
¿Necesita...? (Do you need...?) __________
¿Quisiera...? (Would you like...?) __________
¿Desea...? (Do you wish...?)__________

¡Yo recuerdo!

Not all of the one-liners in Spanish are found in this guidebook, which means you've got to hit the streets and find the translations by yourself. If possible, get help from a native speaker!

¡Cállese!	______	**¡Ojalá!**	______
¡Cálmese!	______	**Siguiente**	______
Otra vez	______	**¡Vamos!**	______
Casi	______	**Por lo menos**	______
No hay	______	**O sea**	______
Creo que si	______	**¡Despiértese!**	______
¡Qué suerte!	______	**¡Siéntese!**	______
No me di cuenta	______	**En general**	______
Todo	______	**Sobre todo**	______
¡Con razón!	______	**A la vez**	______
Yo también	______	**¡Caramba!**	______
Es muy cierto	______	**Así**	______
¡Démelo!	______	**No sé**	______
Por fin	______	**Al revés**	______
Poco a poco	______	**No sabía**	______
Nada	______	**¡Qué chiste!**	______
No me interesa	______	**Es muy terrible**	______
Por supuesto	______	**No comprendo**	______
Después	______	**No me gusta**	______

The list of creative ways to acquire Spanish is endless. We all learn differently, so go with whatever works best for you. And remember—no idea is too far-fetched or crazy. If it helps, use it!

BEFORE YOU GO
Antes de irse

After twenty years of teaching Spanish, I've discovered that most learners at this level often get frustrated, slow down, and decide to quit. Many end up stuck forever at the beginner's level. I hope that the following twelve suggestions will help eliminate some of the walls, blocks, or hindrances that get in your way. Remember this page number. It's not a bad idea if you refer to this list whenever you feel overwhelmed:

1. Don't worry if you cannot understand what other people are saying, in Spanish. Believe me—if you're out there listening to the language regularly, your ear will become attuned to Spanish speech in a surprisingly short time.

2. If you are not fluent in Spanish after reading this book or taking a language course, don't fret. It takes years of continuous exposure and practice before you can speak like a native.

3. Feeling comfortable around people from Spanish-speaking countries will make a difference! The more you know about the Hispanic culture, the closer you'll be to understanding their language.

4. Not all Spanish speakers from different countries agree! It's not uncommon for them to clash over meanings of words, customs, or historical events. That's why it's important to be aware of the differences between Hispanic dialects.

5. If you struggle with self-confidence, try to unwind before you say anything. Apply any relaxation techniques you know prior to conversing in Spanish. Giggle, and then go for it.

6. Assertive, outgoing students usually pick up Spanish faster than others. They tend to guess, take chances and experiment whenever they're unsure. A carefree attitude wins over a careful one.

7. Courtesy is king in Spanish. The more respectful you are, the more Spanish you'll learn. So practice polite words and phrases every day. And, as always, be patient and sincere.

8. Practice Spanish every day. Whether it's reading your watch, exchanging greetings, or calling out items throughout the house—try to practice and improve at every chance you get!

9. Bear in mind that being close in grammar and pronunciation is usually good enough. People will understand you as long as the key words are there. Avoid stopping to translate everything during a conversation. Roll with the general idea, and assess the damage later.

10. For those moments of silence when you're desperately trying to recall words and form a response, try muttering one of these "pause" words:

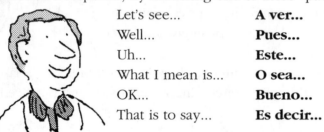

Let's see...	**A ver...**
Well...	**Pues...**
Uh...	**Este...**
What I mean is...	**O sea...**
OK...	**Bueno...**
That is to say...	**Es decir...**

11. When you are in an embarrassing situation, stuck, confused, or at a loss for Spanish words, rely on these phrases for help:
    Lo siento (I'm sorry.)
    No recuerdo la palabra. (I don't remember the word.)
    Estoy estudiando español. (I'm studying Spanish.)

12. Add your own ideas on how to practice and improve! This guidebook only establishes a base for your entire Spanish learning experience. Ask around, listen, and build from here.

THE GRAMMAR WORDS
Las palabras gramaticales

Eventually, you will be forced to communicate using grammar words commonly found in textbooks. They're a bore, but any real student of languages needs to know them. Fortunately, many of these look like English:

irregular	irregular	**el futuro**	future
plural	plural	**el gerundio**	gerund
radical	radical	**la gramática**	grammar
regular	regular	**el habla**	speech
singular	singular	**el idioma**	language
		el imperativo	imperative
femenino	feminine	**el imperfecto**	imperfect
masculino	masculine	**el indicativo**	indicative
		el infinitivo	infinitive
la letra	letter	**la lección**	lesson
el adjetivo	adjective	**la lectura**	the reading
el adverbio	adverb	**la mayúscula**	capital letter
la base	base	**el método**	method
el cambio	change	**la minúscula**	lower case letter
el capítulo	chapter	**el modelo**	model
el cognado	cognate	**el objetivo**	object
el condicional	conditional	**la página**	page
la conjugación	conjugation	**la palabra**	word
la consonante	consonant	**el participio**	participle
el diálogo	dialog	**el pasado**	past
el ejemplo	example	**el perfecto**	perfect
el ejercicio	exercise	**la persona**	person
la escritura	writing	**el posesivo**	possessive
la estructura	structure	**la práctica**	practice
el estudio	study	**la pregunta**	question
el examen	test	**el presente**	present
el final	ending	**el pretérito**	preterite
la forma	form	**el progresivo**	progressive
la frase	sentence	**el pronombre**	pronoun

la pronunciación	pronunciation	**el sujeto**	subject
el reflexivo	reflexive	**el sustantivo**	noun
el repaso	review	**la tarea**	homework
el significado	meaning	**el tema**	theme
la sílaba	syllable	**el tiempo**	tense
el símbolo	symbol	**el verbo**	verb
el sinónimo	synonym	**el vocabulario**	vocabulary
el sonido	sound	**la vocal**	vowel
el subjuntivo	subjunctive	**la voz pasiva**	passive voice

¡HASTA LUEGO, AMIGOS, Y VAYAN CON DIOS!

Good-byes are never pleasant, but we've run out of things to say! All that's left is a hearty handshake, a warm embrace, and a sincere farewell. Our travels together have taught us many new and exciting lessons. We began as beginners and have ended up advanced. So what's next? Well, you know which direction to go from here—¡Adelante!

Su amigo y profesor,

Bill

English-Spanish Verb Infinitives

absorb, to absorber
accept, to aceptar
acquire, to adquirir
add, to añadir
adhere, to adherir
adjust, to ajustar
advance, to avanzar
advise, to advertir
affirm, to afirmar
agree, to convenir
alienate, to alienar
allow, to dejar
alter, to alterar
analyze, to analizar
anger, to enojar
annul, to anular
answer, to contestar
appear, to aparecer
appreciate, to apreciar
argue, to discutir
arrange, to arreglar
arrest, to arrestar
arrive, to llegar
ascend, to ascender
ask, to preguntar
ask for, to pedir
assist, to atender
attack, to atacar
attend, to asistir
attract, to atraer
authorize, to autorizar
balance, to balancear
be, to estar (condition, location)
be, to ser
be able to, to poder
be born, to nacer
be missing, to faltar
be worth, to valer
bear, to aguantar
beat, to batir
beg, to suplicar
begin, to comenzar, empezar
believe, to creer
belong, to pertenecer
bend, to doblar
bet, to apostar
bite, to morder
bleed, to sangrar
block, to impedir
blow, to soplar
boil, to hervir
break, to quebrar, romper
breathe, to respirar
bring, to traer
build, to construir
burst, to estallar
buy, to comprar
call, to llamar
calm, to calmar
caress, to acariciar
carry, to llevar
catch, to atrapar
cause, to causar
change, to cambiar
charge, to cargar
chat, to platicar
choose, to escoger
circulate, to circular
clean, to limpiar
climb, to subir
close, to cerrar
collect, to coleccionar
come, to venir
communicate, to comunicar
compensate, to compensar
compete, to competir
concede, to conceder
conceive, to concebir
concentrate, to concentrar
conclude, to concluir
confuse, to confundir
consent, to consentir
conserve, to conservar
consider, to considerar
consist, to consistir
consult, to consultar
contain, to contener
contract, to contraer
contribute, to contribuir
control, to controlar
converse, to conversar
convert, to convertir
convince, to convencer
cook, to cocinar
correct, to corregir
cost, to costar
count, to contar
cover, to cubrir, tapar
crash, to chocar
cross, to cruzar
cry, to llorar
cure, to curar
cut, to cortar
dance, to bailar
decide, to decidir
declare, to declarar
dedicate, to dedicar
defend, to defender
deliver, to entregar
deny, to negar
depend, to depender
describe, to describir
desire, to desear
destroy, to destruir
detain, to detener
die, to morir
dig, to escarbar
diminish, to disminuir
direct, to dirigir
discover, to descubrir
discuss, to conversar
dissolve, to disolver
distinguish, to distinguir
distract, to distraer
distribute, to distribuir
divide, to dividir
do, to hacer
draw, to dibujar
dream, to soñar
drink, to beber, tomar
drive, to manejar
dry, to secar
earn, to ganar
eat, to comer
eliminate, to eliminar
empty, to vaciar
end, to acabar, terminar
enter, to entrar
entertain, to entretener
escape, to huir
evacuate, to evacuar
evaluate, to evaluar
examine, to examinar
exchange, to cambiar
exist, to existir
explain, to explicar
explore, to explorar
facilitate, to facilitar
fall, to caer
fear, to temer
feed, to alimentar
feel, to sentir
fight, to pelear
fill, to llenar
find, to encontrar
find out, to averiguar
finish, to acabar
fish, to pescar
fit, to caber
fix, to componer
flee, to huir
fly, to volar
follow, to seguir
forget, to olvidar
forgive, to perdonar
form, to formar
freeze, to congelar
frighten, to espantar
function, to funcionar
get, to obtener
get down, to bajar
get near, to acercar
give, to dar
go, to ir
go out, to salir
grind, to moler
grow, to crecer
hang, to colgar
happen, to pasar
hate, to odiar
have, to (perfect tenses) haber
have, to tener
hear, to oír
help, to ayudar
hide, to esconder
hire, to contratar
hit, to pegar
hold, to detener
hug, to abrazar
hunt, to cazar
hurt, to doler
imagine, to imaginar
include, to incluir
indicate, to indicar
inform, to informar
inhibit, to inhibir
injure, to herir
insert, to meter
insist, to insistir
install, to instalar
interpret, to interpretar
invest, to invertir

investigate, to investigar
involve, to comprometer
judge, to juzgar
jump, to saltar
keep, to guardar
kick, to patear
kiss, to besar
know someone, to conocer
know something, to saber
lay, to colocar
lead, to guiar
learn, to aprender
leave, to salir
lend, to prestar
let, to permitir
lie, to mentir
lift, to levantar
light, to encender
like, to gustar
listen, to escuchar
live, to vivir
look, to mirar
loosen, to soltar
lose, to perder
love, to amar
maintain, to mantener
make, to hacer
mark, to marcar
mean, to significar
measure, to medir
meet, to encontrar
melt, to derretir
move, to mover
need, to necesitar
note, to notar
notify, to notificar
obey, to obedecer
oblige, to obligar
observe, to observar
obstruct, to obstruir
obtain, to obtener
occur, to ocurrir
offend, to ofender
offer, to ofrecer
omit, to omitir
open, to abrir
operate, to operar
oppose, to oponer
order, to ordenar
owe, to deber
park, to estacionar
pay, to pagar
perceive, to percibir
permit, to permitir
persist, to persistir
pick up, to recoger
plant, to plantar
play, to jugar
plug in, to enchufar
polish, to pulir
practice, to practicar
pray, to rezar
prefer, to preferir
prepare, to preparar
present, to presentar
prevent, to prevenir
proceed, to proceder
produce, to producir
progress, to progresar
prohibit, to prohibir
promise, to prometer
pronounce, to pronunciar
propose, to proponer
protect, to proteger
prove, to probar
publish, to publicar
pull, to jalar
push, to empujar
put, to poner
quit, to renunciar
rain, to llover
reach, to alcanzar
read, to leer
receive, to recibir
recognize, to reconocer
recommend, to recomendar
reduce, to reducir
refer, to referir
remember, to recordar
rent, to alquilar
repair, to reparar
repeat, to repetir
require, to requerir
resent, to resentir
resolve, to resolver
respect, to respetar
respond, to responder
rest, to descansar
retire, to jubilar
return, to regresar
return something, to devolver
ride, to montar
ring, to sonar
run, to correr
sail, to navegar
save, to ahorrar
say, to decir
scratch, to rascar
search, to buscar
see, to ver
seem, to parecer
select, to seleccionar
sell, to vender
send, to enviar, mandar
separate, to separar
serve, to servir
set, to colocar
sew, to coser
shake, to sacudir
share, to compartir
shine, to brillar
shoot, to disparar
shout, to gritar
show, to mostrar
sing, to cantar
skate, to patinar
sleep, to dormir
smoke, to fumar
sneeze, to estornudar
snow, to nevar
speak, to hablar
spend, to gastar
stay, to quedar
stick, to pegar
stir, to batir, revolver
stop, to parar
study, to estudiar
subtract, to substraer
suffer, to sufrir
suppose, to suponer
surprise, to sorprender
surrender, to rendir
swallow, to tragar
sweat, to sudar
sweep, to barrer
swim, to nadar
take, to tomar
take care of, to cuidar
take out, to sacar
talk, to hablar
teach, to enseñar
tell, to decir
thank, to agradecer
think, to pensar
threaten, to amenazar
throw, to tirar
tire, to cansar
touch, to tocar
translate, to traducir
transmit, to transmitir
travel, to viajar
trim, to podar
try, to provocar
turn, to voltear
turn off, to apagar
turn on, to prender
twist, to torcer
uncover, to destapar
understand, to comprender
use, to usar
utilize, to utilizar
visit, to visitar
vote, to votar
walk, to andar, caminar
want, to querer
wash, to lavar
wear, to llevar
win, to ganar
wish, to desear
work, to trabajar
worry, to preocupar
write, to escribir
yawn, to bostezar

Spanish-English Verb Infinitives

abrazar hug, to
abrir open, to
absorber absorb, to
acabar finish, to
acariciar caress, to
aceptar accept, to
acercar get near, to
adherir adhere, to
adquirir acquire, to
advertir advise, to
afirmar affirm, to
agradecer thank, to
aguantar bear, to
ahorrar save, to
ajustar adjust, to
alcanzar reach, to
alienar alienate, to
alimentar feed, to
alquilar rent, to
alterar alter, to
amar love, to
amenazar threaten, to
añadir add, to
analizar analyze, to
andar walk, to
anular annul, to
apagar turn off, to
aparecer appear, to
apostar bet, to
apreciar appreciate, to
aprender learn, to
arreglar arrange, to
arrestar arrest, to
ascender ascend, to
asistir attend, to
atacar attack, to
atender assist, to
atraer attract, to
atrapar catch, to
autorizar authorize, to
avanzar advance, to
averiguar find out, to
ayudar help, to
bailar dance, to
bajar get down, to
balancear balance, to
barrer sweep, to
batir beat, to; stir, to
beber drink, to
besar kiss, to
bostezar yawn, to
brillar shine, to
buscar search, to
caber fit, to
caer fall, to
calmar calm, to
cambiar change, to; exchange, to
caminar walk, to
cansar tire, to
cantar sing, to
cargar charge, to
causar cause, to
cazar hunt, to
cerrar close, to
chocar crash, to
circular circulate, to
cocinar cook, to
coleccionar collect, to
colgar hang, to
colocar lay, to; set, to
comenzar begin, to
comer eat, to
compartir share, to
compensar compensate, to
competir compete, to
componer fix, to
comprar buy, to
comprender understand, to
comprometer involve, to
comunicar communicate, to
concebir conceive, to
conceder concede, to
concentrar concentrate, to
concluir conclude, to
confundir confuse, to
congelar freeze, to
conocer know someone, to
consentir consent, to
conservar conserve, to
considerar consider, to
consistir consist, to
construir build, to
consultar consult, to
contar count, to
contener contain, to
contestar answer, to
contraer contract, to
contratar hire, to
contribuir contribute, to
controlar control, to
convencer convince, to
convenir agree, to
conversar discuss, to
convertir convert, to
corregir correct, to
correr run, to
cortar cut, to
coser sew, to
costar cost, to
crecer grow, to
creer believe, to
cruzar cross, to
cubrir cover, to
cuidar take care of, to
curar cure, to
dar give, to
deber owe, to
decidir decide, to
decir say, to; tell, to
declarar declare, to
dedicar dedicate, to
defender defend, to
dejar allow, to
depender depend, to
derretir melt, to
descansar rest, to
describir describe, to
descubrir discover, to
desear desire, to; wish, to
destapar uncover, to
destruir destroy, to
detener detain, to; hold, to
devolver return something, to
dibujar draw, to
discutir argue, to
disminuir diminish, to
disolver dissolve, to
disparar shoot, to
distinguir distinguish, to
distraer distract, to
distribuir distribute, to
dividir divide, to
doblar bend, to
doler hurt, to
dormir sleep, to
eliminar eliminate, to
empezar begin, to
empujar push, to
encender light, to
enchufar plug in, to
encontrar find, to; meet, to
enojar anger, to
enseñar teach, to
entender understand, to
entrar enter, to
entregar deliver, to
entretener entertain, to
enviar send, to
escarbar dig, to
escoger choose, to
esconder hide, to
escribir write, to
escuchar listen, to
espantar frighten, to
estacionar park, to
estallar burst, to
estar (condition, location) be, to
estornudar sneeze, to
estudiar study, to
evacuar evacuate, to
examinar examine, to
existir exist, to
explicar explain, to
explorar explore, to
facilitar facilitate, to
faltar be missing, to
formar form, to
fumar smoke, to
funcionar function, to
ganar earn, to; win, to
gastar spend, to
gritar shout, to
guardar keep, to
guiar lead, to
gustar like, to
haber have, to (perfect tenses)
hablar speak, to; talk, to
hacer do, to; make, to
herir injure, to
hervir boil, to
huir escape, to; flee, to
imaginar imagine, to
impedir block, to
incluir include, to
indicar indicate, to
informar inform, to
inhibir inhibit, to
insistir insist, to
instalar install, to
interpretar interpret, to

invertir invest, to
investigar investigate, to
ir go, to
jalar pull, to
jugar play, to
jubilar retire, to
juzgar judge, to
lavar wash, to
leer read, to
levantar lift, to
limpiar clean, to
llamar call, to
llegar arrive, to
llenar fill, to
llevar carry, to; wear, to
llorar cry, to
llover rain, to
mandar send, to
manejar drive, to
mantener maintain, to
marcar mark, to
medir measure, to
mentir lie, to
meter insert, to; put inside, to
mirar look, to
moler grind, to
montar ride, to
morder bite, to
morir die, to
mostrar show, to
mover move, to
nacer be born, to
nadar swim, to
navegar sail, to
necesitar need, to
negar deny, to
nevar snow, to
notar note, to
notificar notify, to
obedecer obey, to
obligar oblige, to
observar observe, to
obstruir obstruct, to
obtener get, to; obtain, to
ocurrir occur, to
odiar hate, to
ofender offend, to
ofrecer offer, to
oír hear, to
olvidar forget, to
omitir omit, to
operar operate, to
oponer oppose, to
ordenar order, to
pagar pay, to
parar stop, to
parecer seem, to
pasar happen, to
patear kick, to
patinar skate, to
pedir ask for, to
pegar hit, to; stick, to
pelear fight, to
pensar think, to
percibir perceive, to
perder lose, to
perdonar forgive, to
permitir let, to; permit, to
persistir persist, to
pertenecer belong, to
pescar fish, to
plantar plant, to
platicar chat, to
podar trim, to
poder be able to, to
poner put, to
practicar practice, to
preferir prefer, to
preguntar ask, to
prender turn on, to
preocupar worry, to
preparar prepare, to
presentar present, to
prestar lend, to
prevenir prevent, to
probar prove, to
proceder proceed, to
producir produce, to
progresar progress, to
prohibir prohibit, to
prometer promise, to
pronunciar pronounce, to
proponer propose, to
proteger protect, to
provocar try, to
publicar publish, to
pulir polish, to
quebrar break, to
quedar stay, to
querer want, to
rascar scratch, to
recibir receive, to
recoger pick up, to
recomendar recommend, to
reconocer recognize, to
recordar remember, to
reducir reduce, to
referir refer, to
regresar return, to
rendir surrender, to
renunciar quit, to
reparar repair, to
repetir repeat, to
requerir require, to
resentir resent, to
resolver resolve, to
respetar respect, to
respirar breathe, to
responder respond, to
rezar pray, to
romper break, to
saber know something, to
sacar take out, to
sacudir shake, to
salir go out, to; leave, to
saltar jump, to
sangrar bleed, to
secar dry, to
seguir follow, to
seleccionar select, to
sentir feel, to
separar separate, to
ser be, to
servir serve, to
significar mean, to
soltar loosen, to
soñar dream, to
sonar ring, to
soplar blow, to
sorprender surprise, to
subir climb, to
substraer subtract, to
sudar sweat, to
sufrir suffer, to
suplicar beg, to
suponer suppose, to
tapar cover, to
temer fear, to
terminar end, to
tirar throw, to
tocar touch, to
tomar drink, to; take, to
torcer twist, to
trabajar work, to
traducir translate, to
traer bring, to
tragar swallow, to
transmitir transmit, to
usar use, to
utilizar utilize, to
vaciar empty, to
valer be worth, to
vender sell, to
venir come, to
ver see, to
viajar travel, to
visitar visit, to
vivir live, to
volar fly, to
voltear turn, to
volver return, to
votar vote, to

English-Spanish Reflexive Verbs

bathe, to bañarse
become, to hacerse
behave, to portarse
brush, to cepillarse
change address, to mudarse
comb, to peinarse
complain, to quejarse
dress, to vestirse
drown, to ahogarse
fall asleep, to dormirse
fall down, to caerse
farget about, to olvidarse
get angry, to enojarse
get better, to mejorarse
get ill, to enfermarse
get married, to casarse
get ready, to arreglarse
get tired of, to cansarse
get up, to levantarse
have fun, to divertirse
hurry up, to apurarse
laugh, to reírse
leave, to irse
lie down, to acostarse
make a mistake, to equivocarse
make fun of, to burlarse
put on, to ponerse
realize, to darse cuenta de
remember, to acordarse
remove, to quitarse
say goodbye, to despedirse
shave, to afeitarse
sit down, to sentarse
stand up, to pararse
stay, to quedarse
wake up, to despertarse
wash, to lavarse
worry about, to preocuparse

Spanish-English Reflexive Verbs

acordarse remember, to
acostarse lie down, to
afeitarse shave, to
ahogarse drown, to
apurarse hurry up, to
arreglarse get ready, to
bañarse bathe, to
burlarse make fun of, to
caerse fall down, to
cansarse get tired of, to
casarse get married, to
cepillarse brush, to
darse cuenta de realize, to
despedirse say goodbye, to
despertarse wake up, to
divertirse have fun, to
dormirse fall asleep, to
enfermarse get ill, to
enojarse get angry, to
equivocarse make a mistake, to
hacerse become, to
irse leave, to
lavarse wash, to
levantarse get up, to
mejorarse get better, to
mudarse change address, to
olvidarse forget about, to
pararse stand up, to
peinarse comb, to
ponerse put on, to
portarse behave, to
preocuparse worry about, to
quedarse stay, to
quejarse complain, to
quitarse remove, to
reírse laugh, to
sentarse sit down, to
vestirse dress, to

English-Spanish Vocabulary

The gender of Spanish adjectives or pronouns shown here is always masculine. To switch the gender to feminine, change the ending to **a** (aburrid**o** = aburrid**a,** much**o** = much**a**).

A.M. de la mañana
above sobre; encima
abuse abuso, el
abused abusado
action acción, la
actor actor, el
actress actriz, la
address dirección, la
adult adulto, el
advice consejo, el
African-American afroamericano, el
after después
again otra vez
age edad, la
ago hace
AIDS SIDA, el
air conditioner acondicionador de aire, el
airport aeropuerto, el
alarm alarma, la
all todo
alley callejón, el
almost casi
along a lo largo
although aunque
always siempre
ambulance ambulancia, la
amusement park parque de atracciones, el
and y
angel ángel, el
Anglo-Saxon anglosajón, el
angry enojado
animal animal, el
ankle tobillo, el
anniversary aniversario, el
answer respuesta, la
answering machine contestador telefónico, el
ant hormiga, la
anxious ansioso
anyone cualquier persona
anything cualquier cosa
anywhere en cualquier parte
apartment apartamento, el
apathetic apático
apple manzana, la
appliance electrodoméstico, el
appointment cita, la
apricot albaricoque, el
April abril
aquarium acuario, el
architect arquitecto, el
area área, el
arena anfiteatro, el
arm brazo, el
armchair sillón, el
armoire armario, el
around alrededor
arrow flecha, la
art arte, el
artichoke alcachofa, la
artist artista, el
ashamed avergonzado
ashtray cenicero, el
Asian asiático
asparagus espárrago, el
assistant asistente, el
astrology astrología, la
astronaut astronauta, el, la
at en
at the bottom en el fondo
atheist ateo, el
athlete atleta, el
attic desván, el
August agosto
aunt tía, la
available disponible
avenue avenida, la
ax hacha, el
baby bebé, el
babysitter niñero, el
back espalda, la
backwards al revés
bacon tocino, el
bad malo
bag bolsa, la
bail fianza, la
balcony balcón, el
bald calvo
ball pelota, la
balloon globo, el
banana plátano, el
bandage vendaje, el
bank banco, el
bannister baranda, la
bar bar, el
barbeque grill parrilla, la
barefoot descalzo
bark corteza, la
bartender cantinero, el
baseball béisbol, el
basement sótano, el
basket canasta, la
basketball básquetbol, el
bat bate, el
bathing suit traje de baño, la
bathroom baño, el
bathroom sink lavabo, el
bathtub tina, la
battery batería, la
beach playa, la
beach chair silla de playa, la
bean frijol, el
bear oso, el
beautiful bello
beauty salon salón de belleza, el
beaver castor, el
because porque
bed cama, la
bedroom dormitorio, el
bee abeja, la
beer cerveza, la
beet betabel, el
beetle escarabajo, el
before antes
behind detrás
belief creencia, la
bellhop botones, el
belt cinturón, el
benefit beneficio, el
besides además
better mejor
between entre
Bible Biblia, la
bicycle bicicleta
big grande
billboard letrero, el
birch abedul, el
bird pájaro, el
birth nacimiento
birthday cumpleaños, el
bitter amargo
black negro
blackboard pizarrón, el
bladder vejiga, la
blame culpa, la
blender licuadora, la
blind ciego
blonde rubio
blood sangre, la
blouse blusa, la
blue azul
boat barco, el
boating paseo en bote, el
body cuerpo, el
bolt perno, el
bone hueso, el
book libro, el
bookshelf librero, el
bookstore librería, la
boot bota, la
border frontera, la
bored aburrido
boss jefe, el
both ambos
bottle botella, la
bottom fondo, el
boulevard bulevar, el
bow arco, el
bowl plato hondo, el
bowling boliche, el
bowling alley bolera, la
box (container) caja, la
boxing boxeo, el
boyfriend novio, el
brain cerebro, el
brake freno, el
branch rama, la
brassiere sostén, el
brave valiente
breakfast desayuno, el
breakfast room antecomedor, el
breast seno, el
breath aliento, el
bridge puente, el
broccoli brócoli, el
broken quebrado
broth caldo, el
brother hermano, el

brother-in-law cuñado, el
brown café
bruise contusión, la
brunette moreno
bucket balde, el
buckle hebilla, la
bud botón, el
Buddist budista
buddy compañero, el
budget presupuesto, el
building edificio, el
bulb (electric) foco, el
bullring plaza de toros, la
bulldozer niveladora, la
bumper parachoques, el
burn quemadura, la
bus autobús, el
bus station estación de autobús, la
bus stop parada de autobús, la
bush arbusto, el
business (commerce) comercio, el
business (deals) negocios, los
busy ocupado
but pero; sino
butter mantequilla, la
buttock nalga, la
button botón, el
by por
cabbage repollo, el
cabinet gabinete, el
cactus cacto, el
calf pantorrilla, la
calm calmado
camper cámper, el
campgrounds campamento, el
can lata, la
can opener abrelatas, el
canary canario, el
candelabra candelabro, el
candy dulce, el
cantaloupe melón, el
cap gorra, la
car carro, el
card tarjeta, la
career carrera, la
careful cuidado
carnation clavel, el
carpenter carpintero, el
carrot zanahoria, la
cartoon dibujo animado, el
cashier cajero, el
cassette player tocador de casetes, el
cat gato, el
cathedral catedral, la
Catholic católico
cave cueva, la
CD disco compacto, el
cedar cedro, el
ceiling techo, el
celery apio, el
cemetery cementerio, el
cent centavo, el
chain cadena, la
chair silla, la
chalk tiza, la
chapel capilla, la
charge acusación, la
chauffeur chofer, el
check cheque, el
cheek mejilla, la
cheese queso, el
cherry cereza, la
chess ajedrez, el
chest (body) pecho, el
chest (storage) baúl, el
chewing gum chicle, el
chicken gallina, la
chicken (hen) pollo, el
child niño, el
chimney chimenea, la
chin barbilla, la
china loza de porcelana, la
chore tarea, la
Christian cristiano
Christmas navidad, la
church iglesia, la
cigarette cigarrillo, el
cinnamon canela, la
circus circo, el
citizen ciudadano, el
city ciudad, la
city block cuadra, la
city hall municipio, el
clarinet clarinete, el
class clase, la
clean limpio
clear claro
clear (weather) despejado
clearly claramente
clerk dependiente, el
client cliente, el
clock reloj, el
closed cerrado
closet ropero, el
clothing ropa, la
cloudy nublado
clown payaso, el
clutch embrague, el
coast costa, la
coconut coco, el
coffee café, el
coin moneda, la
cold frío
cold (illness) resfriado, el
collarbone clavícula, la
college colegio, el
color color, el
comedian comediante, el
comedy comedia, la
comet cometa, la
comfortable cómodo
commerce comercio, el
community comunidad, la
computer computadora, la
concert concierto, el
condiments condimentos, los
condominium condominio, el
conference conferencia, la
confession confesión, la
confident seguro
confused confundido
congratulations felicitaciones
constellation constelación, la
consultant consultor, el
contest concurso, el
contractor contratista, el
contruction construcción, la
cook cocinero, el
cookie galleta, la
copier copiadora, la
corn maíz, el
corner esquina, la
costume disfraz, el
counter mostrador, el
county condado, el
court (sports) cancha, la
court (law) tribunal, el
cousin primo, el
cow vaca, la
coward cobarde
coyote coyote, el
crab cangrejo, el
cracker galleta salada, la
crazy loco
creation creación, la
cricket grillo, el
crime crimen, el
crooked torcido
crop cosecha, la
cross cruz, la
cross-eyed bizco
crow cuervo, el
crutches muletas, las
cucumber pepino, el
cuff puño, el
cult culto, el
cup taza, la
curious curioso
curtains cortinas, las
curve curva, la
cut corte, el
daily diario
dancing baile, el
dark oscuro
dark-skinned prieto
data processor procesador de datos, el
date cita, la
date (calendar) fecha, la
daughter hija, la
daughter-in-law nuera, la
dawn amanecer, el
day día, el
deaf sordo
December diciembre
decoration decoración, la
deep profundo
deer venado, el
defendant acusado, el
defense defensa, la
degree grado, el
den sala de familia, la
dentist dentista, el
depressed deprimido
description descripción, la
desert desierto, el
desk escritorio, el
dessert postre, el
detour desviación, la
difficult difícil
dimple hoyuelo, el
dining room comedor, el

dinner cena, la
dirt tierra, la
dirty sucio
disabled incapacitado, el
disciple discípulo, el
dish plato, el
dishwasher lavaplatos, el
distance distancia, la
district distrito, el
divorced divorciado
dizzy mareado
doctor doctor, el
dog perro, el
doghouse perrera, la
doll muñeca, la
door puerta, la
doorbell timbre, el
doorknob perilla, la
dot punto, el
double doble
doubt duda, la
down abajo
downtown centro, el
dozen docena, la
dragonfly libébula, la
draperies colgaduras, las
drawer cajón, el
drawing dibujo, el
dream sueño, el
dress vestido, el
dresser tocador, el
dressing room vestuario, el
drill taladro, el
driveway entrada para carros, la
drizzling lloviznando
drug droga, la
drum tambor, el
dry seco
dryer secadora, la
duck pato, el
dull romo
dumb tonto
dump truck volquete, el
during durante
dust polvo, el
dustpan pala de recoger basura, la
dwarf enano, el
each cada
ear oreja, la
early temprano
easily fácilmente
east este, el
Easter Pascuas
easy fácil
egg huevo, el
eggplant berenjena, la
eighth octavo
elbow codo, el
elderly person anciano, el
electrical outlet enchufe, el
electricity electricidad, la
elephant elefante, el
elevator ascensor, el
elm olmo, el
embroidery bordado, el
employee empleado, el
employer empresario, el
empty vacío
enemy enemigo, el
engine motor, el
engineer ingeniero, el
entrance entrada, la
envelope sobre, el
equipment equipo, el
eraser borrador, el
errand mandado, el
escalator escalera mecánica, la
European europeo
evening noche, la
everyone todo el mundo
everything todo
everywhere en todas partes
evidence evidencia, la
evolution evolución, la
example ejemplo, el
excited emocionado
excuse me con permiso; disculpe; perdón
exercise ejercicio, el
exhausted agotado
exit salida, la
expensive caro
eye ojo, el
eyebrow ceja, la
eyelid párpado, el
face cara, la
factory fábrica, la
faint desmayado
faithful fiel
fall otoño, el
family familia, la
fan ventilador, el
far lejos
far-sighted présbita
farmer campesino, el
fast rápido
fat gordo
father padre, el
father-in-law suegro, el
faucet grifo, el
fault culpa, la
favorite favorito
fax fax, el
feather duster plumero, el
February febrero
female femenino
fence cerca, la
fender guardabarro, el
fern helecho, el
fertilizer abono, el
fever fiebre, la
field campo, el
fifth quinto
fig higo, el
file archivo, el
film película, la
fine bien
finger dedo, el
fire fuego
fire department departamento de bomberos, el
fire extinguisher extintor, el
firefighter bombero, el
fireplace fogón, el
firewood leña, la
fireworks fuegos artificiales, los
first primero
first aid primeros auxilios, los
fish (fished) pescado, el
fish (swimming) pez, el
fishing pesca, la
fixtures instalaciones, las
flea pulga, la
flesh carne, la
flight vuelo, el
floor piso, el
flour harina, la
flower flor, la
flowerpot maceta, la
flu influenza, la
fly mosca, la
folder cuaderno, el
foliage follaje, el
food comida, la
food procesor procesador de comida, el
foot pie, el
football fútbol americano, el
for para
forearm entebrazo, el
foreigner extranjero, el
forest bosque, el
fork tenedor, el
form formulario, el
fountain fuente, la
fourth cuarto
fox zorro, el
frame marco, el
freckles pecas, las
free libre
freedom libertad, la
freezer congelador, el
frequently frecuentemente
Friday viernes
friend amigo, el
friendly amistoso
frog sapo, el
from de
frown ceño, el
fruit fruta, la
frustrated frustrado
full lleno
fun diversión, la
funnel embudo, el
funny chistoso
furious furioso
furniture muebles, los
fuse fusible, el
fusebox caja de fusibles, la
gain ganancia, la
galaxy galaxia, la
gallbladder vesícula, la
gallon galón, el
game juego, el
gang pandilla, la
garage garaje, el
garage door opener abridor de garajes, el
garbage disposal triturador de basura, el
garden jardín, el
gardener jardinero, el
garlic ajo, el
gas gasolina, la
gas meter medidor de gas, el
gas station gasolinera, la
gate portón, el
gauge indicador, el
gear engranaje, el
gentleman caballero, el
geranium geranio, el
giant gigante
gift regalo, el

giraffe jirafa, la
girdle faja, la
girlfriend novia, la
glass vaso, el
glasses lentes, los
gloves guantes, los
glue pegamento, el
goat chivo, el
God Dios
Goddaughter ahijada, la
Godson ahijado, el
Godfather padrino, el
Godmother madrina, la
gold oro
golf course campo de golf, el
good bueno
good afternoon buenas tardes
good evening buenas noches
good morning buenos días
good night buenas noches
good-bye adiós
gossip chisme, el
government gobierno, el
grain grano, el
granddaughter nieta, la
grandfather abuelo, el
grandmother abuela, la
grandson nieto, el
grape uva, la
grapefruit toronja, la
grass pasto, el
grasshopper saltamontes, el
gravel grava, la
gravity gravedad, la
gray gris
green verde
griddle comal, el
ground beef carne molida, la
grove arboleda, la
guest huésped, el
guide guía, el
guilty culpable
guitar guitarra, la
gulch barranca, la
gums encías, las
gym gimnasio, el
hair pelo, el
hair dryer secador de pelo, el
haircut corte de pelo, el
half medio; mitad, la
hallway pasillo, el
ham jamón, el
hamburger hamburguesa, la
hammer martillo, el
hammock hamaca, la
hamster hámster, el
hand mano, la
handle tirador, el
handsome guapo
happy feliz
hard duro
hatch portillo, el
hate odio, el
hated odiado
hawk halcón, el
hay heno, el
he él
head cabeza, la
headache dolor de cabeza, el
headlight faro delantero, el
health salud, la
healthy saludable
heart corazón, el
heat calor
heater calentador, el
heating calefacción, la
heaven cielo, el
heavy pesado
height altura, la
helicopter helicóptero, el
hell infierno, el
her su
here aquí
hero héroe, el
hers suya
hi hola
highway carretera, la
hiking caminata, la
hill cerro, el
hip cadera, la
hippopotamus hipopótamo, el
Hispanic hispano
hobby pasatiempo, el
hoe azadón, el
homeless desamparado, el
honey miel, la
honeymoon luna de miel, la
hood capot, el
hope esperanza, la
horn bocina, la
hornet avispón, el
horse caballo, el
horseback riding equitación, la
hose manguera, la
hospital hospital, el
hostile hostil
hot caliente
hot dog perrito caliente, el
hour hora, la
house casa, la
house trailer coche habitación, el
housecleaning limpieza de la casa, la
how cómo
how many cuántos
how much cuánto
however sin embargo
hubcap tapacubo, el
hug abrazo, el
hundred cien
hungry hambre
husband esposo, el
I yo
ice cream helado, el
ice maker hielera, la
if si
immigrant inmigrante, el
impatient impaciente
in en
in front enfrente
inch pulgada, la
industry industria, la
inexpensive barato
ingredient ingrediente, el
innocence inocencia, la
insecure inseguro
inside adentro
interested interesado
interesting interesante
interview entrevista, la
intestine intestino, el
intoxicated intoxicado
investment inversión, la
invoice factura, la
it lo
ivy hiedra, la
jacket chaqueta, la
jail cárcel, la
janitor conserje, el
January enero
jaw mandíbula, la
jealous celoso
jealousy celos, los
jeep jip, el
jello gelatina, la
Jesus Christ Jesucristo
Jew judío, el
job trabajo, el
jogging trote, el
joke chiste, el
judge juez, el
juice jugo, el
July julio
June junio
jungle selva, la
jury jurado, el
kidney riñón, el
kindness bondad, la
king rey, el
kiss beso, el
kitchen cocina, la
kitchen sink fregadero, el
kite cometa, la
knee rodilla, la
knife cuchillo, el
laborer obrero, el
ladder escalera, la
ladle cucharón, el
lady dama, la
ladybug mariquita, la
lagoon laguna, la
lake lago, el
lamb cordero, el
lame cojo
lamp lámpara, la
lampshade pantalla, la
land terreno, el
last fin
last name apellido
late tarde
later más tarde
laughter risa, la
law ley, la
lawn césped, el
lawn chair silla de patio, la
lawn mower cortadora de césped, la
lawsuit pleito, el
lawyer abogado, el
lazy perezoso
leaf hoja, la
leash traílla, la
left izquierda
left-handed zurdo
leg pierna, la
lemon limón, el
lemonade limonada, la

length largo, el
less menos
letter carta, la
letter (alphabet) letra, la
lettuce lechuga, la
library biblioteca, la
lie mentira, la
life vida, la
light luz, la
light (weight) ligero
light bulb foco, el
light switch interruptor, el
lion león, el
lip labio, el
little poco
liver hígado, el
living room sala, la
lizard lagarto, el
lobby salón, el
lobster langosta, la
lock cerradura, la
logic lógico
long largo
loose flojo
loss pérdida, la
lost perdido
love amor, el
lover amante, el
luck suerte
lunch almuerzo, el
lung pulmón, el
machine máquina, la
magazine revista, la
magic magia, la
maid criado, el
mail correo, el
mail carrier cartero, el
mailbox buzón, el
male masculino
man hombre, el
manager gerente, el
maple arce, el
marbles canicas, las
March marzo
margarine margarina, la
market mercado, el
marmalade mermelada, la
marriage matrimonio, el
married casado
mask máscara, la
mat tapete, el
matches fósforos, los
mature maduro
May mayo
maybe quizás
mayonnaise mayonesa, la
meat carne, la
meatball albóndiga, la
mechanic mecánico, el
medicine medicina, la
medicine chest botiquín, el
meeting reunión, la
message mensaje, el
microwave horno de microonda, el
middle medio
mile milla, la
military militar, el
milk leche, la
mine mío
minister pastor, el
mint menta, la
minute minuto, el
mirror espejo, el
Miss Señorita
mitt guante, el
mittens mitones, los
mixer batidora, la
mobile home casa rodante, la
mold molde, el
mole lunar, el
mole (animal) topo, el
Monday lunes
money dinero, el
monkey mono, el
month mes, el
moon luna, la
moose alce, el
mop trapeador, el
more más
Moslem musulmán, el
mosquito zancudo, el
mosquito screen mosquitero, el
moth polilla, la
mother madre, la
mother-in-law suegra, la
motorcycle motocicleta, la
mountain montaña, la
mouse ratón, el
mouth boca, la
movie theater cine, el
Mr. Señor
Mrs. Señora
mud lodo, el
muffler silenciador, el
muscle músculo, el
museum museo, el
mushroom champiñón, el
music música, la
musician músico, el
mustard mostaza, la
mute mudo
my mi
myself yo mismo
nail clavo, el
naked desnudo
name nombre, el
napkin servilleta, la
narrow estrecho
nature naturaleza, la
near cerca
near-sighted miope
neck cuello, el
necklace collar, el
neighbor vecino, el
neighborhood vecindario, el
neither tampoco
nephew sobrino, el
nerve nervio, el
nervous nervioso
net red, la
never nunca
new nuevo
newspaper periódico, el
next próximo
next to al lado
nice simpático
niece sobrina, la
nightstand mesita de noche, la
ninth noveno
no one nadie
none ninguno
noodle fideo, el
noon mediodía
north norte, el
nose nariz, la
nostril fosa nasal, la
not well mal
nothing nada
November noviembre
now ahora
nowhere en ninguna parte
numb adormecido
number número
nurse enfermero, el
nut tuerca, la
nuts nueces, las
oak roble, el
ocean océano, el
October octubre
of de
of course por supuesto
office oficina, la
often a menudo
oil aceite, el
OK bueno
old viejo
older mayor
olive aceituna, la
on en
on top encima
one-eyed tuerto
onion cebolla, la
open abierto
opossum zarigüeya, el
opportunity oportunidad, la
or o
orange naranja, la
orange (color) anaranjado
orbit órbita, la
orchard huerta, la
organ órgano, el
ornament ornamento, el
ounce onza, la
our nuestro
outside afuera
outskirts afueras, las
oven horno, el
overcoat abrigo, el
owl buho, el
owner dueño, el
P.M. de la tarde
package paquete
pain dolor, el
paint pintura, la
painter pintor, el
painting pintura, la
pair par, el
pajamas pijama, la
pale pálido
palm palmera, la
pan sartén, el
panties bragas, las
pants pantalones, los
paper papel, el
parade desfile, el
parakeet perico, el
parents padres, los
park parque, el
parking lot estacionamiento, el; lote de carros, el
parsley perejil, el
partner socio, el

party fiesta, la
path senda, la
patience paciencia, la
patient paciente, el
pea arvejita, la
peace paz, la
peach melocotón, el
peanut butter crema de maní, la
pear pera, la
pen lapicero, el
pencil lápiz, el
people gente, la
pepper pimienta, la
percent por ciento, el
person persona, la
pharmacy farmacia, la
photograph foto, la
piano piano, el
pick pico, el
pickle encurtido, el
pickup camioneta, la
picture cuadro, el
pie pastel, el
piece pedazo, el
pier muelle, el
pig puerco, el
pilot piloto, el
pine pino, el
pineapple piña, la
pink rosado
pitcher jarro, el
place lugar, el
planet planeta, el
plant planta, la
plate plato, el
platter fuente, la
play drama, el
playground campo de recreo, el
pleasant agradable
please por favor
pliers pinzas, las
plum ciruela, la
plumber plomero, el
plumbing tubería, la
pocket bolsillo, el
poison veneno, el
pole poste, el
police policía, la
police station estación de policía, la
polite cortés
political party partido político, el
pollution contaminación, la
pond charca, la
pool piscina, la
poor pobre
poorly mal
popcorn palomitas, las
population población, la
porch portal, el
porcupine puercoespín, el
pork cerdo, el
portrait retrato, el
position puesto, el
post card tarjeta postal, la
post office correo, el
pot olla, la
potato papa, la
pottery alfarería, la
poverty pobreza, la
power poder, el
practice práctica, la
prayer rezo, el
president presidente, el
pretty bonito
priest sacerdote, el
prince príncipe, el
princess princesa, la
printer impresora, la
prison prisión, la
prize premio, el
problem problema, el
product producto, el
program programa, el
promise promesa, la
prompt puntual
property propiedad, la
prune ciruela pasa, la
psychology psicología, la
pump bomba, la
pumpkin calabaza, la
punishment castigo, el
puppet títere, el
purchase compra, la
purple morado
puzzle rompecabezas, el
quarter cuarto
queen reina, la
question pregunta, la
quickly rápidamente
quiet quieto
rabbit conejo, el
raccoon mapache, el
race carrera, la
rack estilador, el
racket raqueta, la
radio radio, el
radish rábano, el
rag trapo, el
railroad ferrocarril, el
railroad track vía del ferrocarril, la
rain lluvia, la
raincoat impermeable, el
raise aumento, el
raisin pasta, la
rake rastrillo, el
raquetball ráquetbol, el
rat rata, la
ready listo
real verdad
reason razón, la
receipt recibo, el
red rojo
red-headed pelirrojo
refrigerator refrigerador, el
relative pariente, el
relaxed relajado
religion religión, la
resident residente, el
respect respeto, el
responsible responsable
rest descanso, el
restless inquieto
restrooms servicios sanitarios, los
rhinoceros rinoceronte, el
rib costilla, la
rice arroz, el
rich rico
riddle adivinanza, la
right derecha
right now ahorita
right-handed diestro
rights derechos, los
river río, el
road camino, el
roast beef rosbif, el
robin petirrojo, el
rock piedra, la
rocket cohete, el
roll panecillo, el
roof tejado, el
room cuarto, el
roommate compañero de cuarto, el
root raíz, la
rope soga, la
rose rosa, la
rough áspero
route ruta, la
rude rudo
rug alfombra, la
rule regla, la
sacrifice sacrificio, el
sad triste
safety seguridad, la
sailing navegación a vela, la
salad ensalada, la
salary salario, el
sale venta, la
salesman vendedor, el
salt sal, la
sand arena, la
sandals sandalias, las
sandpaper papel de lija, el
sane cuerdo
satellite satélite, el
Saturday sábado
sauce salsa, la
saucepan cacerola, la
saucer platillo, el
sausage salchicha, la
saw serrucho, el
saxophone saxófono, el
scale báscula, el
scar cicatriz, la
scared espantado
scarf bufanda, la
schedule horario, el
school escuela, la
science ciencia, la
scissors tijeras, las
screw tornillo, el
screwdriver atornillador, el
sea mar, el
seafood marisco, el
season estación, la
seat asiento, el
second segundo
secret secreto, el
secretary secretario, el
security seguridad, la
seed semilla, la
seldom casi nunca
sensitive sensible
September septiembre
seventh séptimo
several varios
sewing machine máquina de coser, la
shallow bajo
shame vergüenza, la
sharp afilado
she ella
sheep oveja, la
shelf repisa, la
shirt camisa, la
shoe zapato, el
short (in height) bajo

short (in length) corto
shorts calzoncillos, los
shoulder hombro, el
shovel pala, la
shower ducha, la
shrimp camarón, el
shutters postigos, los
shy tímido
sick enfermo
side lado, el
sidewalk acera, la
sight vista, la
sign letrero, el
silver plata, la
silverware cubiertos, los
since desde
sincere sincero
single soltero
sister hija, la
sister-in-law cuñada, la
site sitio, el
sixth sexto
size tamaño, el
skateboard patineta, la
skates patines, los
skiing esquí, el
skin piel, la
skirt falda, la
skunk zorrino, el
sky cielo, el
skyscraper rascacielos, el
sled trineo, el
sleeve manga, la
slippers zapatillas, las
slow lento
slowly lentamente
slug babosa, la
small chico
smart inteligente
smell olor, el
smile sonrisa, la
smooth liso
snack merienda, la
snail caracol, el
snake culebra, la
snow nieve, la
so así que
soccer fútbol, el
socks calcetines, los
sofa sofá, el
soft blando
soft drink refresco, el
solar system sistema solar, el
soldier soldado, el
some unos
some algunos
someone alguien
something algo
sometimes a veces
somewhere en alguna parte
son hijo, el
son-in-law yerno, el
song canción, la
soon pronto
sore dolorido
soul alma, el
sound sonido, el
soup sopa, la
south sur, el
spa balneario, el
space espacio, el
Spanish español
spark plug bujía, la
sparrow gorrión, el
spatula espátula, la
speedometer velocímetro, el
spices especias, las
spider araña, la
spinach espinaca, la
spine espinazo, el
spleen bazo, el
sponge esponja, la
spoon cuchara, la
sportcoat saco, el
sports deportes, los
sprain torcedura, la
spring primavera, la
squirrel ardilla, la
stable establo, el
stadium estadio, el
stairs escaleras, las
stamps estampillas, las
staple grapa, la
stapler engrapadora, la
star estrella, la
state estado, el
statue estatua, la
steak bistec, el
steering wheel volante, el
stem tallo, el
step paso, el
stepdaughter hijastra, la
stepson hijastro, el
stepfather padrastro, el
stepmother madrastra, la
steps escalones, los
stereo estéreo, el
still aún
stockings medias, las
stomach estómago, el
stool banquillo, el
stop parada, la
store tienda, la
stories cuentos, los
stove estufa, la
straight recto
strange extraño
strap correa, la
strawberry fresa, la
stream arroyo, el
street calle, la
streetcar tranvía, el
strike huelga, la
strong fuerte
student estudiante, el
subway metro, el
success éxito, el
suffering sufrimiento, el
suit traje, el
summer verano, el
sun sol, el
Sunday domingo
sunflower girasol, el
sunglasses lentes de sol, los
sure cierto
surgeon cirujano, el
surprise sorpresa, la
suspicious sospechoso
swamp pantano, el
swan cisne, el
sweater suéter, el
sweatsuit sudadera, la
sweet potato camote, el
swing columpio, el
synagogue sinagoga, la
system sistema, el
T-shirt camiseta, la
table mesa, la
tall alto
tape cinta, la
tape deck casetera, la
tapestry tapiz, el
taste sabor, el
tatoo tatuaje, el
tea té, el
tea kettle tetera, la
teacher maestro, el
tears lágrimas, las
teenager adolescente, el
telephone teléfono, el
television televisor, el
temple templo, el
tennis tenis, el
tenth décimo
terrace terraza, la
territory territorio, el
thank you gracias
that (adj. dem) ese; aquel
that (conj.) que
theater teatro, el
their su
then entonces
there allí
there are hay
there is hay
therefore por eso
thermos termo, el
thermostat termostato, el
these estos
they ellos
thick grueso
thief ladrón, el
thigh muslo, el
thin delgado
thing cosa, la
third tercero
thirsty sed, la
this este
those esos
those aquellos
thought pensamiento, el
thousand mil
throat garganta, la
Thursday jueves
tie corbata, la
tiger tigre, el
tight apretado
time tiempo, el
tire neumático, el
tired cansado
to a
toaster tostadora, la
today hoy
toe dedo del pie, el
together juntos
toilet excusado, el
toll booth caseta de peaje, la
tomato tomate, el
tomorrow mañana
ton tonelada, la
tongs tenazas, las
tongue lengua, la
too también
too much demasiado
tools herramientas, las
tooth diente, el
top trompo, el
touch tacto, el
tourism turismo, el
tow truck grúa, la
towards hacia
towel toalla, la
tower torre, el

town pueblo, el
toy juguete, el
tractor tractor, el
traffic tráfico, el
traffic light semáforo, el
tragedy tragedia, la
train tren, el
training entrenamiento, el
trash basura, la
trash-can basurero, el
tray bandeja, la
treasure tesoro, el
tree árbol, el
trial juicio, el
trip viaje, el
trowel llana, la
truck camión, el
truck driver camionero, el
trumpet trompeta, el
trunk tronco, el
trunk (auto) maletera, la
trust confianza, la
truth verdad, la
Tuesday martes
tulip tulipán, el
tuna atún, el
tunnel túnel, el
turkey pavo, el
turnip nabo, el
turtle tortuga, la
twig ramita, la
typewriter máquina de escribir, la
ugly feo
umbrella sombrilla, la
uncle tío, el
under debajo
underwear ropa interior, la
universe universo, el
university universidad, la
unless a menos que
until hasta
up arriba
upholstery tapicería, la
vacations vacaciones, las
vacuum cleaner aspiradora, la
valley valle, el
value valor, el
valve válvula, la
vanilla vainilla, la
vase florero, el
VCR videocasetera, la
veal ternera, la
vegetables vegetales, los
vein vena, la
verdict veredicto, el
vest chaleco, el
village villa, la
vinegar vinagre, el
violet violeta, la
violin violín, el
visitor visitante, el
voice voz, la
waiter mesonero, el
wall pared, la
walnut nogal, el
war guerra, la
warehouse almacén, el
washer lavadora, la
wasp avispa, la
wastebasket cesto de papeles, el
water agua, el
way paseo, el
we nosotros
weak débil
weapon arma, la
weather tiempo, el
wedding boda, la
Wednesday miércoles
weed hierba, la
week semana, la
weekend fin de semana, el
weight peso, el
welcome bienvenido
west oeste, el
wet mojado
what qué
whatever cualquiera
wheel rueda, la
wheelbarrow carretilla, la
wheelchair silla de ruedas, la
when cuándo
where dónde
wherever dondequiera
which cuál
while mientras
white blanco
who quién
whoever quienquiera
whose de quién
why por qué
wide ancho
widowed viudo
width ancho, el
wife esposa, la
wig peluca, la
wild salvaje
willow sauce, el
wind viento, el
window ventana, la
windshield parabrisas, el
wine vino, el
winter invierno, el
wise sabio
with con
without sin
witness testigo, el
wolf lobo, el
woman mujer, la
wonderful maravilloso
woodpecker picaposte, el
word palabra, la
work trabajo, el
world mundo, el
worm gusano, el
worse peor
worship adoración, la
wren reyezuelo, el
wrench llave inglesa, la
wrinkles arrugas, las
wrist muñeca, la
writer escritor, el
wrong equivocado
yard patio, el
year año, el
yellow amarillo
yesterday ayer
yet todavía
you (formal) usted
you (informal) tú
you (plural) ustedes
young joven
younger menor
youngster muchacho, el
your su
your (informal) tu
yours suyo
zebra cebra, la
zipper cierre, el
zone zona, la
zoo zoológico, el

Spanish-English Vocabulary

The gender of Spanish adjectives or pronouns shown here is always masculine. To switch the gender to feminine, change the ending to **a** (aburrid**o** = aburrid**a**, much**o** = much**a**).

a to
a lo largo along
a menos que unless
a menudo often
a veces sometimes
abajo down
abedul, el birch
abeja, la bee
abierto open
abogado, el lawyer
abono, el fertilizer
abrazo, el hug
abrelatas, el can opener
abridor de garajes, el garage door opener
abrigo, el overcoat
abril April
abuela, la grandmother
abuelo, el grandfather
aburrido bored
abusado abused
abuso, el abuse
acción, la action
aceite, el oil
aceituna, la olive
acera, la sidewalk
acondicionador de aire, el air conditioner
actor, el actor
actriz, la actress
acuario, el aquarium
acusación, la charge
acusado, el defendant
además besides
adentro inside
adiós good-bye
adivinanza, la riddle
adolescente, el teenager
adoración, la worship
adormecido numb
adulto, el adult
aeropuerto, el airport
afilado sharp
afroamericano, el African-American
afuera outside
afueras, las outskirts
agosto August
agotado exhausted
agradable pleasant
agua, el water
ahijada, la Goddaughter
ahijado, el Godson
ahora now
ahorita right now
ajedrez, el chess
ajo, el garlic
al lado next to
al revés backwards
alarma, la alarm
albaricoque, el apricot
albóndiga, la meatball
alcachofa, la artichoke
alce, el moose
alfarería, la pottery
alfombra, la rug
algo something
alguien someone
algunos some
aliento, el breath
allí there
alma, el soul
almacén, el warehouse
almuerzo, el lunch
alrededor around
alto tall
altura, la height
amanecer, el dawn
amante, el lover
amargo bitter
amarillo yellow
ambos both
ambulancia, la ambulance
amigo, el friend
amistoso friendly
amor, el love
anaranjado orange (color)
ancho wide
ancho, el width
anciano, el elderly person
anfiteatro, el arena
ángel, el angel
anglosajón, el Anglo-Saxon
animal, el animal
aniversario, el anniversary
año, el year
ansioso anxious
ante-comedor, el breakfast room
antes before
apartamento, el apartment
apático apathetic
apellido last name
apio, el celery
apretado tight
aquel that (adj. dem)
aquellos those
aquí here
araña, la spider
árbol, el tree
arboleda, la grove
arbusto, el bush
arce, el maple
archivo, el file
arco, el bow
ardilla, la squirrel
área, el area
arena, la sand
arma, la weapon
armario, el armoire
arquitecto, el architect
arriba up
arroyo, el stream
arroz, el rice
arrugas, las wrinkles
arte, el art
artista, el artist
arvejita, la pea
ascensor, el elevator
así que so
asiático Asian
asiento, el seat
asistente, el assistant
áspero rough
aspiradora, la vacuum cleaner
astrología, la astrology
astronauta, el astronaut
ateo, el atheist
atleta, el athlete
atornillador, el screwdriver
atún, el tuna
aumento, el raise
aún still
aunque although
autobús, el bus
avenida, la avenue
avergonzado ashamed
avispa, la wasp
avispón, el hornet
ayer yesterday
azadón, el hoe
azul blue
babosa, la slug
baile, el dancing
bajo shallow; short (in height)
balcón, el balcony
balde, el bucket
balneario, el spa
banco, el bank
bandeja, la tray
baño, el bathroom
banquillo, el stool
bar, el bar
baranda, la bannister
barato inexpensive
barbilla, la chin
barco, el boat
barranca, la gulch
báscula, el scale
básquetbol, el basketball
basura, la trash
basurero, el trash-can
bate, el bat
batería, la battery
batidora, la mixer
baúl, el chest (storage)
bazo, el spleen
bebé, el baby
béisbol, el baseball
bello beautiful
beneficio, el benefit
berenjena, la eggplant
beso, el kiss
betabel, el beet
Biblia, la Bible
biblioteca, la library
bicicleta bicycle
bien fine
bienvenido welcome
bistec, el steak
bizco cross-eyed
blanco white
blando soft
blusa, la blouse
boca, la mouth
bocina, la horn
boda, la wedding
bolera, la bowling alley
boliche, el bowling
bolsa, la bag

bolsillo, el pocket
bomba, la pump
bombero, el firefighter
bondad, la kindness
bonito pretty
bordado, el embroidery
borrador, el eraser
bosque, el forest
bota, la boot
botella, la bottle
botiquín, el medicine chest
botón, el bud; button
botones, el bellhop
boxeo, el boxing
bragas, las panties
brazo, el arm
brócoli, el broccoli
budista Buddist
buenos días good morning
buenas noches good night; good evening
buenas tardes good afternoon
bueno good; OK
bufanda, la scarf
buho, el owl
bujía, la spark plug
bulevar, el boulevard
buzón, el mailbox
caballero, el gentleman
caballo, el horse
cabeza, la head
cacerola, la saucepan
cacto, el cactus
cada each
cadena, la chain
cadera, la hip
café brown
café, el coffee
caja de fusibles, la fusebox
caja, la box (container)
cajero, el cashier
cajón, el drawer
calabaza, la pumpkin
calcetines, los socks
caldo, el broth
calefacción, la heating
calentador, el heater
caliente hot
calle, la street
callejón, el alley
calmado calm
calor heat
calvo bald
calzoncillos, los shorts
cama, la bed
camarón, el shrimp
caminata, la hiking
camino, el road
camión, el truck
camionero, el truck driver
camioneta, la pickup
camisa, la shirt
camiseta, la T-shirt
camote, el sweet potato
campamento, el campgrounds
cámper, el camper
campesino, el farmer
campo de golf, el golf course
campo de recreo, el playground
campo, el field
canario, el canary
canasta, la basket
cancha, la court (sports)
canción, la song
candelabro, el candelabra
canela, la cinnamon
cangrejo, el crab
canicas, las marbles
cansado tired
cantinero, el bartender
capilla, la chapel
capot, el hood
cara, la face
caracol, el snail
cárcel, la jail
carne molida, la ground beef
carne, la flesh; meat
caro expensive
carpintero, el carpenter
carrera, la career; race
carretera, la highway
carretilla, la wheelbarrow
carro, el car
carta, la letter
cartero, el mail carrier
casa rodante, la mobile home
casa, la house
casado married
caseta de peaje, la toll booth
casetera, la tape deck
casi almost
casi nunca seldom
castigo, el punishment
castor, el beaver
catedral, la cathedral
católico Catholic
cebolla, la onion
cebra, la zebra
cedro, el cedar
ceja, la eyebrow
celos, los jealousy
celoso jealous
cementerio, el cemetery
cena, la dinner
cenicero, el ashtray
ceño, el frown
centavo, el cent
centro, el downtown
cerca near
cerca, la fence
cerdo, el pork
cerebro, el brain
cereza, la cherry
cerrado closed
cerradura, la lock
cerro, el hill
cerveza, la beer
césped, el lawn
cesto de papeles, el wastebasket
chaleco, el vest
champiñón, el mushroom
chaqueta, la jacket
charca, la pond
cheque, el check
chicle, el chewing gum
chico small
chimenea, la chimney
chisme, el gossip
chiste, el joke
chistoso funny
chivo, el goat
chofer, el chauffeur
cicatriz, la scar
ciego blind
cielo, el heaven; sky
cien hundred
ciencia, la science
cierre, el zipper
cierto sure
cigarrillo, el cigarette
cine, el movie theater
cinta, la tape
cinturón, el belt
circo, el circus
ciruela, la plum
ciruela pasa, la prune
cirujano, el surgeon
cisne, el swan
cita, la appointment
cita, la date
ciudad, la city
ciudadano, el citizen
claramente clearly
clarinete, el clarinet
claro clear
clase, la class
clavel, el carnation
clavícula, la collarbone
clavo, el nail
cliente, el client
cobarde coward
coche habitación, el house trailer
cocina, la kitchen
cocinero, el cook
coco, el coconut
codo, el elbow
cohete, el rocket
cojo lame
colegio, el college
colgaduras, las draperies
collar, el necklace
color, el color
columpio, el swing
comal, el griddle
comedia, la comedy
comediante, el comedian
comedor, el dining rooom
comercio, el commerce
cometa, la comet; kite
comida, la food
cómo how
cómodo comfortable
compañero de cuarto, el roommate
compañero, el buddy
compra, la purchase
computadora, la computer
comunidad, la community
con with
con permiso excuse me
concierto, el concert
concurso, el contest
condado, el county
condimentos, los condiments
condominio, el condominium
conejo, el rabbit
conferencia, la conference
confesión, la confession

confianza, la trust
confundido confused
congelador, el freezer
consejo, el advice
conserje, el janitor
constelación, la constellation
construcción, la contruction
consultor, el consultant
contaminación, la pollution
contestador telefónico, el answering machine
contratista, el contractor
contusión, la bruise
copiadora, la copier
corazón, el heart
corbata, la tie
cordero, el lamb
correa, la strap
correo, el mail
correo, el post office
cortadora de césped, la lawn mower
corte, el cut
corte de pelo, el haircut
cortés polite
corteza, la bark
cortinas, las curtains
corto short (in length)
cosa, la thing
cosecha, la crop
costa, la coast
costilla, la rib
coyote, el coyote
creación, la creation
creencia, la belief
crema de maní, la peanut butter
criado, el maid
crimen, el crime
cristiano Christian
cruz, la cross
cuaderno, el folder
cuadra, la city block
cuadro, el picture
cuál which
cualquier cosa anything
cualquier persona anyone
cualquiera whatever
cuándo when
cuánto how much
cuántos how many
cuarto fourth; quarter
cuarto, el room
cubiertos, los silverware
cuchara, la spoon
cucharón, el ladle
cuchillo, el knife
cuentos, los stories
cuerdo sane
cuerpo, el body
cuervo, el crow
cueva, la cave
cuidado careful
culebra, la snake
culpa, la blame; fault
culpable guilty
culto, el cult
cumpleaños, el birthday
cuñada, la sister-in-law
cuñado, el brother-in-law
curioso curious
curva, la curve
dama, la lady
de from; of
de la mañana A.M.
de la tarde P.M.
de quién whose
debajo under
débil weak
décimo tenth
decoración, la decoration
dedo del pie, el toe
dedo, el finger
defensa, la defense
delgado thin
demasiado too much
dentista, el dentist
departamento de bomberos, el fire department
dependiente, el clerk
deportes, los sports
deprimido depressed
derecha right
derechos, los rights
desamparado, el homeless
desayuno, el breakfast
descalzo barefoot
descanso, el rest
descripción, la description
desde since
desfile, el parade
desierto, el desert
desmayado faint
desnudo naked
despejado clear (weather)
después after
desván, el attic
desviación, la detour
detrás behind
día, el day
diario daily
dibujo animado, el cartoon
dibujo, el drawing
diciembre December
diente, el tooth
diestro right-handed
difícil difficult
dinero, el money
Dios God
dirección, la address
discípulo, el disciple
disco compacto, el CD
disculpe excuse me
disfraz, el costume
disponible available
distancia, la distance
distrito, el district
diversión, la fun
divorciado divorced
doble double
docena, la dozen
doctor, el doctor
dolor de cabeza, el headache
dolor, el pain
dolorido sore
domingo Sunday
dónde where
dondequiera wherever
dormitorio, el bedroom
drama, el play
droga, la drug
ducha, la shower
duda, la doubt
dueño, el owner
dulce, el candy
durante during
duro hard
edad, la age
edificio, el building
ejemplo, el example
ejercicio, el exercise
él he
electricidad, la electricity
electrodoméstico, el appliance
elefante, el elephant
ella she
ellos they
embrague, el clutch
embudo, el funnel
emocionado excited
empleado, el employee
empresario, el employer
en at; in; on
en alguna parte somewhere
en cualquier parte anywhere
en el fondo at the bottom
en ninguna parte nowhere
en todas partes everywhere
enano, el dwarf
enchufe, el electrical outlet
encías, las gums
encima above; on top
encurtido, el pickle
enemigo, el enemy
enero January
enfermero, el nurse
enfermo sick
enfrente in front
engranaje, el gear
engrapadora, la stapler
enojado angry
ensalada, la salad
entebrazo, el forearm
entonces then
entrada para carros, la driveway
entrada, la entrance
entre between
entrenamiento, el training
entrevista, la interview
equipo, el equipment
equitación, la horseback riding
equivocado wrong
escalera, la ladder
escalera mecánica, la escalator
escaleras, las stairs
escalones, los steps
escarabajo, el beetle
escritor, el writer
escritorio, el desk
escuela, la school
ese that (adj. dem.)
esos those
espacio, el space
espalda, la back
español Spanish

espantado scared
espárrago, el asparagus
espátula, la spatula
especias, las spices
espejo, el mirror
esperanza, la hope
espinaca, la spinach
espinazo, el spine
esponja, la sponge
esposa, la wife
esposo, el husband
esquí, el skiing
esquina, la corner
establo, el stable
estación, la season
estación de autobús, la bus station
estación de policía, la police station
estacionamiento, el parking lot
estadio, el stadium
estado, el state
estampillas, las stamps
estatua, la statue
este this
este, el east
estéreo, el stereo
estilador, el rack
estómago, el stomach
estos these
estrecho narrow
estrella, la star
estudiante, el student
estufa, la stove
europeo European
evidencia, la evidence
evolución, la evolution
excusado, el toilet
éxito, el success
extintor, el fire extinguisher
extranjero, el foreigner
extraño strange
fábrica, la factory
fácil easy
fácilmente easily
fax, el fax
factura, la invoice
faja, la girdle
falda, la skirt
familia, la family
farmacia, la pharmacy
faro delantero, el headlight
favorito favorite
febrero February
fecha, la date (calendar)
felicitaciones congratulations
feliz happy
femenino female
feo ugly
ferrocarril, el railroad
fianza, la bail
fideo, el noodle
fiebre, la fever
fiel faithful
fiesta, la party
fin last
fin de semana, el weekend
flecha, la arrow
flojo loose
flor, la flower
florero, el vase
foco, el light bulb
fogón, el fireplace
follaje, el foliage
fondo, el bottom
formulario, el form
fosa nasal, la nostril
fósforos, los matches
foto, la photograph
frecuentemente frequently
fregadero, el kitchen sink
freno, el brake
fresa, la strawberry
frijol, el bean
frío cold
frontera, la border
frustrado frustrated
fruta, la fruit
fuego, el fire
fuegos artificiales, los fireworks
fuente, la fountain; platter
fuerte strong
furioso furious
fusible, el fuse
fútbol americano, el football
fútbol, el soccer
gabinete, el cabinet
galaxia, la galaxy
galleta, la cookie
galleta salada, la cracker
gallina, la chicken (hen)
galón, el gallon
ganancia, la gain
garaje, el garage
garganta, la throat
gasolina, la gas
gasolinera, la gas station
gato, el cat
gelatina, la jello, gelatin
gente, la people
geranio, el geranium
gerente, el manager
gigante giant
gimnasio, el gym
girasol, el sunflower
globo, el balloon
gobierno, el government
gordo fat
gorra, la cap
gorrión, el sparrow
gracias thank you
grado, el degree
grande big
grano, el grain
grapa, la staple
grava, la gravel
gravedad, la gravity
grifo, el faucet
grillo, el cricket
gris gray
grúa, la tow truck
grueso thick
guante, el mitt
guantes, los gloves
guapo handsome
guardabarro, el fender
guerra, la war
guía, el guide
guitarra, la guitar
gusano, el worm
hace ago
hacha, el ax
hacia towards
halcón, el hawk
hamaca, la hammock
hambre hungry
hamburguesa, la hamburger
hámster, el hamster
harina, la flour
hasta until
hay there are; there is
hebilla, la buckle
helado, el ice cream
helecho, el fern
helicóptero, el helicopter
heno, el hay
hermano, el brother
héroe, el hero
herramientas, las tools
hiedra, la ivy
hielera, la ice maker
hierba, la weed
hígado, el liver
higo, el fig
hija, la daughter; sister
hijastra, la stepdaughter
hijastro, el stepson
hijo, el son
hipopótamo, el hippopotamus
hispano Hispanic
hoja, la leaf
hola hi
hombre, el man
hombro, el shoulder
hora, la hour
horario, el schedule
hormiga, la ant
horno, el oven
horno de microonda, el microwave
hospital, el hospital
hostil hostile
hoy today
hoyuelo, el dimple
huelga, la strike
huerta, la orchard
hueso, el bone
huésped, el guest
huevo, el egg
iglesia, la church
impaciente impatient
impermeable, el raincoat
impresora, la printer
incapacitado, el disabled
indicador, el gauge
industria, la industry
infierno, el hell
influenza, la flu
ingeniero, el engineer
ingrediente, el ingredient
inmigrante, el immigrant
inocencia, la innocence
inquieto restless
inseguro insecure
instalaciones, las fixtures
inteligente smart
interesado interested

interesante interestin
interruptor, el light switch
intestino, el intestine
intoxicado intoxicated
inversión, la investment
invierno, el winter
izquierda left
jamón, el ham
jardín, el garden
jardinero, el gardener
jarro, el pitcher
jefe, el boss
Jesucristo Jesus Christ
jip, el jeep
jirafa, la giraffe
joven young
judío, el Jew
juego, el game
jueves Thursday
juez, el judge
jugo, el juice
juguete, el toy
juicio, el trial
julio July
junio June
juntos together
jurado, el jury
labio, el lip
lado, el side
ladrón, el thief
lago, el lake
lagarto, el lizard
lágrimas, las tears
laguna, la lagoon
lámpara, la lamp
langosta, la lobster
lapicero, el pen
lápiz, el pencil
largo long
largo, el length
lata, la can
lavabo, el bathroom sink
lavadora, la washer
lavaplatos, el dishwasher
leche, la milk
lechuga, la lettuce
lejos far
leña, la firewood
lengua, la tongue
lentamente slowly
lentes de sol, los sunglasses
lentes, los glasses
lento slow
león, el lion
letra, la letter (alphabet)
letrero, el billboard
letrero, el sign
ley, la law
libébula, la dragonfly
librería, la bookstore
libertad, la freedom
libre free
librero, el bookshelf
libro, el book
licuadora, la blender
ligero light (weight)
limón, el lemon
limonada, la lemonade
limpieza de la casa, la housecleaning
limpio clean
liso smooth
listo ready
llana, la trowel
llave inglesa, la wrench
lleno full
lloviznando drizzling
lluvia, la rain
lo it
lobo, el wolf
loco crazy
lodo, el mud
lógico logic
lote de carros, el car lot
loza de porcelana, la china
lugar, el place
luna, la moon
luna de miel, la honeymoon
lunar, el mole
lunes Monday
luz, la light
maceta, la flowerpot
madrastra, la stepmother
madre, la mother
madrina, la Godmother
maduro mature
maestro, el teacher
magia, la magic
maíz, el corn
mal not well; poorly
maletera, la trunk (auto)
malo bad
mañana tomorrow
mandado, el errand
mandíbula, la jaw
manga, la sleeve
manguera, la hose
mano, la hand
mantequilla, la butter
manzana, la apple
mapache, el raccoon
máquina, la machine
máquina de coser, la sewing machine
máquina de escribir, la typewriter
mar, el sea
maravilloso wonderful
marco, el frame
mareado dizzy
margarina, la margarine
mariquita, la ladybug
marisco, el seafood
martes Tuesday
martillo, el hammer
marzo March
más more
más tarde later
máscara, la mask
masculino male
matrimonio, el marriage
mayo May
mayonesa, la mayonnaise
mayor older
mecánico, el mechanic
medias, las stockings
medicina, la medicine
medidor de gas, el gas meter
medio half; middle
mediodía noon
mejilla, la cheek
mejor better
melocotón, el peach
melón, el cantaloupe
menor younger
menos less
mensaje, el message
menta, la mint
mentira, la lie
mercado, el market
merienda, la snack
mermelada, la marmalade
mes, el month
mesa, la table
mesonero, el waiter
mesita de noche, la nightstand
metro, el subway
mi my
miel, la honey
mientras while
miércoles Wednesday
mil thousand
militar, el military
milla, la mile
minuto, el minute
mío mine
miope near-sighted
mitad, la half
mitones, los mittens
mojado wet
molde, el mold
moneda, la coin
mono, el monkey
montaña, la mountain
morado purple
moreno brunette
mosca, la fly
mosquitero, el mosquito screen
mostaza, la mustard
mostrador, el counter
motocicleta, la motorcycle
motor, el engine
muchacho, el youngster
mudo mute
muebles, los furniture
muelle, el pier
mujer, la woman
muletas, las crutches
mundo, el world
muñeca, la doll; wrist
municipio, el city hall
músculo, el muscle
museo, el museum
música, la music
músico, el musician
muslo, el thigh
musulmán, el Moslem
nabo, el turnip
nacimiento birth
nada nothing
nadie no one
nalga, la buttock
naranja, la orange
nariz, la nose
naturaleza, la nature
navegación a vela, la sailing
navidad, la Christmas
negocios, los business
negro black
nervio, el nerve
nervioso nervous
neumático, el tire
nieta, la granddaughter
nieto, el grandson

nieve, la snow
niñero, el babysitter
ninguno none
niño, el child
niveladora, la bull dozer
noche, la evening
nogal, el walnut
nombre, el name
norte, el north
nosotros we
noveno ninth
novia, la girlfriend
noviembre November
novio, el boyfriend
nublado cloudy
nueces, las nuts
nuera, la daughter-in-law
nuestro our
nuevo new
número number
nunca never
o or
obrero, el laborer
océano, el ocean
octavo eighth
octubre October
ocupado busy
odiado hated
odio, el hate
oeste, el west
oficina, la office
ojo, el eye
olla, la pot
olmo, el elm
olor, el smell
onza, la ounce
oportunidad, la opportunity
órbita, la orbit
oreja, la ear
órgano, el organ
ornamento, el ornament
oro gold
oscuro dark
oso, el bear
otoño, el fall
otra vez again
oveja, la sheep
paciencia, la patience
paciente, el patient
padrastro, el stepfather
padre, el father
padres, los parents
padrino, el Godfather
pájaro, el bird
pala, la shovel
pala de recoger basura, la dustpan
palabra, la word
pálido pale
palmera, la palm
palomitas, las popcorn
pandilla, la gang
panecillo, el roll
pantalla, la lampshade
pantalones, los pants
pantano, el swamp
pantorrilla, la calf
papa, la potato
papel, el paper
papel de lija, el sandpaper
paquete package
par, el pair
para for
parabrisas, el windshield
parachoques, el bumper
parada de autobús, la bus stop
parada, la stop
pared, la wall
pariente, el relative
párpado, el eyelid
parque de atracciones, el amusement park
parque, el park
parrilla, la barbeque grill
partido político, el political party
pasatiempo, el hobby
paseo en bote, el boating
paseo, el way
pasillo, el hallway
pasa, la raisin
paso, el step
Pascuas Easter
pastel, el pie
pasto, el grass
pastor, el minister
patines, los skates
patineta, la skateboard
patio, el yard
pato, el duck
pavo, el turkey
payaso, el clown
paz, la peace
pecas, las freckles
pecho, el chest (body)
pedazo, el piece
pegamento, el glue
película, la film
pelirrojo red-headed
pelo, el hair
pelota, la ball
peluca, la wig
pensamiento, el thought
peor worse
pepino, el cucumber
pera, la pear
pérdida, la loss
perdido lost
perdón excuse me
perejil, el parsley
perezoso lazy
perico, el parakeet
perilla, la doorknob
periódico, el newspaper
perno, el bolt
pero but
perrera, la doghouse
perrito caliente, el hot dog
perro, el dog
persona, la person
pesado heavy
pesca, la fishing
pescado, el fish (fished)
peso, el weight
petirrojo, el robin
pez, el fish (swimming)
piano, el piano
picaposte, el woodpecker
pico, el pick
pie, el foot
piedra, la rock
piel, la skin
pierna, la leg
pijama, la pajamas
piloto, el pilot
pimienta, la pepper
piña, la pineapple
pino, el pine
pintor, el painter
pintura, la paint; painting
pinzas, las pliers
piscina, la pool
piso, el floor
pizarrón, el blackboard
planeta, el planet
planta, la plant
plata, la silver
plátano, el banana
platillo, el saucer
plato hondo, el bowl
plato, el dish; plate
playa, la beach
plaza de toros, la bullring
pleito, el lawsuit
plomero, el plumber
plumero, el feather duster
población, la population
pobre poor
pobreza, la poverty
poco little
poder, el power
policía, la police
polilla, la moth
pollo, el chicken
polvo, el dust
por by
por ciento, el percent
por eso therefore
por favor please
por qué why
por supuesto of course
porque because
portal, el porch
portillo, el hatch
portón, el gate
poste, el pole
postigos, los shutters
postre, el dessert
práctica, la practice
pregunta, la question
premio, el prize
présbita far-sighted
presidente, el president
presupuesto, el budget
prieto dark-skinned
primavera, la spring
primero first
primeros auxilios, los first aid
primo, el cousin
princesa, la princess
príncipe, el prince
prisión, la prison
problema, el problem
procesador de comida, el food procesor
procesador de datos, el data processor
producto, el product
profundo deep
programa, el program
promesa, la promise
pronto soon
propiedad, la property
próximo next
psicología, la psychology
pueblo, el town

puente, el bridge
puerco, el pig
puercoespín, el porcupine
puerta, la door
puesto, el position
pulga, la flea
pulgada, la inch
pulmón, el lung
puño, el cuff
punto, el dot
puntual prompt
que that (conj.)
qué what
quebrado broken
quemadura, la burn
queso, el cheese
quién who
quienquiera whoever
quieto quiet
quinto fifth
quizás maybe
rábano, el radish
radio, el radio
raíz, la root
rama, la branch
ramita, la twig
rápidamente quickly
rápido fast
raqueta, la racket
ráquetbol, el raquetball
rascacielos, el skyscraper
rastrillo, el rake
rata, la rat
ratón, el mouse
razón, la reason
recibo, el receipt
recto straight
red, la net
refresco, el soft drink
refrigerador, el refrigerator
regalo, el gift
regla, la rule
reina, la queen
relajado relaxed
religión, la religion
reloj, el clock
repisa, la shelf
repollo, el cabbage
resfriado, el cold (illness)
residente, el resident
respeto, el respect
responsable responsible
respuesta, la answer
retrato, el portrait
reunión, la meeting
revista, la magazine
rey, el king
reyezuelo, el wren
rezo, el prayer
rico rich
rinoceronte, el rhinoceros
riñón, el kidney
río, el river
risa, la laughter
roble, el oak
rodilla, la knee
rojo red
romo dull
rompecabezas, el puzzle
ropa, la clothing
ropa interior, la underwear
ropero, el closet
rosa, la rose
rosado pink
rosbif, el roast beef
rubio blonde
rudo rude
rueda, la wheel
ruta, la route
sábado Saturday
sabio wise
sabor, el taste
sacerdote, el priest
saco, el sportcoat
sacrificio, el sacrifice
sal, la salt
sala de familia, la den
sala, la living room
salario, el salary
salchicha, la sausage
salida, la exit
salón de belleza, el beauty salon
salón, el lobby
salsa, la sauce
saltamontes, el grasshopper
salud, la health
saludable healthy
salvaje wild
sandalias, las sandals
sangre, la blood
sapo, el frog
sartén, el pan
satélite, el satellite
sauce, el willow
saxófono, el saxophone
secador de pelo, el hair dryer
secadora, la dryer
seco dry
secretario, el secretary
secreto, el secret
sed, la thirsty
segundo second
seguridad, la safety; security
seguro confident
selva, la jungle
semáforo, el traffic light
semana, la week
semilla, la seed
senda, la path
seno, el breast
Señor Mr.
Señora Mrs.
Señorita Miss
sensible sensitive
septiembre September
séptimo seventh
serrucho, el saw
servicios sanitarios, los restrooms
servilleta, la napkin
sexto sixth
si if
SIDA, el AIDS
siempre always
silenciador, el muffler
silla, la chair
silla de patio, la lawn chair
silla de playa, la beach chair
silla de ruedas, la wheelchair
sillón, el armchair
simpático nice
sin without
sin embargo however
sinagoga, la synagogue
sincero sincere
sino but
sistema solar, el solar system
sistema, el system
sitio, el site
sobre above
sobre, el envelope
sobrina, la niece
sobrino, el nephew
socio, el partner
sofá, el sofa
soga, la rope
sol, el sun
soldado, el soldier
soltero single
sombrilla, la umbrella
sonido, el sound
sonrisa, la smile
sopa, la soup
sordo deaf
sorpresa, la surprise
sospechoso suspicious
sostén, el brassiere
sótano, el basement
su her; their; your
sucio dirty
sudadera, la sweatsuit
suegra, la mother-in-law
suegro, el father-in-law
sueño, el dream
suerte luck
suéter, el sweater
sufrimiento, el suffering
sur, el south
suya hers
suyo yours
tacto, el touch
taladro, el drill
tallo, el stem
tamaño, el size
también too
tambor, el drum
tampoco neither
tapacubo, el hubcap
tapete, el mat
tapicería, la upholstery
tapiz, el tapestry
tarde late
tarea, la chore
tarjeta, la card
tarjeta postal, la post card
tatuaje, el tatoo
taza, la cup
té, el tea
teatro, el theater
techo, el ceiling
tejado, el roof
teléfono, el telephone
televisor, el television
templo, el temple
temprano early
tenazas, las tongs
tenedor, el fork
tenis, el tennis
tercero third
termo, el thermos
termostato, el thermostat
ternera, la veal
terraza, la terrace
terreno, el land
territorio, el territory
tesoro, el treasure

testigo, el witness
tetera, la tea kettle
tía, la aunt
tiempo, el time; weather
tienda, la store
tierra, la dirt
tigre, el tiger
tijeras, las scissors
timbre, el doorbell
tímido shy
tina, la bathtub
tío, el uncle
tirador, el handle
títere, el puppet
tiza, la chalk
toalla, la towel
tobillo, el ankle
tocador, el dresser
tocador de casetes, el cassette player
tocino, el bacon
todavía yet
todo all; everything
todo el mundo everyone
tomate, el tomato
tonelada, la ton
tonto dumb
topo, el mole (animal)
torcedura, la sprain
torcido crooked
tornillo, el screw
toronja, la grapefruit
torre, el tower
tortuga, la turtle
tostadora, la toaster
trabajo, el job; work
tractor, el tractor
tráfico, el traffic
tragedia, la tragedy
traílla, la leash
traje, el suit
traje de baño, la bathing suit
tranvía, el streetcar
trapeador, el mop
trapo, el rag
tren, el train
tribunal, el court (law)
trineo, el sled
triste sad
triturador de basura, el garbage disposal
trompeta, el trumpet
trompo, el top
tronco, el trunk
trote, el jogging
tu your (informal)
tú you (informal)
tubería, la plumbing
tuerca, la nut
tuerto one-eyed
tulipán, el tulip
túnel, el tunnel
turismo, el tourism
universidad, la university
universo, el universe
unos some
usted you (formal)
ustedes you (plural)
uva, la grape
vaca, la cow
vacaciones, las vacations
vacío empty
vainilla, la vanilla
valiente brave
valle, el valley
valor, el value
válvula, la valve
varios several
vaso, el glass
vecindario, el neighborhood
vecino, el neighbor
vegetales, los vegetables
vejiga, la bladder
velocímetro, el speedometer
vena, la vein
venda bandage
venado, el deer
vendedor, el salesman
veneno, el poison
venta, la sale
ventana, la window
ventilador, el fan
verano, el summer
verdad real
verdad, la truth
verde green
vergüenza, la shame
veredicto, el verdict
vesícula, la gallbladder
vestido, el dress
vestuario, el dressing room
vía del ferrocarril, la railroad track
viaje, el trip
vida, la life
videocasetera, la VCR
viejo old
viento, el wind
viernes Friday
villa, la village
vinagre, el vinegar
vino, el wine
violeta, la violet
violín, el violin
visitante, el visitor
vista, la sight
viudo widowed
volante, el steering wheel
volquete, el dump truck
voz, la voice
vuelo, el flight
y and
yerno, el son-in-law
yo I
yo mismo myself
zanahoria, la carrot
zancudo, el mosquito
zapatillas, las slippers
zapato, el shoe
zarigüeya, el opossum
zona, la zone
zoológico, el zoo
zorrino, el skunk
zorro, el fox
zurdo left-handed